...omen *are* committing more crimes than eve.. ...efore. And more violent ones—homicide, armed ...bbery, aggravated assault, gang violence. ...nd this crime wave is growing at an alarming ...te.

... this powerful, eloquent book that distin-
...uished reviewers have called "a profound
...ork," "a landmark in the study of female
...ime," Freda Adler overcomes a decade of re-
...stance from traditional theorists, police chiefs,
...dges, and probation officers to take account of
...ew social facts. Her total reassessment of the
...ope, depth, and implications of female crime
...ows that the exception has become the rule
... thousands of women are stepping across the
...naginary boundary line which once separated
...imes into "masculine" and "feminine" cate-
...ories. She reveals the dramatic entrance of
...omen into the major leagues of crime with top
...illing on the FBI's list of wanted criminals.
...ased on original research conducted over sev-
...al years, she explains how the rising tide of
...emale assertiveness has led women to break out
...f the traditional limits of prostitution and shop-
...fting into grand larceny, embezzlement, bank
...obbery, and sky-rocketing crimes of violence
...hat are increasing at rates six and seven times
... great as those for men.

...he author's fascinating account goes far beyond
...eadline journalism into a brilliant exploration
...f the new breed of female criminal and her re-
...ation to the larger social forces in our society.
...er book challenges a variety of stereotypes of
...omen and crime, of race and class, and of
...ealth and power, and reveals qualitative
...hanges in female juvenile delinquents. Her re-
...earch shatters the time-honored myth of the
...enetic basis of the passive female, as well as
...he alleged psychopathology of the prostitute,
...whom she finds increasingly "better educated,
...etter accepted, and increasingly independent of
...en." The author has written a work that is as
...rilliant and eloquent in its overall analysis as it
...s human and sensitive in its individual examples.

sisters in crime

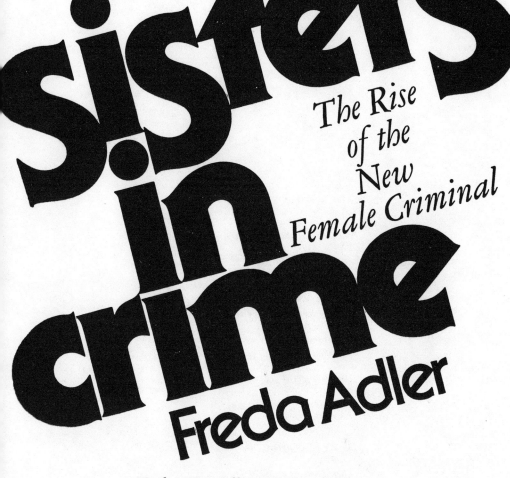

sisters in crime

The Rise of the New Female Criminal

Freda Adler

Herbert M. Adler, M.D., collaborator
Hoag Levins, interviewer

McGraw-Hill Book Company

New York   St. Louis   San Francisco   Düsseldorf   London
Mexico   Sydney   Toronto

Book design by Milton Jackson

123456789   BPBP   798765

Library of Congress Cataloging in Publication Data

Adler, Freda.
    Sisters in crime.

    1. Female Offenders—United States.   I.   Title.
HV6791.A55   364.3'74   74-31403
ISBN 0-07-000415-3

To Marvin E. Wolfgang,

Kind friend and wise mentor

Unless otherwise noted, all case studies and interviews with administrators, criminal "sisters," and other consumers of the criminal justice system were conducted exclusively for this book over a three-year period from 1971 to 1974.

Acknowledgments

It is with great pleasure that I acknowledge the considerable support I have received from my professional colleagues. Thorsten Sellen, Otto Pollak, and, particularly, Marvin E. Wolfgang played a significant role in the conception of this book. By conducting much of the field work and editing portions of the manuscript, Hoag Levins has been of invaluable assistance to me. Before I felt each chapter to be presentable I called on the advice of colleagues renowned for their work in specific fields: Don M. Gottfredson, Cherif Bassiouni, Nicholas N. Kittrie, C. Ray Jeffery, G. O. W. Mueller, Richard F. Sparks, John Decker, and John P. Reid.

My family was forced to live with this project for three years. I would like to acknowledge my indebtedness to Herbert M. Adler, a psychiatrist by training, a scholar by temperament, and a talented writer. Without his efforts the work would not have been possible. My children, Jill, Nancy, and Mark, have helped their mother through thoughtfulness and understanding. To them I owe a very special debt of gratitude.

I also want to thank two very special ladies who have helped me throughout this endeavor. Bonnie Edington worked tirelessly as research assistant and Mary Connolly as secretary.

Lastly, McGraw-Hill's editor-in-chief, Frederic W. Hills, deserves more than the customary acknowledgment. He saw the book through the editorial and production process with extraordinary devotion. To all those who have thus contributed to the completion of this work, I extend my sincere appreciation.

Freda Adler

Contents

Prologue 1

1
Changing Patterns 5

2
Female Passivity: Genetic Fact or Cultural Myth? 31

3
The Oldest and Newest Profession 55

4
Minor Girls and Major Crimes 85

5
Women in Wonderland:
The Psychotropic Connection 111

6
The Link Between Opportunity and Offense: Race 133

7
The Link Between Opportunity and Offense: Class 155

8
New Crimes and Old Corrections 171

9
Ladies and the Law 203

Epilogue—Liberation and Beyond 247

References 255

Index 279

Prologue

There is a tide in the affairs of women as well as men, and in the last decade it has been sweeping over the barriers which have protected male prerogatives and eroding the traditional differences which once nicely defined the gender roles. The phenomenon of female criminality is but one wave in this rising tide of female assertiveness—a wave which has not yet crested and may even be seeking its level uncomfortably close to the high-water mark set by male violence. On the surface there seems to be little connection between the "masculinization" of female behavior and the civil-rights movement of the 1950s, but in perspective they appear to be twin aspects of an assault on the separate-but-equal philosophy which has maintained the white and male power structure. Recognition by the courts and the Congress of the inherent inequality of artificial separateness was not only, as legislators in the 1960s proclaimed, "an idea whose time had come." It was also itself an *ex post facto* acknowledgment of the profound social changes which had already occurred. In fact, so far-reaching is this movement in both its civil and criminal aspects that it may be as portentous for the quality of our social life as the industrial revolution was for our material standard of living.

There was a time, not so long ago, when women knew their place and men knew women's place, and while women had little direct access to power, they were accorded a certain compensatory status for abiding by a nonaggression pact. For eschewing violence and most kinds of male assertiveness, women were deferred to and given certain privileges. In consequence, society sanctioned two distinct styles of behavior, differentiated by sex. Males were supposed to be active, powerful, and chivalrous, and females passive, weak, and receptive. This was represented to be the normal expression of physiological sex differences, and scientific observations, such as the activity of the sperm versus the passivity of the ovum, were cited to support the biological foundation of this social scheme. More recent anthropological and ethological evidence, however, indicates that this order rests as much on male cultural domination as on female genetic destiny. While it is true that androgen, the male hormone, mediates aggression in lower animals, human females also have androgen in their blood; but regardless, there is no direct correlation—in humans of either sex—between the level of androgen and the level of aggression. There are, for example, many passive men with normal androgen levels who are less aggressive than women. Furthermore, the human cerebral capacity for abstraction and symbol formation renders the behavior more dependent on psychic than physiological determinants. Even though American males are in general more aggressive than American females, there is no reason to assume that it is because females lack aggressive drives. Historically, it appears that society has capitalized on what is at most a degree of difference between the sexes in order to institutionalize the polarization of aggression. At the individual level, not only are women more aggressive than their social role would suggest, but men are less aggressive than their role expectation. The innocence of women, to paraphrase St. Augustine, appears to reside more in the weakness of their limbs than in the passivity of their drives. It is just in this area of physical and political weakness that technology and the women's liberation movement have equalized the capacity for male crimes, including violence. A frail woman with a pistol is just as threatening to a bank teller as a burly man, and a demure female bank executive has the same opportunity and inclination for embezzlement as her male counterpart.

If old concepts die hard, new ones have a difficult time aborning—and the resistance in recognizing the changing pattern of female criminality is no exception. Reflecting the strong male orientation of the news media and of the scientific community as well as the security inherent in established mental sets, the scope, depth, and implications of female crime have been minimized or ignored. At first there was a reluctant recognition that idiosyncratic females did occasionally venture into such areas of male crime as burglary, robbery, assault, and gang violence, but this was chivalrously dismissed as individual aberrations. Gradually, as the exceptions multiplied, police chiefs, judges, and probation officers across the land began to question the basic rule that limited females to prostitution and shoplifting. Once the question was asked, the answer was nothing short of a revelation. Women are indeed committing more crimes than ever before. Those crimes involve a greater degree of violence, and even in prison this new breed exhibits a hitherto unmatched pugnacity.

In this book I propose to document the extent and nature of the changing pattern of female crime in America. In addition, I believe there is enough information to plot its course and project its future direction. Further, the book offers a psychosocial perspective through which female criminal behavior can be understood as a natural extension of normal female behavior, which is itself both a product and producer of the larger forces which mediate all human interaction.

1

Changing Patterns

I am Woman, hear me roar,
In numbers too big to ignore,
And I know too much
To go back and pretend.

—Helen Reddy
"I Am Woman"

Characteristically, major social movements are spawned in obscurity at the periphery of public awareness, seem to burst suddenly and dramatically into public view, and eventually fade into the landscape not because they have diminished but because they have become a permanent part of our perceptions and experience. Thus it has been with the liberation of the female criminal, whose coming was foretold in song and foreshadowed in unisexual styles of dress and hair and attitude long before it appeared on police blotters. The portrait of the breathless, squeaky-voiced, empty-headed female professing awed admiration over some incredibly routine male accomplishment began to look less like a stereotype than a caricature. Even motherhood, in an era of zero-population goals and the diminishing status of homemaking, has been too closely linked with antiquated male domination to remain forever sacred. In spite of the cultural lag of white-male bias, the *Zeitgeist* of liberation has been moving irresistibly across the land. A generation militantly young, black, and female has stirred to storm and controversy previously whispered plaints whose answer, as Bob Dylan so eloquently lyricized, "is blowing in the wind." The term "social movement" is a useful abstraction to describe the distillation

5

of innumerable events which together form a trend. But in another sense there are no social movements, only individuals reacting to the immediacy of their own felt experience. Such an individual is Marge.

Marge is forty-three years old, with brown hair headed for gray and muscular legs somewhat the worse for wear. Soft-spoken and hovering just this side of being quite plump, Marge has spent a good many years on those legs earning a living. Since her husband disappeared one day eighteen years ago, she has worked a total of fifteen years either as a waitress or a barmaid. During those years, she supported and raised two sons, one of whom eventually worked his way through a small state college and is currently a teacher. The other one, younger, died four years ago as a result of a bad bag of heroin he pumped into his arm.

Deserted, with two small children, Marge was forced to get the first job she had ever had. It was as a barmaid in a small restaurant-lounge. Not long afterward, she gave her first serious thought to being a prostitute—like a fellow barmaid who was developing a very lucrative following among the bar's male clientele.

But soon Marge gave up the idea of prostitution—partly because of her figure, which she didn't feel was suited for the trade, and partly because of her "strong Catholic upbringing." She explained, "I just never felt right in that kind of thing. Now it didn't bother me that other girls I knew were turning tricks; I just couldn't bring myself to stay with it. I guess underneath it all, I was more strait-laced than I knew."

In place of prostitution, Marge found a more acceptable degree of reprehensibility in shoplifting. "Boosting" from department stores became a regular habit with her. At first she began by putting small items, like watches, into her pocket. Later, she progressed to more sophisticated methods. She wore large baggy coats which could conceal things like toasters and radios, then began to sew large bag-like pockets inside the coats to facilitate even larger load handling. She shoplifted for years, and was caught only once. On that occasion she was allowed to go free on her own recognizance and, although threatened with further prosecution, never heard of the incident again.

Five years ago Marge robbed her first bank. The planning took her some months. "It was something that came to me all of a sudden. . . . I had a couple of big debts and I was getting tired of working like I was. . . . I wanted a bit of easy time. I mean, the kids were getting older and I was still working and, after all those years, I needed a break. I guess maybe I got the idea from watching TV or something, I don't remember. But it surprised me; like, I first thought of it seriously and thought, 'No, I couldn't do that . . . I'm a woman,' you know? But when I thought more about it, what the hell, it didn't seem so bad. The other girls I knew were boosting or [credit] carding. They said I must be crazy when we talked about it one day. We never really thought about a woman hitting a bank before . . . but then soon after that, I heard on the radio of a lady who hit a bank and got away and I figured, what the hell, if she can do it, why can't I?"

After many months of careful planning and observation, Marge attempted to rob one particular bank. That first attempt was a failure. She walked in and approached the teller's window, but was unable to go through with the robbery. "I just asked for change for a ten-dollar bill and felt like a real smacked-ass to myself." Two months later, though, she went through with it and went on to rob two more banks before she was finally caught. After the first one it seemed easy to her. "I just walked in, walked out, and went home to count the money. I always thought it would be a lot harder . . . a lot more dangerous. I did take a gun each time, but it was never loaded and I only really had to show it to one teller. The others just put the money in the bag when I asked them to. . . . I remember that first job. It was like a cheap high afterward. I went home and turned on the radio to see what they would say about me on the news."

To her disappointment, after that first heist, police described her to the news media as a "male dressed in women's clothing." That upset Marge a bit. "Well, I mean, I know I'm no beauty queen, but I didn't think I was that bad . . . and who the hell ever saw a man with plucked eyebrows?"

During her third try, Marge was stopped on her way out of the bank by policemen responding to a silent alarm. She gave up peacefully. ("What the hell else could I do, the gun wasn't loaded or anything.") She is currently serving an indefinite prison term for robbery.

In a number of ways, Marge is typical of a new breed of women criminals making their appearance across America. She, along with thousands of others, has stepped across the imaginary boundary line which once separated crimes into "masculine" and "feminine" categories. Marge is a member of the new "liberation movement" which is spreading through the ranks of the nation's female offenders, but Marge would be the last person in the world to accredit her actions to any sort of a "liberation." She, like the majority of incarcerated women throughout the country, comes from a lower socioeconomic level and tends to identify with a value code embracing the "traditional" image of women.

"Most of the women we've gotten in the past have had what you could call a 'traditional' view of themselves as women," explained one female counselor who has worked for nearly two decades in a major East Coast correctional institution for women. "They have very strong feelings about what a woman 'should be' and that image has to do with the woman mostly as a homebody who has babies, gratifies her man's sexual wishes and otherwise keeps her mouth shut. Despite the fact that they themselves may have been quite aggressive, they hold a view that 'good' women are passive.

"I don't mean that in a derogatory way, but they tend to be from lower socioeconomic backgrounds and, among other things, they are not particularly well read or educated. Their thinking about a woman's place is even more strongly stereotyped than other women in their same age bracket who have broader, more sophisticated backgrounds.

"Prisons are just a microcosm of larger society, so, like everywhere else, there is a great deal of friction between the older women and the new 'lib' type we are currently getting. Perhaps that friction is a bit more intense here than on the outside."

Marge will not tolerate the mention of women's liberation; she considers it synonymous with lesbian. She feels that "women's lib" is an organization of "kooks," and scoffs at the mention of any connection between her latest criminal actions and the beliefs of the female emancipation movement. Ironically, her feelings are similar to those expressed by countless prison administrators, police officials, and other law-enforcement authorities who believe that the women's liberation movement is in no way connected to the sharply rising crime rate of women in America. Indeed, many of them won't admit that such a female crime wave even exists. The facts, however, show not only that it exists, but also that it is growing at an alarming rate.

Part of the difficulty in understanding changes in female crime stems from the blind spots which have obstructed society's vision of women in general. Throughout centuries of male domination, even men of good will have persistently tried to unravel the mystery of women as if women were a species apart, as if women did not share the male need for status and security. If mystery there is, it is why men have been unaware that women have the same basic motivations as men; why they have exaggerated whatever natural differences may exist between the sexes; and why they have all the while pretended in their most self-righteous Henry Higgins manner that they really wanted women to be like men. The understanding of women has been unnecessarily mystified because we have reasoned backward from the observation that their techniques and approaches (wiles, if you will) are different from men's, to the unwarranted conclusion that they have basically different motivations and goals.

Once such mental sets become established, they are difficult to eradicate, for several reasons: they preserve the power structure of the male hierarchy; they form a thought pattern which tends to limit observations and speculations to preformed notions; and they are inherently satisfying as security mechanisms even to the disadvantaged group. It is little wonder that women are an enigma, if not anathema, to themselves and others.

"The fundamental fault of the female character," declared Schopenhauer, "is that it has no sense of justice." Women have been presented as being childish, devious, indirect, petty, seductive, inappropriately domineering, and incomprehensibly manipulative. It is not difficult to see that, aside from total submission, these are the only options available to the weak in dealing with the strong. To believe that these techniques are preferred by women when the more direct masculine approaches are available is to miss the point of female psychology—namely, that there is no female psychology different from the human psychology which also governs men. Ibsen's Nora said it simply and completely: "I believe that before all else, I am a human being." Not surprisingly, it took a woman, Karen Horney, to dispute Sigmund Freud's assumption that women labored through life under the spell of penis envy. It is not man's penis that a woman strives for but his power, and until recently the only way to achieve that has been through apparently paradoxical indirection. The phrase "she stoops to conquer," from the title of Oliver Goldsmith's play, perhaps sums up the method and the madness of women.

Interesting analogies to traditional man-woman relationships may be seen in the behavior of our closest animal relatives, the social primates. Like humans, and perhaps in response to similar biological imperatives,[1] they form structured social organizations in which emotional security and high status appear to be synonymous. Among subhuman primates where size and muscle mass usually determine dominance,[2] mature males are the dominant sex and the position of females is primarily determined by their ability to consort with and maintain relationships with high-ranking males. This is necessarily so where muscle is the arbiter of power. The parallels to human society are clear; but so are the differences, for technology has been redefining the criteria for power.

Men have historically achieved individual status through their domination of other men, labeling them in such a way that they could be perceived as not fully human and, therefore, not entitled to human rights and dignity. Men as a group have done the same to women. The primary access that women have had to status has been through men, and the price they paid was conformity to male standards for femininity—not only in how they should act, but also in how they should think and feel. For her pains, a woman was often allowed to stand close, but rarely high. Tragically, she was playing a game of submission she could not win. The more closely she approximated the mold of femininity, the less she was respected as a person in her own right. Tennyson paternalistically dubbed her "the lesser man," and La Bruyère contemptuously declared that "women have no moral sense; they rely for their behavior upon the men they love." This notion was as injurious as it was uncharitable because it led the woman as well as the man into thinking about her as an inexplicable and irrational contradiction. What other choice did she have?

All that is changing. Women are no longer behaving like subhuman primates with only one option. Medical, educational, economic, political, and technological advances have freed women from unwanted pregnancies, provided them with male occupational skills, and equalized their strength with weapons. Is it any wonder that once women were armed with male opportunities they should strive for status, criminal as well as civil, through established male hierarchial channels? The fact that women are surging so readily into male positions suggests that role playing is no more congenial to their nature than it is to men's. As with the landmark judicial decisions which broadened civil liberties for whites as well as blacks, the liberation of women has necessarily liberated men from fixed and unnatural postures.

The question we should be asking is not why women are committing male crimes, but what has taken them so long to start and why is the time now propitious. From this perspective, women are no more enigmatic than men. Like other oppressed classes they have always had the same aspirations as the dominant class but, lacking direct means, have utilized ploys, ruses, and indirection.[3] Their resort to petty social gambits and petty crimes was a reflection more of their petty strengths than their petty drives.

"It was the radios that changed things for me: like I got a whole new look at what I was doing," said a female inmate at a California prison. Sentenced in connection with a number of drug and drug-related charges, she said that she had supported her drug addiction in part by working as a prostitute. And, according to her account, she had also moonlighted as a shoplifter . . . for a start.

"I needed more money, you know, and I was always taking these small transistor radios because there was this guy who would take all the radios I could give him for five or ten dollars each. So I needed more money for drugs, and the only thing I could think of at first was 'take more radios.' Then one day it hit me. Wow! It was weird. What the hell was I doing just taking radios all these months? I was knocking myself out for a bunch of five-buck radios. I don't know what it was at the time, but like, I couldn't see myself taking anything other than that. Like I had a block or something. Then it was like a flash. I got with a friend—she was strung out too—and we started taking color-TV sets. We got them from the loading docks of a couple of stores which left them sitting there for a while if you caught the trucks just right. We just picked one up and pushed it into the trunk and drove off. I got about a dozen of them until I got busted, you know, on the drug thing.

"I can see it now . . . how dumb I was. I mean, if I was going to rip something off, why the hell didn't I take Cadillacs for all that time instead of some goddamned radios? It took me a long while to see that. A long while."

Women are no longer indentured to the kitchens, baby carriages, or bedrooms of America. The skein of myths about women is unraveling, the chains have been pried loose, and there will be no turning back to the days when women found it necessary to justify their existence by producing babies or cleaning houses. Allowed their freedom for the first time, women—by the tens of thousands—have chosen to desert those kitchens and plunge exuberantly into the formerly all-male quarters of the working world.

There are now female admirals, longshorewomen, stevedores, and seagoing sailors (tattoos and all); there are policewomen patrolling in one-person cars, women FBI agents, and female sky marshals. Women can now be found clinging to telephone poles as installers and line workers; peering from behind acetylene welding torches and seated behind the wheels of over-the-road tractor-trailer trucks. They can be found at work as fork-lift drivers and crane operators, pipe fitters and carpenters, mail carriers and morticians, commercial airline pilots and jet-engine mechanics. Women now serve as Congressional pages. They have run for, and won, a substantial number of powerful positions throughout the American political system; and ever-increasing numbers of women continue to become judges, lawyers, and high-level executives in industry and government.

On the lighter side, many women have produced an almost carnival-like atmosphere in breaking through the discrimination barriers in such bastions of male supremacy as the Clam Broth House of Hoboken and McSorley's Old Ale House in Manhattan. They have burned their bras and staged hundreds of theater-of-the-absurd antics to dramatize their point. But these stag-bar crashers and sign-wavers are few compared with the waves of women who have quietly and effectively set up shop in a wide variety of job fields across the nation.

To be sure, the gains grow slowly, and sometimes painfully, but nevertheless women are pushing their way into—and succeeding at—innumerable jobs, occupations, and positions traditionally thought to be "for men only"! Between 1900 and 1972 the percentage of females in the total labor force has risen from 18 per cent to 37 per cent, remaining stable at about 23 per cent between 1900 and 1940, but rapidly accelerating during World War II and continuing to rise at a steady rate.[4]

But women, like men, do not live by bread alone. Almost every other aspect of their life has been similarly altered. The changing status of women as it affects family, marriage, employment, and social position has been well documented by all types of sociologists.[5] But there is a curious hiatus: the movement for full equality has a darker side which has been slighted even by the scientific community. In a recent issue of a respected sociology journal devoted entirely to the changing role of females in a changing society, not one of the twenty-one papers dealt with female criminality.[6] Therefore, it should not be surprising that this shady aspect of liberation has also escaped the scrutiny of the media, of the general public, and even of the law-enforcement agencies which have the advantage of early contact.

In the same way that women are demanding equal opportunity in fields of legitimate endeavor, a similar number of determined women are forcing their way into the world of major crimes.

· A Florida female parolee: "I don't think women are sitting down and saying, 'Oh, gee, I'll be liberated. I'll rob a bank.' Things are different today. I was living alone for years. It wasn't any real thought of 'liberation' that had to do with what I was doing. I wanted the money. If I was going to put myself out, I intended to aim as high as I could. I got caught, but a lot of others don't. Off the record I'll tell you, they'd never pinch me again because I've learned a lot now. I'd be a lot more careful."

· A Pennsylvania female inmate: "I'm not the only one. I know a lot of sisters who got tired of hanging with some dude who took all their money while they took all the heat that was coming down. I know one sister—she cut her pimp up over a five-dollar bill. It wasn't the money, see. It just got to be too much for her. I get out of here and you better believe that no man's going to do a thing on me again. I don't need them. I got it together for myself now. I can handle my own action."

· A Chicago female inmate: "It's like what they say, you know, about mountains. You climb them because they're there. Well, that's the way it is with banks and department stores; that's where the money is.

It's not a question of whether you're a man or a woman. It's a question of money. That's it. Money."

It is this segment of women who are pushing into—and succeeding at—crimes which were formerly committed by males only. Females like Marge are now being found not only robbing banks single-handedly, but also committing assorted armed robberies, muggings, loan-sharking operations, extortion, murders, and a wide variety of other aggressive, violence-oriented crimes which previously involved only men.

Like her sisters in legitimate fields, the female criminal is fighting for her niche in the hierarchy, for, curiously enough, the barriers of male chauvinism in some areas of criminal activity are no less formidable than those which confront female newcomers in the world of business. There is, perhaps, no more macho group than the traditional "family" units of organized crime. "It was just a while ago that we got our first female loan shark here in the city," said a New York assistant district attorney. "That was something new. That was strictly an organized crime thing in the past. She was a free-lancer, though. Even today, you don't get women operating on that level with the mob. They wouldn't stand for it. In a lot of ways they are a very conservative bunch of guys."

In a book which probes the inner logistics of the Mafia, Nicholas Gage points out the strict roles which are currently allowed for women with syndicate families:

> In the Mafia a woman may be a means to a profitable alliance with another Mafia "family"; a showcase for displaying her husband's wealth, status, and power; a valuable piece of property; a loyal helpmate; a good cook; a showy and ego-boosting mistress. But what she may never be is a liberated woman.[7]

Given the status of women in the Mafia, the organization clearly has a long way to go before it can be considered an equal-opportunity employer. While it is not likely that we will see the ascension of a family "Godmother" in the near future, it does appear certain that the status of women in the Mafia may well change, if only for purely pragmatic reasons. The mob, like other successful organizations, reacts to competition and accomplishment. They are not likely to ignore the increasing numbers of women who are using guns, knives, and wits to establish themselves as full human beings, as capable of violence and aggression as any man.

By every indicator available, female criminals appear to be surpassing males in the rate of increase for almost every major crime. Although males continue to commit the greater absolute number of offenses, it is the women who are committing those same crimes at yearly rates of increase now running as high as six and seven times faster than males.[8]

Like her legitimate-based sister, the female criminal knows too much to pretend, or return to her former role as a second-rate criminal confined to "feminine" crimes such as shoplifting and prostitution. She has had a taste of financial victory. In some cases, she has had a taste of blood. Her appetite, however, appears to be only whetted.

"Crime is like anything else; the people learn and explore wider areas as they go along and gain confidence," explained a Los Angeles police lieutenant, who was openly dismayed while speaking of the increasing numbers of women being brought into his station house. "You know how it is with a child . . . you can watch it grow and develop. It's like that with women we're getting. First it was a shock to be getting so many females. Now it's repeaters. You can see them grow in confidence. Like they opened a new door and realized all of a sudden that they can walk through it. The second time, they don't hesitate; they barge right in. The only way I can think to describe it is that it's like a lion cub. O.K., it gets its first taste of red meat. It doesn't wait to be fed any longer. It goes out and begins to learn how to hunt. That is what I see with a lot of these women. They've had the taste. It's not as hard as they thought to hit a drugstore or whatever. They'll go into the slammer with others and they learn to be better as criminals. It's started now and you can't break the cycle. You can only wish it hadn't started."

The extent to which women have thrown themselves into criminal endeavors can be approximated from the FBI's yearly Uniform

Crime Reports, the closest thing the United States has to a comprehensive national statistical overview of its crime situation. In spite of a number of methodological problems [9]—such as a variability in number and distribution of sources, erratic reporting, and inconsistencies in adhering to a universal code of crime definitions—these statistics nevertheless suggest broad trends of criminal behavior on a national scale. During the twelve years from 1960 through 1972, the FBI monitored 2430 law-enforcement agencies across the country, recording the number and causes for all arrests. While arrests are not synonymous with crimes, they are generally a reliable indication that a crime has been committed. As one might expect, the absolute number of males arrested exceeds that of females, but what is noteworthy is that the arrest rate among females is rising nearly three times faster than males. During the twelve-year period between 1960 and 1972 the number of women arrested for robbery rose by 277 per cent, while the male figure rose 169 per cent. Dramatic differences are found in embezzlement (up 280 per cent for women, 50 per cent for men), larceny (up 303 per cent for women, 82 per cent for men), and burglary (up 168 per cent for women, 63 per cent for men).[10] Except for parity in the categories of murder and aggravated assault, the picture of female arrest rates rising several times faster than male arrest rates is a consistent one for all offenses.

Murder and aggravated assault, curiously, remain the exceptions. In these categories, the rates of men are not significantly different from those of women, although both are rising. Since these are primarily crimes of passion in which well over half of the victim-offender relationships are interpersonal,[11] as opposed to the economically motivated offenses, it would appear that the liberated female criminals, like their male counterparts, are chiefly interested in improving their financial circumstances and only secondarily in committing violence.

A thirty-eight-year-old Miami, Florida, woman currently on parole explains: "I had a gun when I went into this one place . . . it was a motel. But I never would have used it. I wanted the cash. I didn't want to hurt anyone. Most places employees understand that. They give you the cash quietly. They understand what's going on . . . you're not out to get them, you just want the money. It's a transaction between you and a large institution. There is no reason why they should get hurt. I think most of the people in the joint [jail] work the same way. It's not like they get a gun and decide to kill someone to get some money. Most are sorry that they even had a gun with them. It's harder that way when you get busted. There are some who are into the guns; who'll blast someone just for the hell of it, but they're a separate breed. Most of us are just in it for the bread. That's all. Guns, knives, and the rest are a sort of necessary window dressing . . . which at times can get out of hand."

Reports from other countries confirm the American experience that as the social and economic disparity between the sexes diminishes, there is a reciprocal increase in female crime.[12] Western Europe and New Zealand, for example, where women enjoy a high degree of equality with men, also report a rise in female criminality. The disparities between the male and female crime rate are now even narrowing in developing countries such as India, where the social distance between the sexes has traditionally been greater.

Some criminologists [13] believe that this principle applies equally well to different groups within a nation. Black males and females, for instance, are more similar in their crime rates than their white counterparts, and they are also closer in their social standing to each other than are white males and females. Black women never fought for this position of parity vis-à-vis their men —economic necessity dictated the terms of the pecking order. These examples serve to verify the proposition that women are psychologically more similar to than different from men and that they are best understood as fellow humans than as a group apart.

If the adult arrest rates say anything about what is happening now, the crime rates for persons under eighteen say something perhaps even more about the woman of the future. The criminal behavior of the female juvenile closely parallels that of her adult sister,[14] portending a protracted association between females and crime. During the period between 1960 and 1972 the number of females under eighteen arrested for robbery jumped by 508 per cent, while the juvenile male figure rose 250 per cent. Likewise, other figures mounted: larceny (up 334 per cent for girls, 84 per cent for boys), burglary (up 177 per cent for girls, 70 per cent for boys), auto theft (up 110 per cent for girls, 38 per cent for boys). In this area, at least, there is no generation gap. Similar to their adult counterparts, there was no significant difference in the arrest increase for murder between males and females, suggesting that economic goals take precedence over violent ones for little sister also.

Aside from the victims, the people most directly and dangerously involved with criminals are the police. They work at the crossroads of the criminal world and society at large, and therefore give us a unique perspective, which has the advantage of being formed from direct contact with the events.

Lieutenant Peter Quinn has spent the last fifteen years with the New York City police force. Quinn's is a city notorious for having the worst happen first. What occurs criminally, as well as culturally, in New York City has an uncanny habit of being a harbinger of things to come in the rest of the country.

"Oh, it's been very obvious to me over these last years that something is happening out there," said the lieutenant, motioning toward the window in his office at the 77th Precinct Headquarters. Outside, the Bedford-Stuyvesant section was teeming in the noonday sun. "We're seeing more and more women all the time. I never really thought much about it . . . as a trend, I mean. I suppose it has to do with women's own image of themselves . . . you know, women know more about what they want, and they want more of the things that men used to have. Whatever the reasons, we see a lot more women purse snatchers, robbers, and a lot more mixed robbery teams, with men and women working as equal partners. Before, it would be only men.

"Even so," Quinn continued, "we're all still a bit less suspicious of women than we are of men. That may change, though, in the future. . . . Like I remember a few years ago, when you would have hesitated to ever put handcuffs on a woman. Not today . . . you *have* to put cuffs on them now. They'll get you just like any man will, if you don't. They've proved that to me."

A less official, perhaps, but no less authoritative view of what is happening to women can be heard from the taxi drivers who must drive in Quinn's area, as well as throughout the rest of the city. "Now I don't come here during the night," explained one driver headed out of Bedford-Stuyvesant. "I know the law says you gotta take fares anywhere, but not me. I don't get killed to collect a salary for nobody. And it ain't just men. Twice I've had women trying to pull something on me in the last year. They had guns, the whole works. And that ain't just me talking. Go see the other drivers around town . . . see if they ain't been hit by women. It's gotten awful here lately. You can't trust nobody. Men, women, they're all the same. Don't trust none of them."

In midtown New York, at the police administration building on Broome Street, Lieutenant Lucy Acerra told a similar story. The lieutenant is coordinator of the eight precincts in the city which have female police officers. In her twenty years on the force she has come in contact with innumerable woman offenders.

"Now today, the majority of women you see are narcotic addicts. But even they have changed . . . their attitude about themselves, the world. Years ago, you'd have a female addict, she'd be docile, almost embarrassed. Very quiet. Today . . . they come in the door screaming and never let up. They are much more demanding than ever before."

Not far away from Acerra's office, another lieutenant in the district attorney's office shook his head while telling how the city recently apprehended its first female loan shark. It is an indication that women are getting into the nitty-gritty, big-time underworld type of operation.

During the 1971–1972 period, 3742 cities across the country reported figures similar to those which troubled New York.[15] Each had its regional peculiarities, but the basic theme was the same. In that year, arrests for index crimes (those crimes considered by the FBI to be serious and to have high reportability) of urban males under eighteen decreased by 1 per cent, while female juveniles increased by 6 per cent. For adults, the picture was similar— males dropping by 0.1 per cent and females rising by 6 per cent. Nor was this trend confined to the cities. Out past the suburbs into the traditionally conservative areas, female arrests for major crimes increased by 14 per cent, while males declined by 0.2 per cent.[16] Clearly, the same drama was playing to different crowds, city by city and section by section, across the country—and the villain in each case was the female.

In 1968, the women of America passed something of a milestone in their criminal development: while their crime rate on all fronts was quietly increasing, the first of their number made her way onto the FBI's infamous "ten most wanted" list.[17] The list had been in existence since 1950 and had never included a woman before. So on December 28, 1968, it was a novelty to see Ruth Eisemann-Schier's name added for her part in a ransom-kidnaping. But the novelty soon wore off. Five months later the second woman, Marie Dean Arrington, appeared on the list. A convicted murderer, she was sought for escaping from a Florida prison farm—she had scaled two barbed-wire fences and disappeared. Since that time, the inclusion of women on the "ten most wanted" list has become normal procedure. During the past few years, women included on the list have been wanted for murder, bank robbery, kidnaping, and a variety of violent, revolutionary acts.[18]

This new national wave crested early in 1974 with the alleged kidnaping of newspaper heiress Patricia Hearst, who was later apparently converted into an enthusiastic member of the Symbionese Liberation Army. The bizarre, tumultuous, and seemingly short-lived era of the SLA may have marked a major turning point for American women. It was the peak of the movement of radically politicized females away from the historical quiescence which so characterized the preceding "silent generation" of the 1950s. In the 1960s, America became aware that increasing numbers of women were involved in the tide of social revolution that was spreading across the country, often in the form of riots, student strikes, and other types of urban guerrilla warfare. By the 1970s, it had become even more apparent that what was occurring was a revolution within a revolution. Despite their broad political pronouncements, what the new revolutionaries wanted was not simply urban social gains, but sexual equality. With a good deal of humor, the media noted that the notorious and highly violence-prone "weathermen" of the late 1960s changed their name to the unisexual "Weather Underground" in the 1970s. It was no longer humorous, however, when that same revolutionary feminism began to manifest itself in the persons of such women as Nancy Ling Perry, Patricia Soltysik, and Camilla Hall.

These three women—all white, middle-class, and highly educated—were the formative core of the Symbionese Liberation Army, a group of no more than a dozen, which distinguished itself with an ongoing demolition derby of blazing guns and falling bodies up and down the California coast. Along with their barrage of volatile rhetoric, their actions included ravaging banks, robbing commercial establishments, and assassinating victims with cyanide-tipped bullets. While the entire world watched on TV, the SLA surfaced for its criminal activities seemingly at will, only to sink into hiding again, easily evading one of the largest and most intense manhunts ever organized in the country's history. Curiously, the national reaction to the SLA's maniacal escapades seemed to focus less on the actual violence than on the group's truly unique sexual emphasis. While "Field Marshal Cinque" was initially heralded as the "leader" of the SLA, authorities soon came to believe otherwise. Cinque was quickly identified as Donald DeFreeze, a black man who had recently escaped from jail. As police uncovered some of the former hiding places of the SLA, it became apparent that the women who had organized the group had decided that it was a symbolic necessity for a Third World revolutionary cadre to be headed by a black male. DeFreeze was the chosen figurehead. But proof of the feminine leadership was found in much of the voluminous written material recovered from various hideouts of the SLA —the phrase "men and women" in various literary tracts was edited to read "women and men."

The group's chief theorist was Patricia Soltysik, who, in background and temperament, was quite typical of other SLA women. The daughter of a well-to-do pharmacist, an honor student in high school prior to winning a scholarship to Berkeley, she was described by former teachers as "a born leader," "a tough competitor," and "unstoppable." [19] By traditional standards of scholastic achievement and physical charm, she was an All-American Girl before she was radicalized. That such women turned so drastically toward a new and highly volatile identity caused a good portion of the nation to ask incredulously, "How could women do this sort of thing?" Perhaps the question itself was the very point of the episode. The fires which consumed the ramshackle Los Angeles house where the small band staged its last shoot-out also burned away a large part of the prevailing American illusions about women.

Women's unaccustomed involvement in crimes which require high levels of violence or potential violence is not limited to the sensational, but can be seen in other, less publicized areas. In the cities, for instance, young girls are now taking to the streets just as boys have traditionally done. It has now become quite common for adolescent girls to participate in muggings, burglaries, and extortion rings which prey on schoolmates. Perhaps the most telling sign of change on this level can be found in a closer inspection of the gangs which have terrorized cities for years. Gang activity is no longer the all-male domain it once was. Girls can now be found participating in all gang activities with a greater degree of equality. Indeed, in New York City there are currently two all-girl gangs.[20] In London, where British statistics reflect a similar female crime wave, female adolescents have become a problem of major proportions.[21]

In one Piccadilly Circus incident, several young women attacked and severely beat a business executive. After taking the man's wallet and watch, the females—described later as being "in their late teens or early twenties"—attacked another man who attempted to aid the victim. That man fled. Finally, the women were approached by a lone, uniformed law officer whom they also managed to knock unconscious before they made their successful escape from the scene. Scotland Yard and public officials have recently been voicing alarm and dismay about these gangs of young girls, now numbering in the dozens, who roam the city streets.[22] Armed with switchblades, razors, clubs, and fists, their members are known to delight in "granny bashing," the attack of elderly ladies, usually at night.

Throughout the United States also, it appears that other ladies of the streets are assuming a more aggressive attitude toward the world. Prostitutes—formerly considered docile body-peddlers—are now taking a much harder line toward their work and clients. In

New York City and other major urban areas, hookers who have taken to mugging people on the sidewalk have become a substantial police problem. Streetwalkers from coast to coast—a large percentage of whom are now narcotic addicts—are demonstrating a new willingness to moonlight on their primary occupation and supplement their income by "rolling" their "marks" or sticking up innocent passersby.

In recent years, the prostitutes of New York have been in the headlines for a number of sensational crimes: Pasquale Bottero, an Italian glass-company executive, was stabbed to death by prostitutes outside the New York Hilton; Charles Addams, the cartoonist, rebuffed two streetwalkers' advances and received a splash of acid in his face; Franz Josef Strauss, the former defense minister of West Germany, was severely beaten and robbed near the Plaza Hotel by hookers. And these are only the headline-worthy instances.

Aside from such obvious examples of the changing way that women relate to the world, numerous other signs, somewhat more subtle but no less important, indicate where women are going. For one thing, along with killing other people more often than before, women are now taking their own lives at a steadily increasing rate. Women accounted for 35 per cent of the successful suicide attempts in Los Angeles in 1960; [23] by 1970, the figure had risen to 45 per cent, and it continues to rise.

The suicide rate is just one indicator of the inner conflicts which women are undergoing at this time, conflicts which affect their propensities toward behavior patterns which are, if not fully criminal, at least marginally deviant. In a recent study of women's role in modern society and its relation to stress, it was found that women were suffering higher rates of mental illness than men.[24] Apparently, they are having a more difficult time coping with the new status for which they strive. This is also evident in the number of women who are now dying from, or being treated for, coronary and other stress-related ailments previously thought to be "male diseases." These inner conflicts are also causing more women to involve themselves not only in divorces, but also in an unprecedented number of family desertions. Marriage counselors, psychiatrists, and detective agencies report that more women than ever before are simply walking out and leaving husband and children behind. A mother who deserted her family was unheard of a decade ago, although the practice was quite frequent among men.

Thus it is that in the middle third of the twentieth century, we are witnessing the simultaneous rise and fall of women. Rosie the Riveter of World War II vintage has become Robin the Rioter or Rhoda the Robber in the Vietnam era. Women have lost more than their chains. For better and worse, they have lost many of the restraints which kept them within the law.

The forces that have propelled females into parity with males have been as blind as justice to which side of the law they landed on. The increase in the incidence of suicide and of previously "male" psychosomatic illnesses, such as ulcers and hypertension, are some indication of the price in stress and stress-induced breakdowns that women have paid for this rite of passage. Women —criminals and legitimate workers alike—are caught up in the gears of a society which is skidding into a drastic turn, and, inevitably, some of those gears—and their cogs—are going to be broken before the turn is completed and a steady course is once again established. Increasing numbers of broken gears and bits of flying debris will be found leaping from bridges, wandering desolate city streets, and entering banks with pistols in their pockets. If our society is going to protect itself from them—as well as offer them any meaningful help once they are apprehended—it must make an effort to understand what makes females criminal. It must understand that criminal women are first human, second female, and third criminal. No one of these facets of their existence can b⁻ properly understood without the other.

• An inmate at Muncy prison which has recently gone coed, integrating males into a formerly all-female population: "I felt a real change when they brought men here. I think the whole place did. After a while, I was starting to feel like a machine. Sometimes I didn't even take a shower for days. It wasn't that I wanted to be dirty, but after a while you get to feeling, like who really gives a shit what you look like in this joint. It was like I had given up on myself. Then they brought some men in. Now I got a husband outside, so it's not like I'm going to try to make one of the new guys. But just being around them made me feel alive again. I even began with the make-up and all again. I felt, well, like a human instead of a machine or something."

A counselor at Purdy prison in Washington State, where the female inmates are regularly taken to outside social affairs to mingle with males from a nearby prison farm: "It's like a breath of life to the girls. You can see it. That's what has to be remembered. O.K., these people are criminals, but they are also humans and women with a very strong need to feel like women. It can make or break their whole attitude for the rest of their life."

The women of America underwent soul-shaking changes in the 1960s. By the end of that decade, the drive which began as sporadic protests had become a trend—"women's liberation" emerged as a well-publicized, well-organized movement, complete with slogans, dues, and membership cards. Most of the country came to identify the entire female emancipation effort with that organized and highly vocal group known as "women libbers," but the actual "lib" organizations are only the tip of the iceberg. The impetus for women's rights and equality of the sexes began in earnest in that decade. At that time it was unheralded as a movement, unseen as an organizational process, and unappreciated as a social revolution. Such a trend did not gain its popularity or momentum because of a sudden, spontaneous recognition of the oppression of women. Rather, the new, broad-based awareness of women's place and potential developed side by side with the civil-rights and antiwar movements, confirming Karl Marx's contention that "social progress can be measured with precision by the social position of the female sex."

In the early sixties, civil-rights actions swirled across the country with the fervor of a revitalization movement, challenging Americans to reaffirm their commitment to equality before the law, and redefining that equality to include those previously alienated by color or age or sex. Man's characteristic tendency to assign other people—whether they were Asians, blacks, young, poor, or women

—to a subhuman status which barred them from equal protection under law was the real issue of the civil-rights movements, and women were now ready to recognize their stake in it. Why this moment was propitious for recognition is difficult to say. The theme of women as a suppressed social class had been carefully documented in 1953 by Simone de Beauvoir in her book *The Second Sex*, but it failed to develop as a serious national concern until the mid-sixties. America of the mid-sixties was rife with disillusionment and ripe for change. We were fighting what Omar Bradley called "the wrong war at the wrong place at the wrong time, and with the wrong enemy"—liberals were adding, "for the wrong reason." In this climate of disillusionment with leadership that was white, male, and over thirty, change was inevitable, and the seeds of liberation rooted in fertile soil. By the decade's end, large numbers of American women in all walks of life had begun to see themselves as Betty Friedan had portrayed them in *The Feminine Mystique:* a systematically and subtly suppressed majority whose real security lay in the strength of their own right arm, and whose time of delivery had arrived.

Many of these believers gravitated to organizations such as NOW, the National Organization for Women, which has a current membership of 18,000 in 255 chapters in 48 states.[25] The women's liberation movements suffered several distortions in the press and, at the same time, added a few bruises to its own image via the actions of a few of its more outspoken members. Hence, "women's lib" came to designate—perhaps for the majority of Americans— organized groups of women who were primarily shrill-voiced witches with clenched fists and slovenly, unloosed breasts. Not so today.

There was, and is, more to women's lib. Much more. And the portrait is changing. The organization and its goals are becoming separated from its antiquated image. There is an ever-growing national awareness of women's rights which is perhaps best described as the "new feminism." The new feminism is not an organized movement, it does not hold meetings or press conferences. It is an all-pervasive consciousness which has permeated to virtually every level of womanhood in America.

The new feminism pertains to the women who may deny any sympathy for the formalized action, but who have recently secured their first job since marriage or decided to go back to school. It applies to the women who stanchly defend their "right to be feminine," and their right to define "feminine" as a variety of human rather than as a complement of masculine. They are standing up and speaking without apology at parent-teacher meetings, they are organizing demonstrations, walking picket lines, and influencing decisions at all levels of their community. It includes the nuns who are asking for rights more closely aligned with the rights which priests enjoy, and the housewives who have come to expect their husbands to share more of the duties of the home. It also means sexually honest women who expect the same orgastic satisfaction as men, and who are requiring that men do something about it. And most relevant to our subject, it describes the women who have concluded that prostitution and shoplifting are not their style: embezzlement, robbery, and assault are more congenial to their self-image.

"You wouldn't catch me doing no boosting," said one female inmate in New York who was somewhat offended by the inference that she might have been a shoplifter. The woman—in her late twenties—found the idea of shoplifting or "boosting" undignified. She did not like "small stuff." Records say she was involved in a robbery of a large movie-theater ticket office. Other inmates privately related that the same woman was nearly killed in recent underworld warfare which broke out when she was thought to have "ripped off" a local heroin dealer for a few thousand dollars' worth of his product. The others spoke of her escapades with envy and obvious admiration.

The entrance of women into the major leagues of crime underscores the point that the incidence and kinds of crime are more closely associated with social than sexual factors. This is so for at least three reasons. First, while cupidity may be universal, ability and opportunity are less evenly distributed. Housewives might pilfer from the supermarket while doing the grocery shopping, but could not embezzle from a corporation unless they work out of the executive office. Secondly, since a crime is a transgression as socially defined by the group in power, authorities are prone to overlook upper-class practices and lean a bit too heavily on the lower class. "The law," declared Anatole France, "forbids the rich as well as the poor from sleeping under bridges and stealing bread in the marketplace." Arrests for prostitution are a pertinent example. If sex on the open market is an illegal commodity, then penalties should fall on the buyer as well as the seller, particularly if it can be established that the buyer understood the nature of the transaction and was a material participant. But such is not the case. While prostitution continues to be a crime for which a significant number of women are arrested every year, the number of males arrested for consorting with prostitutes is so small that it does not even merit a special category in the Uniform Crime Reports. The third reason why kinds of crimes are more closely linked with social roles than sex has to do with mental sets. According to the group-system hypothesis,[26] behavior is directed by a largely conscious desire to please one's own significant groups, and by a predominantly unconscious tendency to conform to an early ingrained set of attitudes. So decisive is this set for the way we think and feel and act that few people breach its boundaries, even in imagination, even in deviance. We go crazy and we go criminal along the well-worn paths that our "mazeway" has constructed for us. Running amuck is not something that Bostonians do, nor do sex-kittens rob banks—they peddle their bodies as untold generations of sex-kittens before them have done. How else can we understand the female (or, for that matter, male) offender except in the context of her social role? The mother becomes the child-beater, the shopper the shoplifter, and the sex-object the prostitute. Adolescent girls have a particularly difficult task because they are attempting to negotiate puberty with nowhere near the spatial and sexual freedom of males. That they often deviate outside their narrow confines is understandable.

In the emergence of women as a socially rising group, we are witnessing an interesting phenomenon which has implications for other upwardly mobile groups. As they become more visible in positions of prestige and power, they receive more attention from the media, and are thus further bolstered in their rising achievement. Old mental sets of devaluation and self-contempt gradually yield to new ones of pride, and sometimes an overcompensating arrogance. Black shifts from denigration to beautiful. Sexually active bachelor women are no longer "ruined" but "free" or, at the very least, "the ruined Maid," as Thomas Hardy described her, exacts no small tribute of envy from her raw country sister. How quaint seem the fallen women of literature—the Charlotte Temples and Hester Prynnes and Catherine Barkleys—who earned red letters or died in childbirth to mark well for generations of women the evils of extramarital sex. They are quaint because women are increasingly imitating men's attitude toward sex rather than submitting to one he designed for her, and they are quaint because sex is no longer the best road out of the female ghetto. In her education, in her jobs, and in her crimes she has found much faster routes to travel. The journey, relatively speaking, has just begun. While the rate of increase of major crimes for women is surpassing that for males, the data [27] still provide some justification for the epithet "fair sex" in that men continue to commit the majority of crimes, and that the highest proportion of females are still arrested for larceny, primarily shoplifting.[28]

However, even here a comparison of figures for 1960 and 1972 shows an unmistakable across-the-board trend. Females are cutting themselves in for a bigger piece of the pie in every category but murder and, in a few—like the subtotal for major crimes, forgery and counterfeiting, and fraud and embezzlement—that piece is 80 to 100 per cent bigger than it had been twelve years before.

In summary, what we have described is a gradual but accelerating social revolution in which women are closing many of the gaps, social and criminal, that have separated them from men. The closer they get, the more alike they look and act. This is not to suggest that there are no inherent differences. Differences do exist and will be elaborated later in this book, but it seems clear that those differences are not of prime importance in understanding female criminality. The simplest and most accurate way to grasp the essence of women's changing patterns is to discard dated notions of femininity. That is a role that fewer and fewer women are willing to play. In the final analysis, women criminals are human beings who have basic needs and abilities and opportunities. Over the years these needs have not changed, nor will they. But women's abilities and opportunities have multiplied, resulting in a kaleidoscope of changing patterns whose final configuration will be fateful for all of us.

2

Female Passivity:
Genetic Fact or Cultural Myth?

Man for the field and woman for the hearth:
Man for the sword and for the needle she:
Man with the head and woman with the heart:
Man to command and woman to obey;
All else confusion.

—Alfred Lord Tennyson
"The Princess"

It is not only by the questions we have answered that progress may be measured, but also by those we are still asking. The passionate controversies of one era are viewed as sterile preoccupations by another, for knowledge alters what we seek as well as what we find. The apparent dichotomies which separated schools of human behavior into nature vs. nurture, and heredity vs. environment, and innate vs. learned have been shown to rest on simplistic concepts and specious arguments—and now each side is recognized to be an integral part of the other. But it wasn't always so. Early criminologists pursued the elusive biological basis underlying female criminality with the same enthusiasm as knights questing for the Holy Grail—and with the same disheartening results.

In the mid-1800s Caesar Lombroso, an Italian physician, began dragging home bags full of bones from the prisons of Turin in an effort to discover the presumed anatomical distinctions between criminal and normal women. He had postulated identifiable physical characteristics which he expected to find at autopsy. As often happens in uncontrolled studies, he was not disappointed, but his followers were. He believed that women were born with the innate ability and motivation for certain types of crimes in the same way that men were inherently equipped for certain other types of crimes as a fact of their biology. Zealously, he set out to prove that some women were predestined to be criminals from birth and could be so categorized by their bone structure and other physical features. The benefits of such a theory—had it proven true—were considerable. Those females born with telltale craniums or suspicious femurs could easily be weeded out before they had time to develop into prostitutes, street thieves, or murderesses. Poring over the bones and bodies of hundreds of harlots, pickpockets, and other female ne'er-do-wells who had died in prison, Lombroso carefully measured and recorded their bone structures, particularly jaw diameters and cranial capacities.

Understandably, his research was both a child and a prisoner of the times. It was an era of discovery in medicine. Janssen's microscope had opened up unseen vistas. Pasteur had entered them to discover microorganisms and formulate the germ theory. Pathologists like Virchow were coining words like "pathognomonic" to describe specific organic changes linked to the dysfunction preceding disease, and phrenologists were confident that the measurement of cranial bumps would foretell psychological propensities. In the tenor of the times, it seemed reasonable that one might find the cause for female criminality in the specimens on the dissecting table. Special physical characteristics were indeed discovered: "The most important [conclusions]," Lombroso surmised, "are those which relate to the cranial and orbital capacity, and to the weight and diameter of the jaw, to which add observations on the cheek bones." [1]

Unfortunately, his meticulous and grizzly labors could not generate a viable theory of crime, as they were bound to the erroneous assumption of physical determination. The nineteenth-century version of chivalry which found expression in his efforts sought to link female deviancy to a biological degeneration, thus preserving the pristine picture of normal women. Like other pioneers, he is less remembered for what he found (which was misleading) than for his originality in daring to seek, even though he did show a certain prescience in recognizing that female deviancy may be different from male deviancy.

With the turn of the century, the pursuit of the illusory physical symptoms which were thought to characterize female criminals shifted from the autopsy of dead prisoners to the exhaustive cataloguing of live ones.[2] Concentration centered on vital characteristics—such as mental capacity, physical ability, and disease—and their relationship to distinctive criminal features. Unfortunately, here too the conclusions were marred by lack of controls and dependence upon two unsubstantiated assumptions—to wit, that there were physical differences between criminal and noncriminal women and that physical characteristics are the basic determinants of deviancy. Their data reflected more about the structure of their theory than about the nature of female criminality.

But just as a species evolves through adaptive mutations and natural selection, so do theories. Erroneous hypotheses are not likely to survive, nor to produce further ideas. By the 1930s, the style of scientific thinking had changed radically. Social Darwinism, with its biological atavism, was superseded by a new psychosocial awareness; innovators like Freud in psychiatry and Durkheim in sociology were recasting our picture of ourselves. We were, as evolutionists had declared, indeed animals, but animals with ethereal aspirations as well as biological drives, and we were comprehensible only within the social context which sustained us in sickness as in health, in deviancy as in conformity. These new concepts made it possible to ask different questions about female criminality and to search in different ways for the answers to old questions. The female mind and social condition, as well as her body, became criminologically relevant.[3]

The suggestion that women are inherently as criminally capable as men but that the restrictions of their social role and the opportunity differential vis-à-vis men largely account for the behavioral difference was a departure; traditionally, women were seen to have inherent anatomical, physiological, and psychological weaknesses which made them inevitably lesser criminals. This traditional view, whatever the validity of its theoretical base, could always find support in statistical studies. Men, after all, have always been the world's greatest criminals, in seriousness as well as numbers of offenses. Men dominate crime as they do most areas of social endeavor, and this dominance is not dependent on any specific activities. Margaret Mead reminds us that whatever tasks men engage in, whether managerial or domestic, these tasks are accorded the position of dominance and high status in their culture. In all the varied richness of male and female behaviors, regardless of division of labor, there are two constants: women bear the children and men bear the honors.

> In every known human society, the male's need for achievement can be recognized. Men may cook, or weave, or dress dolls, or hunt humming birds, but if such activities are appropriate occupations of men, then the whole society, men and women alike, votes them as important. When the same occupations are performed by women, they are regarded as less important.[4]

How this discrepancy came to be will be explored presently. For now, suffice it to say that there are hardly any universal male and female roles, only universal dominance and submission status. It would be only slightly whimsical to speculate that if men predominated in prostitution and shoplifting and women in armed robbery and violence, the former would be high crimes and the latter peccadillos. Whether females really commit fewer crimes or they are merely less often reported; whether females are really restricted to minor crimes or the crimes are simply labeled as minor, the statistics are clearly weighted toward males. But this seems to be changing. As we have seen, more and more women have penetrated male enclaves in business, education, politics, and, most relevant to our discussion, crime. The question of whether biological or cultural forces were the chief inhibiting factors in the long delay may soon be settled by events. If the women's liberation movement succeeds in its goal of equality of opportunity and women are allowed to seek their own level, then presumably any sex differences which persisted would be attributable to biology. Some would assert that women would still remain passive, dependent, and fearful;[5] others would assert that they would be every bit the equal of men.[6] Until cultural influences become so evenly distributed that the answer may be found in empirical data, we can only review what is known about the physical, psychological, and social differences between the sexes, with particular emphasis on how they account for the difference in their criminality.

Physical Differences

The historical notions of conception were heavily laden with theories about the natural proclivities of men and women. Aristotle, and later Hippocrates, believed that the fetus resulted from the union of products which each sex contributed, but their contributions were very unequal in character: the male supplied force, activity, movement, strength, and life; the female furnished only weak and passive matter. This is of more than incidental historical interest, because their theories survived in one way or another into modern times and were instrumental in providing a biological rationale for female inferiority.[7] It was, therefore, a shock equivalent to a theological declaration that God was a woman when embryologists discovered that the basic pattern of the embryo was neither male nor undifferentiated nor, as Freud believed, bisexual, but female in structure.[8] It is only after the introduction of male hormones that the complicated steps toward male differentiation ensues from the female anlage (the initial development of the embryo). Without this androgenetic influence the embryo would continue to develop as a female. In terms of the biblical model of special creation, it would be like saying that God created Eve first, then added to her body an androgen-soaked rib to produce a belated Adam.

Unlike the embryonic structure, there is no such female bias at the chromosomal level, where sex determination is set at the moment of conception. At conception, there is a chromosomal differentiation between the sexes which will characterize every cell in the body. The sex-determining pair of chromosomes in the female are identical, and are designated by scientific convention XX. The corresponding male pair contains a Y chromosome not found in females and is designated XY.[9] Thus, at the outset, the males have genetic material which may not be found in females, and females have what might be considered an "insurance" chromosome as a possible hedge against genetic defects.[10] Whether or not the latter is a sufficient explanation, females are indeed less prone than males to such genetic flaws and sex-linked disorders as hemophilia and color-blindness, and their mortality rate in every age group from almost every disease is less than that of males.[11] Clearly, the characterization of females as the "weaker sex" is not justified by such elemental considerations as genetic resistance to defects or long-term survival.

While motor development and muscular strength are more advanced in boys by the age of two years, in practically all physical dimensions girls are larger than boys until sometime between ten and a half and thirteen, when the male growth spurt begins.[12] Beyond that, the differences increase with each step toward maturity until they eventuate in adults with the well-known secondary sex characteristics. Men are heavier-boned and -muscled; females are generally only two-thirds as strong as males and have a lighter skeleton and a broader pelvis.[13] While the musculoskeletal system of males is well suited for physical work and that of females for bearing and nurturing children, the utility of other sex differences is not clear: for example, girls develop greater manual dexterity,[14] have a lower metabolism,[15] quicker and more extreme physiological responses to stress,[16] more flexible adaptation to temperature changes,[17] greater auditory sensitivity to high tones,[18] and distinctive electroencephalographic patterns.[19] Of particular significance is the level of circulating hormones: females exceed males in estrogen production,[20] but have only one-half the androgen and one-sixth the testosterone found in males.[21] Over all, the female physiological organization, including endocrine secretions,[22] muscular coordination, and nervous control, is more irregular than the male and lacks his stability.

Clearly, men and women are not created equal. Just what the direct and indirect psychosocial effects of these physical influences are on female criminality remains somewhat veiled. But in reviewing the major physical, psychological, and social characteristics found to distinguish women from men, I emphasize that it is not possible to understand one apart from the others because together they form a mixture which transcends its original ingredients.

Psychological Differences

As we leave those relatively hard and clear parameters—size, shape, growth curves, metabolic rates, etc.—which characterize the physical differences between the sexes and enter the fields of cognition and affect, we advance into an arena which is more complex to measure, more difficult to trace, and in many instances—for example, aggression [23]—too ambiguous to allow accurate comparisons. While Eve was portrayed as simply more curious or more gullible or less virtuous than Adam, subsequent research has revealed a vastly more complex set of differences. A composite of those studies might portray the contemporary American female as follows:

She started talking in a comprehendible manner at age two (when less than half the boys could do the same) [24] and has been chattering on amiably ever since.[25] She appears to be more amiable than she really is, because she is more prone to flight than fight—especially with dominant males like repairmen. Even if she weren't so fearful of aggression,[26] she would in this instance still be uncharacteristically reticent because, although her disinclination to physical activity pushes her to seek more and more labor-saving household appliances, she has little comprehension of how they work.[27] That is not to say that she couldn't make one—her capacity for fine-hand movements and digital dexterity [28] make her an invaluable asset in the assembly of such precision instruments as cameras and watches. It is unfortunate that she cannot get the better-paying job of designing such instruments, because while she is as bright as the male is,[29] she lacks his aptitude for engineering, science, geometry, and certain kinds of spatial tasks.[30] Perhaps she does not try hard enough to learn because she is not particularly achievement-oriented.[31] Perhaps, also, she is too dependent and conforming [32] and too fearful of taking risks [33] to even wish to escape the assembly line to a position of responsibility. This may be, under the circumstances, wise, because while anxiety tends to improve the performance of men, it crushes women.[34] Most likely the person our amiable female is chatting with is another female, and the most likely content of their conversation is gossip. Not that she is uninterested in church [35] or organizational work, but she has been more interested in people than things since infancy [36] and her point of view is still characteristically more dependent upon interpersonal relationships than high philosophical issues.[37] She is as concerned about maintaining friendships [38] as her husband is about maintaining his car, and she weeps at the thought of hurting someone's feelings.[39] She may also be upset because her husband's fears of infidelity restrict her freedom of movement. They are, for the most part, unwarranted not because she is more moral, but because she is less tempted than he is.[40] She is explaining this to her friend over coffee because she has already given up on explaining it to her husband. He does not understand her.

Unfortunately, he is not alone in his puzzlement. More sophisticated men than he have been exasperated, if not infuriated, by the riddle of femininity. Pope declared, "Woman's at best a contradiction still," [41] and Homer darkly opined that "there is no more trusting in women." Less in anger than in thoughtful bewilderment, Freud concluded, "the great question that has never been answered and which I have not yet been able to answer despite my thirty years of research into the feminine soul, is: What does a woman want?" [42]

It is the same unprofitable question that has been asked from time immemorial about all minority groups and betrays the insensitivity that insists such groups disguise their true needs and conform to their expected needs in order to gain acceptance. The question is analogous to the schizophrenogenic double bind [43] whereby two contradictory messages, each at a different level of communication, are conveyed to the hapless victim in such a way that she cannot succeed whichever course she chooses. Shaw's Henry Higgins framed the same question with an implicit answer when he beseeched, "Why can't a woman be more like a man?" The answer, quite simply, is that if she were, she would be rejected by men and spurned by other women; she would receive neither a marriage proposal nor the opportunity to rise independently to the level of her own potential; and finally, she isn't because she knows that men do not really want her to aspire to masculine status and that his needs require that she appear ignorant of what she knows. Freud's efforts to understand women failed for the same reason as Lombroso's: the causes of her femininity reside no more in her unique biological drives than her criminality resides in her unique anatomy. Neither had grasped the significant effect of the social forces on the behavior of an animal so profoundly acculturated as Homo sapiens.

Social Differences

Whatever equality may have existed between Adam and Eve before the Fall, there was a clear distinction in their social roles afterward. Adam was thenceforth required to till the soil and earn his bread by the sweat of his brow; Eve was condemned to painful childbirth and total submission to her husband. In one august decree, her reproductive role and social role were established and fixed. To be a woman, then as now, meant not just to be a distinctive blend of physiological and psychological characteristics. It meant and means that one is perceived differently, treated differently, responded to differently, and the subject of different expectations. Given the varying social forces that weigh unequally on the sexes in creatures as culture-dependent as humans, it seems clear that the resulting differences in behavior owe more to wide disparities in social-role than to the narrow differences in physical and psychological makeup.

The answer to the nursery-rhyme question, "what are little girls made of?" is revealing at several different levels. The list of ingredients—"sugar and spice and everything nice"—contains both a biological theory and a social demand. We are told, first of all, that little girls are good because of their inherent structure, and secondly, that they had better be good if they hope to enjoy the status of femininity and avoid the social disapproval which accompanies deviancy. Little boys, too, are under social pressure, but of a different kind. They are made of "snakes and snails and puppy-dog tails"—a combination designed to contrast mischievously and dynamically with the inert and saccharine constitution of their female counterparts. They, too, are saddled with social and presumed biological imperatives which compress the wide-ranging human potential for variation into the narrow confines of social-role expectation. There is hardly any important individual or social area—play, personal hygiene, manners, discipline, dependency, dress, activity, career, sexual activity, aggressiveness, etc.—which has not been polarized and institutionalized as a sex-role difference.[44] While it is true that men have tended to stigmatize women as a group,[45] deviation from social standards is even worse—e.g., the "effeminate" man and the "masculine" woman.

Traditionally, the little girl and later the woman are confined to a low-level of noise, dirt, disorder, and physical aggression.[46] They must be obedient, dependent, modest about their bodies, and avoid sex play as well as rough and tumble competition.[47] But life is not all no-no's: for her pains she is allowed to turn more readily to others for gratification, to cry when hurt, to be spontaneously affectionate, and to achieve less in school and work.[48] Whatever the natural inclination of the sexes may be, society does not depend on spontaneous acquisition of the profile it considers desirable: besides identification with the parent of the same sex,[49] which is probably the single most important determinant of behavior, it selects out from the random range of childhood activities those certain ones which will be accentuated or discarded. The shaping process includes toys—mechanical and problem-solving for boys, and soft and nonchallenging for girls—social structuring, individual rewards and punishments,[50] and the satisfactions apparently inherent in conforming to role expectations. The development of aggressive and dependent traits, both of which are considered to be sex-related, is a case in point. One research study [51] found that while aggressive boys become aggressive men and dependent girls become dependent women, the reverse was true for dependent boys and aggressive girls: as they approach maturity, they reverse themselves and also become aggressive men and dependent women, respectively. Similarly, there is a greater overlap of sex-role personality traits when the sibling in a two-child family is of the opposite sex, and this effect is greater with the younger siblings than with the older ones.[52] Clearly, learning and social pressure are influential in effecting sex-role expectations. Extending the argument that social roles are related to biological processes only indirectly,[53] presumably a technology which permitted father to nurture the child could result in a complete social-role reversal. In a pithy and accurate observation, Simone de Beauvoir summed up the consensus of current thinking when she said, "One is not born, but rather becomes, a woman." [54]

In the interests of clarity, I have spoken separately of the major physical, psychological, and social characteristics which distinguish women from men, although obviously each molds the final form of the other, both clinically and theoretically. Investigations of animal behavior demonstrate, for example, that rat pups who are psychologically stimulated develop larger and presumably smarter brains than those exposed to sensory isolations; [55] a litter born to a low-status African wild dog is less likely to survive than one born to a high-status female because the pups are less well fed and less protected by the pack; [56] the male offspring of low-status baboon females, regardless of their innate characteristics, are less likely to become dominant than those born to high-status females because the latter spend more time in physical proximity to the inner circle of dominant males and learn dominance behavior; [57] and the ovulatory cycle of a dove is retarded when a glass partition is placed between her and the rest of the flock, and it is stopped altogether if she is isolated in a room, unless there is a mirror.[58] The interdependency between biological drive and learning is described in Konrad Lorenz's formulation of the concept of "instinct-training interlocking behavior": [59] he describes this as a blend of instinctive and learned components, with instinct guaranteeing the readiness for certain kinds of learning and behavior to occur but experience shaping its final form.

In summary, females are smaller and meeker than men, they are less stable physiologically, they produce fewer androgenic hormones, and they have been socially shaped toward passivity, dependency, and conformity. Men are bigger, stronger, more aggressive, achievement-oriented, and more willing to break rules and take risks. This profile of the "normal" male and the "normal" female is consistent with the traditional differences which, until the last few decades, have prevailed for their criminal counterparts. However, the increasing "masculinization" of female social and criminal behavior forces us to re-examine the basis for her previous feminine limitations. A common-sense approach, and one followed by even such uncommon men as Freud and Adler, would suggest that what is natural to the female could be inferred from a factual description of the way the majority of females think and feel and act. Understandably, this is what has been done, and just as understandably it has been wrong.

"Oh, we'll never have to worry about the women becoming just like men . . . girls aren't masculine. They can't be as aggressive. That's how they're made, you know . . . ," explained a lieutenant in the New York City juvenile-aid division. He was explaining casually and confidently that girls would never be as criminal as adolescent boys. But the officer had been at a desk for the last ten years and was unaware that murders by adolescent girls have risen 400 per cent. Convinced that the adolescent crime spurt among girls was only an aberration that would "get back to normal" when the drug or other problems were solved, the lieutenant unshakably held that girls really were innately "more gentle" than boys.

The lieutenant suffers from the assumption which has had, and will probably continue to have, a serious effect on the handling of female criminals: that aggression is an exclusively masculine trait.

In the past, aggression was thought to be chiefly a biologically controlled trait. As a matter of their birth and ongoing internal chemistry, males were assumed to be "naturally aggressive"—hence the explanation of their historic roles as soldiers, hard-boiled businessmen, and merciless criminals. Women, on the other hand, were thought to be innately timid, passive, and conforming. Their general failure to be anything but mothers and housewives was offered as proof of their inability to be aggressive.

Of all the differences between the sexes, only four—size, strength, aggression, and dominance—have been implicated in any way with the overrepresentation of males in the criminal system. The first two are biological givens; the other two are largely, if not entirely, socially learned. Let us examine them separately. In nontechnological societies and in earlier periods in industrial societies, physical strength was often the final arbiter of social interaction, but even so, it was not the only one. In man as well as in the apes,[60] psychological factors including social manipulation, ruses, and group alliances were often decisive for leadership and effective action. In animals as well as men, the battle did not always go to the strong nor the race to the swift. But even if it did, this edge has been diminished by the technology of modern weapons. The deadliness of a gun is not necessarily less dangerous in the hands of a woman—although some have claimed that her lack of aggressiveness makes her a very unlikely and ineffective gunslinger. This is an interesting assumption because it is a common stereotype and is grounded in studies of male hormonal influences on lower animals, which gives it a ring of biological authenticity. There is much truth in this, but it is only a partial truth which, when stretched beyond its limits, conveys a falsehood. The truth is that in lower animals males are characteristically more aggressive, and this aggression is so directly linked to male hormones that if the male is castrated or injected with estrogen (the female hormone) he will stop fighting.[61] Likewise, the prenatal administration of testosterone to pregnant monkeys results in pseudohermaphroditic female offspring who even three years after birth are more aggressive than normal females.[62] However, it would be misleading to formulate the equation androgen = aggression or estrogen = nonaggression for all but the simplest and least socially developed species. Furthermore, it cannot be claimed that aggression is the exclusive prerogative of males. Mature female chimpanzees regularly drive off lower-status males [63] and any female mammal's defense of her cubs is as fierce as it is legendary.

But relevant as this is in establishing that aggression can co-exist with estrogen and can be unrelated to male hormones in mammals, the evidence for hormonal-behavioral detachment is even more compelling in subhuman primates and men. It is not possible to understand the behavior of social animals outside the context of a social situation. For example, an electric shock applied to an animal in a dominant position vis-à-vis another will result in an attack; the same stimulus applied to the same animal who is in a subdominant position vis-à-vis another will result in cringing, submissive behavior.[64] Likewise, the response of anger vs. fear or fight vs. flight depends less on the release of specific chemicals than on whether we perceive the threatening stimulus, in relation to ourselves, to be smaller or larger. The human capacity for abstraction and symbol formulation extends the range of "size" to include factors only remotely related to actual mass, so that characteristics such as wealth, lineage, social connections, skill, and intelligence may be perceived as "big" and accorded dominance. In the evolutionary progression toward higher mammals, there is a decreasing dependency between hormones and behavior, and in humans we find an almost complete cultural "override" of innate drives and tendencies. Thus, while status and dominance appear to be constants throughout the order of social primates, culture defines which characteristics will be labeled as dominant. Likewise, the distinctive sex-appropriate behaviors so rigidly controlled by hormones in lower animals have yielded to a rich variety of gender roles in human societies.

In *Sex and Temperament in Three Primitive Societies,* Margaret Mead described three revealing cultural variations. In one tribe, both sexes acted in the mild, parental, responsive manner we expect of women; in a second, both sexes acted in the fierce initiating fashion we expect of men; in a third, the men were chatty, wore curls, and went shopping in the manner of our stereotype of women, while the women were their unadorned, managerial, energetic partners. She concluded that sex roles were "mere variations of human temperament, to which the members of either or both sexes may, with more or less success in the case of different individuals, be educated to approximate." [65] She also concluded that regardless of what social role the male plays, it is always the lead. Regardless of what his characteristic behavior may be and even when it is imitative of "feminine behavior," it is considered high status when he adopts it. While historically and universally it is indeed a man's world, it does not follow that modern industrial man is innately more dominant than modern woman. It could be argued that the equalizing effects of a technological civilization like ours is without historical parallel and that the universal dominance of men may have resulted more from the institutionalization of man's superior strength than from any innate feminine submissiveness.

Western history is replete with examples of women who have risen above their cultural stereotype to become leaders of vigor and acclaim. Nor has their reign or tenure in office been particularly noteworthy for its tranquillity, peacefulness, or lack of aggressive adventures, all characteristics of their countrywomen in the social role of housewife. These women have, in fact, displayed a remarkable talent for ruthless and highly aggressive leadership. For instance, few world leaders have ever been so renowned for their tyrannical, belligerent rule as the English queens. One can still be stirred by the picture of Elizabeth I attired with her gold crown and shining breastplate, mounted on a white stallion, and moving like an avenging angel through her army of twenty thousand men at Tilbury. Her manner was august, but her words were passionate as she declared that she trusted their loyalty and was not afraid to commit herself to them.

> And therefore I am come amongst you, as you see, resolved in the midst and heat of the battle to live or die amongst you all, to lay down for my God and for my Kingdom, and for my people, my honour and my blood, even in the dust. I know I have the body of a weak and feeble woman, but I have the heart and stomach of a King, and a King of England, too, and I think foul scorn that Parma or Spain or any prince of Europe should dare to invade the borders of my realm. . . .[66]

Cleopatra of ancient Egypt, a biological woman's woman by any standards, was known for her shrewd political manipulations and insatiable appetite for military conquests; Maria Theresa was the founder of the modern Austrian state; the Russian Empress Catherine, who mothered a dozen children during her reign, still found time to annex ever-widening territories and seek new armies to defeat. In the present day, it is noteworthy that the two major countries with female rulers have both been at war within the last few years: Indira Gandhi of India and Golda Meir of Israel have shown no timidity—each, in wars across her border, has wielded political and military might as effectively as any man. Of course, such women as these who have risen to national leadership possess extraordinary characteristics which distinguish them from the mass of women—and the mass of men, for that matter. The very capacity and drive for ascension through a male world involved a selection process which would have discouraged weaker women. Notwithstanding their small numbers, the resoluteness and fortitude of such women challenge the myth of innate female passivity. On a broader scope, and one which encompassed more ordinary women, was the female incursion into criminal areas, previously considered male, during World War II.[67] In law-enforcing as well as law-breaking, it would appear that social position and social-role expectations are more important than sex in determining behavior.

During the early 1940s, the mobilization of males from the civil to the military sector resulted in the necessity for a large number of women to fill positions previously held by men. And fill them they did, in a way not altogether anticipated. It had been known and expected that lesser men often rise to the stature of a role thrust on them by circumstance. It should not have been surprising, therefore, that "lesser men" who happen to be women would do the same thing. What was most portentous, however, about this vocational shift was not that women could assume men's jobs, but that in doing so they could also presume to men's social roles. One need not look to psychological theories to explain the enthusiasm with which women embraced men's esteemed positions. Their own, as housewife and playmate, had been eroding for years and a desperately labor-short male establishment had further devalued it in the interests of national defense, as something akin to indolence, if not disloyalty. "Rosie the Riveter," symbol of the women working for the war, was proclaimed a heroine in song and style by a grateful country. As the residence of female status shifted from the home to the office or factory, a trip that men had made long before, the American woman accommodated so congenially to the change that few people at the time challenged her credentials to perform. However, many were concerned that she was not just commuting to her new-found roles but might settle down to stay. In unprecedented numbers women crossed the sex-role line in their jobs and in their crimes during the war years, 1940 to 1945. In that period, the crimes committed by women almost doubled in number [68] and even began to assume the same patterns as male crime. The trend peaked in 1945 and declined rapidly after the war with the return of men to their jobs, but it could never be the same. Women were now urged to act more like women by a male establishment which wanted to return to the position it had temporarily (it hoped) vacated. But in social evolution as in biological evolution, there is no easy road back, especially since in a very profound sense the women could not go home again. Labor-saving household appliances and the denigration of the domestic work ethic they conveyed rendered her old position untenable. In addition, there was a shift in the male attitude. Men were seeing women as worthy rivals and feeling considerably less charitable and more competitive toward them. Furthermore, in a world grown too full of people, even the once sacrosanct status of motherhood was beginning to bear unhappy resemblances to overproductive pollution. With zero population as a national goal and household drudgery an accepted epithet, where was the woman to go? The road back was blocked, and while the road forward was not completely open it was now more accessible than ever before.

The pressure was all for discarding the separate-but-equal provisions of the old social contract and opting for a chance to compete in the same field and under the same conditions as men. Unfortunately, the men were not as ready for this change as the women. Psychoanalysts, long accustomed to the futile penis envy of women, were now talking about breast envy and womb envy, an example of male jealousy toward women almost unheard of in Freud's day.[69]

While women proceeded to widen their social and criminal roles, many men, especially middle- and lower-class men, who had the least ground to yield in the status hierarchy, resisted in every way they could. Policemen, for example, showed the greatest reluctance to accept the changed women either as criminals or as coworkers.

"I think you find a lot of people in police work who tend to underestimate women," said Patrolman Jim Orman with a shrug of his shoulders. Orman, an officer with the Washington, D.C., police force for the last twelve years, admits that he began police work laboring under the impression that women were "nicer" than men; that they were much less apt to commit violent acts. "I suppose it's a natural thing as a rookie to be less suspicious of a woman; I mean, there is this tendency to let your guard down easier," he said. "But you learn. Let me tell you . . . I learned."

Orman now lives with a constant reminder of the education he received about women—a jagged scar which snakes its way from above his elbow down to his wrist on the underside of his forearm. The scar was put there by a woman who was swinging a straight razor and aiming for Orman's throat. He was able to block it with his arm. "I've been punched in the mouth, grabbed, kicked in the groin, and threatened by women I've had to apprehend. I learned."

This tendency to be a bit less cautious, a bit more open with females, is a common one throughout the various police departments of the country. Females are less likely to be arrested and, when arrested, are far less likely to be convicted than are males involved in exactly the same sort of crime, because policemen suffer from deeply ingrained prejudices which put female criminals at an advantage. In their dealings with females in all walks of life, policemen tend to conform to the traditionally paternalistic attitudes of society in general toward women. That such attitudes and tendencies have remained throughout the various law-enforcement levels in this country in spite of the rising rates of female crime puts it in the category of a prejudice.

That such prejudices have influenced the standard operating procedures in most police departments is well established.[70] Even the way male police officers have related to female members of their own force is a good indication of some of the problems inherent in their dealing with ever-increasing numbers of female offenders. Traditionally, few women were hired by police departments, and those few were assigned primarily to the offices of the youth-aid division, to jockey typewriters, or to take "special" assignments dealing with the apprehension of male sex offenders. In keeping with their general status, women in police departments were paid less than their male counterparts and seldom, if ever, promoted. They were not allowed to wear uniforms, and they were rarely allowed to do any work on their own without male "protection" or supervision.

Within the last few years, however, there have been changes. Pressured by women's groups as well as the general national atmosphere encouraging women's rights, police departments have begun to hire more women. For the first time, a number of cities across the country are experimenting with female officers who receive the same training and perform the same patrol duties as males. Throughout the departments in New York, Philadelphia, Washington, Dallas, and other major cities where women are performing formerly male-only duties, there have been problems. Male officers have been quite consistent in their hostility toward females working with them as equals. Those male officers have often refused to ride with female partners, threatened boycotts, resignations, and picket lines.

"How would you like to ride with a woman?" asked one New York patrolman indignantly. "Women have no right carrying guns . . . and what about when you get into a violent situation . . . is a woman going to be able to respond? Is she really going to be able to shoot or subdue a suspect?"

This antagonism toward policewomen may well be related to the kinds of women who are attracted to police work. Like their male counterparts in the force, they often share many of the aggressive, action-oriented, risk-taking characteristics of the criminals they pursue.[71] In this regard, policewomen would seem to be more compatible with policemen than their own wives. Why, then, would they object so strenuously? Precisely, it is suggested, because of the similarity. It threatens to obliterate the sexual differences and appears to lower his status by redistributing male machismo a bit too liberally. It is not because of her weakness, inability, or lack of effectiveness that the policeman objects to the policewoman. It is more likely because she demonstrably possesses the opposite qualities all too well. This same social defense mechanism probably operates in the suppression of other stigmatized groups. Dominance necessarily requires submissiveness, and "ins" require "outs." Otherwise, how could anybody know the difference?

In light of these obstacles, it is remarkable that women are not only doing their jobs well as patrol officers but, in some cases, drawing enthusiastic praise from police administrators.

"The women have worked out to a degree which many people just didn't expect. I think heir performance has surprised a lot of people," explained a lieutenant in New York City whose precinct now has women patrolling the streets in one- and two-person cars. "In the first place, they have proven themselves very capable of handling the variety of situations in which they routinely come in contact on patrol. They also seem to be a bit better at calming down family disputes; even situations where things have deteriorated to a level of violence, their mere presence has had a calming effect."

In Washington, D.C., one of the first cities to embrace the idea of women patrol officers, females were commended for their performance. Lieutenant Al Hack, a forty-seven-year-old, twenty-four-year veteran of the force, thinks women are working out "fantastically" in his district. "As a matter of fact, we have many women who are, in my opinion, more qualified to be riding in patrol cars than a lot of the men around here. The girls are quick, bright, and physically capable of doing their job. They've proven that. The men are slowly accepting that fact. But full acceptance will take a while . . . the old ways sometimes die hard."

The old ways do indeed die hard, not only because we need our stereotypes and our subdominants, but also because cognitive systems tend to become security blankets to which we cling most tenaciously just when we are most threatened. It is perhaps for these reasons that the coming of age of the Western woman was not forecast by the behavioral scientists who should have known, but instead it caught us unawares and overtook our comfortable prejudices with a *fait accompli*. While most were predicting that it was impossible and many were arguing that it wasn't happening, it had already occurred. It is tempting to think no deeper than an apparent fact, and it must be admitted that the "facts" of female inferiority were apparent to all who could read the figures that supported them. It did not seem productive to search out the reasons behind the figures. They were self-evident because they confirmed what we already knew about the natural superiority of men. If it were otherwise, we surely would have been told by this time. But, indeed, we *were* being told new "facts" in compelling ways by new figures which were challenging old theories.

In the countless indices which measure female output of degrees and income and factory production, and in the Uniform

Crime Reports which tabulate her legal transgressions, these rising figures were intruding not only on our beliefs but on the mores which supported them. At first, the rising crime figures were greeted as an apparition, a mirage; at first, they were dismissed as an aberration which would correct itself by statistical adjustments; at last, they were recognized as ancient female strengths which had always been latent and were just now, at this sociotechnological juncture of history, realizing their potential. Everything we know about the history of woman and everything we see about her current behavior tells us that her past limitations as a worker and law-breaker have been largely, if not entirely, the result of her physical weakness and the cultural institutions which derived from that fact.[72] Save only her inferiority in size and strength, her differences from men are just *that*, differences. Some confer an advantage, others a disadvantage, depending on the particular culture. In our own, given her education, aspirations (these, too, have been liberated), freedom from unwanted pregnancies, healthy assertiveness, and access to labor-saving devices, including guns, she shares the same fortunate or unfortunate criminogenic qualities as men.

I have not contended here that women are equal *to* men, simply that they are potentially the equal *of* men. There are many differences which we have described and no doubt more will be discovered, but all evidence points to two complementary conclusions: First, the small natural differences between the sexes have been polarized and institutionalized in special ways by different cultures to produce a gender disparity which reveals more about the emotional needs of the society than about the innate possibilities of the individual. And second, when size and strength between the sexes are discounted by technology, as they have been within the ranks of men, social expectations and social roles, including the criminal roles, tend increasingly to merge.

There was a time early in the history of the physical sciences, before the concepts of mass and gravity were formulated, when the weight of an object was thought to reside within the physical boundaries of the object. Because weight is palpable and measurable, it was a conclusion which met the requirements of common sense and common experience. But the limitation of common sense is that it owes too much allegiance to the past to permit conceptual breakthroughs to the future. It is a better follower than leader. As physicists later discovered, the weight of an object is not inherent within it but rather the measure of an outside gravitational pull acting upon it. In an analogous manner, scientific thinking about human behavior has evolved in the same centrifugal direction. From the predecessors of Lombroso to the followers of Freud and into modern times, the search for the causes of female criminality have focused on her biology with scant heed to her sociology. We have only recently recognized that the clothes of social-role expectations not only make the man, they also form the woman.

Even if it is established that humans have innate biological drives, and even if it were confirmed that females have a different biogrammar [73] (i.e., a behavioral repertoire of signals) from males, the social forces which impinge on her from without would still be decisive for her conformist as well as her deviant behavior. In the profoundest evolutionary sense, the social factors which sustain and suspend us also create our destiny, and biology must follow where society leads.

3

The Oldest and Newest Profession

". . . there is nothing either good or bad,
but thinking makes it so . . ."

—Shakespeare
Hamlet

The type of fig leaf which each culture employs to cover its social taboos offers a twofold description of its morality. It reveals that certain unacknowledged behavior exists and it suggests the form that such behavior takes.

The appellations "streetwalker" and "call girl" connote a sense of mobility and communication native to our culture. Earlier euphemisms conveyed aspects of other cultures: the word "prostitute" comes from the Latin "to stand in a place"; "whore" is derived from the Indo-European "dear" or "friend"; "hookers," according to one explanation,[1] were those loyal or opportunistic camp followers who attached themselves to the division of Civil War General Joseph Hooker; "brothel" is a public bath which the Crusaders frequented in search of assignation;[2] and "red-light district" conjures up rows of red signal lanterns which brakemen in Western railroad construction camps hung outside the tents of women with whom they were spending the night.[3]

Euphemisms, like fashions, have their day and pass, perhaps to return at another time. Like the guests at a masquerade ball, they enjoy social approval only so long as they retain the capacity for deception. Once common usage renders their disguise too transparent, their vulgarity is revealed and they are banished. But it is not long before the magic of verbal legerdemain allows us again to say what we wish without hearing what we fear. The traditional brothel has largely vanished from the American scene, but in its place one may find "massage parlors" and "vibrator-demonstration offices." Out of deference to social sensibilities, the names have been changed to protect the identity of the vices.

The emphasis of this book is on change, and through the years few things have changed less than sexual behavior or more than sexual attitudes. As some of the derivations suggest, activities similar to those we now consider scandalous were and are accorded a much more respectable position in other times and at other places. The geisha are Japanese females skilled in art; that they also often engaged in sexual intercourse with their patrons was not only acceptable but appropriate. The Hebrews did not strongly disapprove of prostitution [4] and the Greeks elevated the courtesan to a position of esteem. A hetaera was the object of love and respect, an integral part of the religious rites; each temple had its house prostitutes, and the best-connected hetaerae lived in the most beautifully appointed homes in the finest parts of the city.[5] Moreover, they deserved it because in their education, their artistic ability, and their social graces as well as their erotic talents, they exemplified the feminine qualities the Greeks extolled. If they stood near the center of power, it was because they stood at the apex of virtue.

Although with considerably less enthusiasm, the Church in medieval Europe accepted prostitution, regulated it in terms of place and dress, and was partly supported by the houses of prostitution, called lupanars. The fact that the name means she-wolf in Latin conveys an aura of threat, but it was not until the end of the fifteenth century that tolerance of prostitution declined sharply, debilitated by the double impact of a syphillis epidemic and the Protestant Reformation. The Protestant backlash against the sexual permissiveness among the Catholic clergy and laity, together with the Protestants' emphasis on the virtues of hard work, self-discipline, and abstinence, were antithetical to a climate of sexual freedom.

As the fortunes of the Protestant Church rose, the position of the prostitute fell—she became a victim of the constrictive puritanical attitudes toward sex which pervaded middle-class values and behavior.[6]

But like most backlash movements, puritanism lacked the balanced perspective that might have prevented it from careening from the plasticity of license at one extreme to the rigidity of repression at the other. It traded the disadvantages of pushing the limits in one direction for the disadvantages of pushing the limits in the other, without testing the middle ground in between. St. Augustine (A.D. 354–430) would not have made such a mistake: "Suppress prostitution," he warned, "and capricious lusts will overthrow society." Nineteenth-century moralists such as William Lecky were making the same point with the declaration that the prostitute "is ultimately the most efficient guardian of virtue." He contended that but for the social function she performs, the chastity of other women, the stability of the family, and the preservation of the very social institutions dependent on abstinence would be in jeopardy. "She remains," he continued, "while creeds and civilizations rise and fall, the eternal priestess of humanity."[7] Given the sexual freedom men have reserved for themselves and the code of premarital chastity and postmarital fidelity they have imposed on women, prostitution is the only mechanism which would permit the coexistence of these two mutually exclusive and contradictory ideals. Without prostitution, their foundations in fantasy would be exposed, and they would fall of their own weight.

In cultures such as those of the Orient, North Africa, continental Europe, and Latin America, which esteem female virginity, the male desire for premarital coital experience creates the need for prostitution.[8] Its social role is to satisfy the demands for illicit sex in such a way that the integrity of irreconcilable social demands does not seem to be compromised. How else could the needs of strangers, perverts, and armies, to say nothing of normal males, be served? It is because of the persistence and imperiousness of such needs that efforts to eliminate prostitution directed solely at the prostitute are generally fruitless. King Louis IX of France, in a fervor of Christian righteousness, ordered all the brothels closed before setting out on the Crusade. To his dismay, the ranks of his entourage to the Holy Land were swelled by the addition of a troop of camp followers.

Prostitution, then, is a ubiquitous institution existing in modern as well as ancient civilizations, and changing as they change. This change is well documented in more recent times, particularly in the last two decades, a time when acceleration in sexual freedom for women and the loosening of restrictive public attitudes toward sex have increased the frequency of extramarital and premarital sexual activity and diminished the participation of prostitutes in this sphere. Kinsey and his associates [9] found that while the post–World War I generation of males had reduced their contact with prostitutes by about one-half, the total amount of premarital coitus remained nearly constant. Men were merely shifting their sexual activities from prostitutes to nonprofessional females. The changes in female sexual freedom which these findings recorded and presaged have shown a consistent trend toward more premarital intercourse with each generation. Women born after 1900 experienced more than twice the amount of premarital sex than those born before 1900. Furthermore, of those who were still single by age twenty-five, only 14 per cent of the old generation (before 1900) as opposed to 36 per cent a decade later had experienced coitus.[10]

In an era when the easily obtained "pill" provides contraception, penicillin protects against venereal disease, and communes and coed dorms make the girl next door accessible, brothels are at a distinct competitive disadvantage. Likewise, the over-thirty group which has eagerly affected younger styles of dress and mannerisms has shown a similar inclination to be influenced by their sexual mores. The female coworker is now much more available than previously for casual, relatively guilt-free sex. The fact, however, that most of the prostitute's clients are married and between thirty and fifty years of age suggests that these coworkers are not yet as available as coeds.[11]

So it is that the "fallen woman" of a previous era has recently risen to the status of the commonplace, while the term itself has leaped from opprobrium to anachronism in two generations. Such shifts in attitudes toward sexual behavior are nothing but a reflection of shifts in sexual behavior itself. Old standards yield to new ones as conformity stretches to accommodate new proprieties and the virtues of chastity are replaced by the virtues of premarital experience. Language itself cooperates in the sterilization of vice as perversion becomes deviancy, deviancy turns into a normal variation, and normal variations are transformed by the weight of numbers to the normal. These changes are not generated within the adult, nor are they simply extensions of childhood experience. It is during the period of adolescence, at the turbulent growing tip of society, that the moral reappraisals of the establishment are made and the pulse of innovation reverberates throughout every segment of the social web. Here the turmoil begins.

During the last decade when "baby pros," prostitutes under sixteen, were merchandising their precocious sexuality, the baby daughters of their slightly older sisters were playing with full-breasted Barbie dolls, who have as little in common with Raggedy Ann as Lolita has with Mary Jane. At the same time, the mothers of these teen-agers were daring to enter burlesque houses,[12] watching movies rated in multiples of X, and perusing explicit sexual material (profusely illustrated) from the corner newsstand. The proliferation of movies, plays, books, and humor about prostitutes in the last three decades [13] appears paradoxical because it coincides with a period of the most intense suppression of organized prostitution. The explanation is probably of the same order as the reciprocal relationship Kinsey [14] found to exist between the decrease in prostitute contacts and the increase in premarital sex with "proper" women.

The mass media have been reflecting not an interest in prostitution per se, which appears to be declining, but a fascination for what it is the prostitute does for a living. This burgeoning interest has found spokesmen in every field—Alfred C. Kinsey in sociology, William H. Masters and Virginia Johnson in medicine, Morris Ploscowe in law, and D. H. Lawrence and Henry Miller in literature—who have both resonated to and synergized public attitudes. Concurrently, the magazine *Confidential* achieved the largest newsstand circulation in history following a series of articles on the sex life of the famous.[15] The huge circulation of *Playboy* magazine, with its glossy portrayals of generously endowed females, also owed much of its success to what moralists were decrying as prurient interest.

Nor was the quest for sex limited to current productions. *Fanny Hill*, a book about the life of prostitutes first published in 1749 under the title *Memoirs of a Lady of Pleasure*, was rediscovered and allowed, by a New York court ruling in 1963, to be sold openly to the American public. Leading American playwrights have found in the prostitute not a creature apart but a woman of some depth and one with whom it is easy to identify. John Steinbeck (*Tortilla Flat*, 1938), William Saroyan (*The Time of Your Life*, 1940), and Tennessee Williams (*A Streetcar Named Desire*, 1947) portrayed her as sometimes callous, sometimes bizarre, and sometimes touching, but always interesting to the public. Since the mid-1940s, at least one Broadway play featuring prostitution has been offered each season, and during 1961 five plays—*Irma la Douce, The Balcony, The Hostage, A Taste of Honey*, and *Tenderloin*—presented varying and appealing views of the prostitute.[16]

The trip from the back streets to the main thoroughfare is one that has changed the prostitute and educated the public to an awareness that what she is and what she does may reflect very little on each other. To the questions "What does he do?" or "What is he?" one will often get a single reply. This is all the more so with prostitutes, because what they do has traditionally been considered so heinous and inherently evil that only an unworthy person could be so engaged. From Victorian times until recently, sexual behavior has been considered so innately depraved that, like the pornographic literature which described it, it could be tolerated only if it was accompanied by redeeming social values such as reproduction, marriage, or, at the very least, love. Consequently, until World War II, prostitution was lumped together with gambling and alcoholism as a package of social evils and placed beyond the pale.[17] There was a certain validity to this indiscriminate labeling because, although they were very different activities, they shared an illegal or quasi-legal status. Consequently, prostitutes were forced to consort with the illegal and disreputable members of society. Legal status has influenced prostitution by restricting both its range of practice and the kinds of people likely to become practitioners. These kinds of people have changed over time as a result of broad cultural transformations as well as alterations in the position of women. As with any other vendor of a service, prostitutes throughout the centuries have merchandised their product so that it would be most attractive in the marketplace, and this has required them to cater to a need not met elsewhere.

From ancient to modern times, there has been a consistent stratification of prostitutes into three classes whose descriptions have been remarkably constant, although, of course, their designations have changed. In ancient Greece, the brothels were not held in the same low regard as modern red-light districts, but the prostitutes were at the bottom of the professional hierarchy. Ranking just above them were the individual practitioners who stood in the marketplaces and who were equivalent to our streetwalkers. Superseding both were the hetaerae, the intellectual and social equals of the wealthy and powerful men with whom they consorted, and whose portraits and statues appeared alongside their men's.[18] The needs which these three groups of women satisfied extended from simple sexual relations at the lower end to a gratifying total relationship, with sexual relations as an additional but not primary benefit at the highest level. This is consonant with our knowledge of human nature, because humans have always needed both relations and relationships and have been willing to pay a premium either in marriage or money to satisfy whichever was lacking. It should be added that between the two, relationships have consistently been most valued and most highly rewarded. People will commit larger sums of their weal to religion or psychotherapy or to their offspring than they will to a mere sex partner, because it is in the relationship that the most vital human interests reside.

This principle is useful in understanding the connection between prevailing family structure and the type of prostitute who flourishes alongside it. In classical Greece, the strong position of the hetaerae resulted from their ability to supply the stimulating companionship unavailable to men from their wives. Respectable Greek housewives of the citizen class lacked education, lived circumscribed lives of routine domesticity, and could not be the intellectual companions their husbands wished for and found elsewhere.[19] Predictably, where the social structure creates a sharp distinction between domestic women and career women, men will seek from prostitutes what they lack at home—whether it be relations or relationships. The emancipation of women and their increasing education and participation in the economic life during the Renaissance, as well as the antipathy of the Church, discouraged the development of the hetaera class.[20] The extrasexual functions of this class were partly discredited by the Protestant work ethic and partly filled by the new type of woman who was evolving in the industrialized West.[21] As the wife's role rose from one of mere sexual relations to relationships, that of the prostitute fell to encompass only the former.

The question of whether prostitution should be more properly considered a profession or a trade is one that will be answered by the marital contract which each society formulates. Where the wife is a domestic tradeswoman, the prostitute will be a professional; where the wife provides a satisfying relationship but little else, the prostitute will be merely a vendor of almost purely sexual services. There is much profound social philosophy and an important connubial statement in the popular remark, "I love my wife, but oh you kid." It is possible for men to feel love and affection for one and sexual attraction for another because, while both satisfactions are necessary, they can be segregated.

The question of what classical Greek and other housewives did to fulfill their unsatisfied needs is difficult to answer because it was not raised at the time—and might not have been still were it not for the current social revolution. The issue of a woman's right to full satisfaction has until very recently not seemed to be an appropriate or worthwhile subject for public discussion.

Even those enlightened moralists who countenanced prostitution and defended prostitutes did so out of pragmatic considerations for social stability and the importance of finding outlets for men's sexual drives. The prostitute's defenders differed from her detractors in their willingness to be charitable toward her pathology, forgiving of her sinfulness, and tolerant of her vice. What they had in common was their perception of her as a person stigmatized by her sexual permissiveness. But this is a very different frame of reference from that which is being emphasized by modern American women—to wit, sexual freedom should be as much a female as a male prerogative.

• Betty, a college junior: "I don't feel the necessity to be 'coy' or have to pander to the men I go out with. I don't want to sound like a whore, but when I'm horny, I'm horny. I don't feel any shame about it. It's as natural to me as being hungry. When I'm hungry, I run out to the sandwich shop and don't think twice about it."

• A thirty-three-year-old housewife: "My husband is in sales. He's on the road about six months each year. I'm not naïve about what goes on when a man is traveling for a long while alone. We never talk about it. It's just something you know about. The thing that has really started to get me mad is that he insists that I be a homebody. I wanted to take a three-day vacation not long ago. Just go to the shore by myself. He hit the ceiling and accused me of being a nympho or something. It wasn't that I wanted to screw other guys . . . I just wanted the freedom, maybe just to drift around and *think* about it. I'm getting just a little tired of his double standard. It has started to affect our marriage in a big way."

• A microbiology researcher: "When my marriage broke up last year, it was completely because of sex. John and I got along well, otherwise. We had similar tastes, similar living habits, but in bed it was really awful. He was unable to talk about sex at all. He had no consideration at all. It was the same old story. He'd roll me over, climb on top, and get done before rolling off and going to sleep. That was it. For a long while, I thought something was wrong with me. When we tried to talk about it, he became very defensive and in the end he was uptight because I was 'attacking' him. By that time, I had found a lover who understood that sex was a fifty–fifty deal, that women have their little kinky preferences also. I just think that I have a right to get as much pleasure out of sex as any man."

While it may be, as the experience of history suggests, that prostitution will remain with us indefinitely, it is also true that so long as it remains illicit, reliable data on its prevalence will be difficult to obtain. The only hard figures available come from the number of arrests, but we do not have a formula for estimating the ratio of number of offenses to number of arrests. Even if we did, however, victimless crimes such as prostitution generate such an uneven response from the public and law-enforcement agencies that they are subject to considerable variation in criteria for arrest. For example, many are arrested for vagrancy or disorderly conduct instead of the more severe charge of prostitution. Furthermore, arrest rates may reflect fluctuations in the activity of law-enforcement groups as well as fluctuations in offenses. An additional source of error in the arrest figures is the fact that those figures include multiple arrests of the same individual.[22]

According to speculative estimates, there are approximately one hundred thousand full-time prostitutes who work six days a week and service an average of three clients per day.[23] At an assumed average fee of $10, a prostitute grosses about $9300. There is thought to be an even larger but undetermined number of part-time prostitutes. The American Social Health Association has developed an index of commercialized prostitution which makes chronological comparisons possible. Pegging the categories of no commercialized prostitution at "0" and flagrant prostitution at "100," they have compiled the following figures:

Years	Average National Score
1920–1929	99
1930–1938	92
1940–1946	49
1947–1949	74
1950–1959	35
1967	37

It would appear from these figures that, except for a post–World War II flare-up (which was not paralleled by a similar rise after the Korean war), commercial prostitution has shown the steady decline characteristic of a dying business. That is not to say that prostitution is a declining activity—it has, as we have said, attracted a large influx of part-timers—but simply that as an organized business enterprise it is languishing.

The patronage has shifted steadily to the "daytimers"—white, haughty, and businesslike—whose ranks include ex-models, jobless actresses, and bored housewives, who add upward of $60 per contact to their household budget. Police estimate that as many as 10 per cent of the prostitutes cruising Times Square on weekends are housewives from Long Island and New Jersey. There is also a younger set—the long-haired, high-booted, miniskirted amateurs from the suburbs or exurbs—whose carelessness and lack of experience make them easy prey for bulls (plainclothes policemen) and meat salesmen (pimps) alike, both of whom are interested in them but for different reasons. The independent call girls, unattached to pimps or madams, cluster around conventions, seeking the lucrative white-collar end of the business which might net them $1000 a week.

Aside from their common activity, there is little that distinguishes these women as a group. Here great change has occurred. They have not retained the solidarity of the pimp-run stables and madam-hosted brothels, nor have they developed an extensive and identifying argot. They are essentially individual operators unsupported by a social structure within which they can or would necessarily wish to advance. They may be the object of a recruiting campaign by pimps and they may be aware of the advantages of having a man around, but most will opt for individual ownership of their bodies.

The days of the colorful pimps and flamboyant madams, like Detroit's Silver-Tongue Jean and New York's Jennie the Factory, have for the most part passed into history, victims of their high visibility to the vice squad and changing social styles. In the heyday of the brothel, during the decades of the twenties and thirties, the madam served as entrepreneur, talent scout, public-relations agent, liaison officer to the police department, and housemother to her girls and their customers alike.[24] Within the madam's house (which Polly Adler wittily described as not the least bit homely) were "wives," who belonged to or were in the stable of a pimp.

The pimp not only helped prostitutes with the police and posted their bail, but he would also strong-arm obstreperous customers and prostitutes as he deemed appropriate. In 1935 it was estimated that there were sixty-three hundred pimps in Chicago alone.[25] Their ethnic background has tended to be similar to that of their stables, Italian and Jewish in the 1920s and 1930s, and more recently black and Puerto Rican. Sociologically, it would appear that these populations represented immigrant or otherwise disadvantaged groups which were nevertheless rising in social acceptance. Sex, like money, is a medium of exchange which often transcends social barriers, and for many of these girls it was their first contact with the American Establishment. But prostitution, like other labor-intense, service-oriented industries, could not enjoy the economies which ordinarily come with increases in size and concentration. On the contrary, the size of the brothel or stable was a double liability, exposing them to the depredations of both dishonest and honest police work through payoffs and raids, respectively. It was partly because size became counterproductive that the trend since the 1940s has been toward dispersion and individual entrepreneurships, making the role of the pimp largely but not entirely anachronistic.

The place is Sunset Strip, not far from the famed intersection of Hollywood and Vine, and the last bit of daylight is fading behind the mountains. It is just about "git-down time," the hour when the streetwalkers "hit the bricks" in downtown Los Angeles to begin their nocturnal trolling for customers. On one corner, propped jauntily against a bus-stop bench, is Willie. Around the corner is Willie's car. It is a Cadillac, lime-green with large diamond-shaped cutouts in the rear window. Willie is wearing a suede hat with a large green plume. His shoes, which have four-inch heels, are the same color as his car, as well as his pants, which are held in place by a richly rhinestoned belt. Willie likes to talk about his profession, even boast about it. He is a pimp, he says, and has "girls all over the city."

Willie obviously enjoys playing the pimp; the gentleman of leisure who has become such a literary hero in recent years. Willie's talk, however, starts to sound a bit too exaggerated after a while, his claims just a bit too way out. "Got maybe hundred girls all over. Maybe hundred and fifty. I just blink my eyes, man, and I got three chicks going down on me if I want."

"That dude is way out," says another character who has been circulating in the underworld of the Strip for half a dozen years.

The man, also black like Willie, makes a disdainful face as he speaks of the pimp. "He's jiving. He's got maybe four girls. Two split from him last week. Right now he's dealing in dope to keep up the payments on his car and the clothes. It's like that a lot now. You know, the pimp has finally made it in the movies, but on the street, he's going down. You got a lot of chicks coming into town who aren't into dope. They're not putting out for dope. They're strictly into the bread. They want the money. They work their thing free-lance—no pimps, no connections. Some of them get roughed up for cutting into someone's action, but now you have so many of them floating around it's hard to fight it. There are a lot of pimps still going strong, but not like before. It's changing. A lot of dudes have gotten into something else, mostly working drugs or small ripoffs out of town. A couple I know who have made big money are getting into night clubs and stuff like that."

Although he may no longer be their legal and political protector (he may disappear at the first sign of trouble), the pimp may still play an important role in the lives of many prostitutes. For many there is still loneliness, isolation, and need for emotional support, which may make them seek out such a man to fill the aching emptiness of their existence. It is for this reason, some writers feel, that in spite of the diminution of his fiscal and organizational contribution, the pimp will continue to play a significant role in the life of the prostitute. The quality of that life was poignantly portrayed many years ago by Will Levington Comfort, a novelist and reporter, who recorded his impressions of a night-long conversation with a prostitute in police court.

The most tragic sentence I ever heard was from the lips of one of these women. . . . I talked with her through the night. She called it her work; she had an ideal about her work. Every turning in her life had been man-directed. She confessed that she had begun with an unabatable passion; that men had found her sensuousness very attractive when it was fresh. She had preserved a certain sweetness; through such stresses that the upper world would never credit. Thousands of men had come to her; all perversions, all obsessions, all madness, and drunkenness, to her alone in this little room. She told of nights when twenty came. Yet there was something inextinguishable about her—something patient and optimistic. In the midst of it all, it was like a little girl speaking:

"I wake up in the morning, and find a man beside me. I am always frightened, even yet—until I remember. I remember who I am and what I am . . . then I try to think what he is like—what his companions called him—what he said to me. I try to remember how he looked—because you know in the morning, his face is always turned away." [26]

In view of such experiences, which are neither unusual nor exaggerated, the question naturally arises as to how and why women become involved in what has euphemistically, if ironically, been designated as "the life." The reasons are as varied as the personalities of the women themselves and as their goals. It would be a mistake to simply conceptualize prostitution as pathological and search for its etiology or to emphasize its antisocial aspects and attempt to uncover its criminal roots. These may be valid assessments, but they are too limited for such a wide-ranging subject. The most useful approach to understanding this complex behavior might best begin with its definition: "the granting of sexual access on a relatively indiscriminate basis for payment." [27] Some theorists find in prostitution a Marxist example of economic exploitation,[28] while others emphasize its ecologic aspects,[29] social utilitarianism,[30] and disorganization associated with mobility.[31] Addressing themselves to the oft-reported frigidity and homosexuality [32] among prostitutes as well as to antisocial aspects, psychological theorists have understood prostitution primarily in terms of sexual "acting out" of underlying psychopathology.[33] Psychoanalysts have contended that the psychological defense mechanism of isolation which separates tender from sensual feelings is an important factor for both the prostitute and her client.[34] Of a certain group of people it can be said, "they cannot desire where they love, and they cannot love where they desire." [35] For them, prostitution plays an essential role in stabilizing their life because it permits them to isolate this objectionable sensuality from either their marital relationship or any other important interpersonal transactions. Were it not for such outlets, these impulses would have to be either repressed, resulting in psychoneurosis, or expressed, resulting in the disruption of important social institutions.

Apart from the psychosocial, economic interpretations contend that women "resort to sex as a means of redressing the status differential," [36] this being the most accessible route to power and material rewards available to them within our culture. In other words, each gender utilizes whatever biological and social possibilities are available to satisfy either socially disallowed drives or to attain socially approved goals. Philosophically, at least, prostitutes may be only contractually removed from the sexual ploys an alluring and designing wife might use to seduce financial favors from her husband. These approaches are at best partial truths providing only a limited understanding of prostitution. To begin with, women are attracted to or drawn into it for many and conflicting reasons. Furthermore, the forces which sustain them in "the life" may be different from those which facilitated their initial entrance. Like Aesop's six blind men and the elephant, our theorists are describing different segments of a complex body of data. Psychoanalysts deal primarily with psychoneurotics who characteristically repress their impulses and inhibit their actions so that "prostitution fantasies" are as close as most of them ever get to such behavior. In addition, these patients are drawn from a middle and upper socioeconomic group which ordinarily has ample socially approved outlets for both sexual and aggressive drives, as well as financial access to material rewards. When executives steal they do not pilfer apples from fruit stands, nor do upper-class women proffer their sexual favors to strangers for money. Each finds means appropriate to his or her status to satisfy the ends.

Motivations may not differ between classes, but means certainly do. Those investigators who emphasize the masochistic [37] elements in prostitution may be failing to appreciate the financial incentive it offers to women who would otherwise be engaged as waitresses, factory workers, or domestics. As Shaw allowed in *Mrs. Warren's Profession,* society was "underpaying, undervaluing, and overworking women so shamefully that the poorest of them are forced to resort to prostitution to keep body and soul together." What they lose socially may in their view be more than compensated for in terms of both money and freedom from rigid job restrictions. If prostitution is, as one women's liberation placard declared, "men's crime against women," it must be acknowledged that prostitutes are very willing victims who are as eager as their male clients to be partners in crime. Such rebukes against society suggest that these women might be happier as file clerks or domestics, occupations which many of them have voluntarily relinquished for both psychological and financial reasons.

"I didn't get along with my family. I left home after high school. I came down to D.C. [Washington, D.C.] just to get away," said a twenty-four-year-old prostitute who grew up in western Pennsylvania. "I made friends here and I liked the city. I got a job as a typist and I was making $110 before deductions. So I was in with three other girls on this apartment because none of us could really afford a place of our own. I wasn't crazy about the work. I mean, I liked office work, but the sort of thing I wanted to do was work in the Library of Congress or something. That sounds silly, right? But for some reason that idea has always struck me. I was having a hard time with the money I was making. There was this guy in the office—he was married—he was always dropping hints to me. He was very nice. We went out to dinner one night and we walked around for a while and in the conversation I mentioned that I adored cashmere sweaters. It was an innocent remark. Later, we had more drinks and ended up in a motel. That was a Friday. On Monday there was a box on my desk. It was a cashmere sweater. At first I was going to give it right back, but later I thought, What the hell. I kept it.

"We went out a few more times after that. He always gave me something. I began to think about the things I needed. We picked things out together sometimes. It just happened after that. I didn't sleep with just anybody; only people who appealed to me. I got overconfident about it all and I quit my job. I expected to make a million as a high-society call girl, I guess. It's not as easy as you think. The secret between a streetwalker and a successful call girl is connections. I was lucky I ran into Jerry. He's not a 'pimp' in the usual sense of the word. He and I have a straight business arrangement. It's a commission on clients.

"I don't like the hustle of it all at times, but I do like the money and there is a lot of freedom. I read a lot, which I like to do. I mean, Jerry has good connections and the johns are nice guys, not just bums off the sidewalk. What can I say? Where else could I make as much money? How could I ever go back to being a typist after having what I have now? How could I afford this apartment? or the clothes? I don't know . . . one day you wake up and realize that you can't get out of it. The money and everything has you surrounded and maybe, deep down you really don't want to get out of it, because part of you really likes it."

But this is not true of all females, especially the large number of emotionally insecure and socially disoriented runaways who flock to the cities each year. These fragments of social disorganization which precipitate in heaps on the sidewalks of center-city business districts have few of the vocational or human resources which would provide them with viable alternatives to prostitution. "It used to be it was boys running away from home—and they were poor ones leaving the inner city headed outward," explained Sergeant Edward Smith, head of the Washington, D.C., Missing Persons Bureau. "That has changed a lot in the last few years. Now it's the girls who are running away more, and they're running away from the affluent suburbs to the inner city, where they end up as prostitutes or drug addicts or both."

Like Washington, cities across the country have been swamped with runaways. Virtually all major urban areas now tabulate that females comprise more than 50 per cent of the runaways on record. These girls are frequently depressed, have poor school records, and few, if any, family ties. They are quick to gravitate to any group or person who offers some measure of security or identity in an alien city. These are the emotionally vulnerable girls on whom pimps prey.

Explaining how such young girls are initially attracted and "turned out" into prostitutes, a New York pimp declared, "You've got to find out if they've got problems, if they're smart enough to say they are 18 when the cops make a bust . . . you've got to stomp her ass a few times to let her know where you're coming from. You've got to set the rules. . . . Maybe use a coat hanger—depends on what she needs. . . . You watch her close, maybe send another girl out with her. If she turns her first trick and comes back smiling, you've got her." [37A]

A highly successful urban pimp who apparently prided himself on keeping abreast of scientific progress boasted that turning a young girl out is "a brainwashing process. The whole thing is creativity," he said. "When you turn a chick out you take away every set of values and morality she previously had and create a different environment." [38] His approach, while successful, is not nearly so impressive as he believes, because his subjects are as different from those of the Chinese interrogators as fish in a barrel are from fish in the open sea. He is not, as he boasts, cutting their previous ties, for if the ties were at all viable he would have few attractive inducements to tempt them into his stable. It is the very absence of those ties and the vulnerability inherent to the non-adapted state [39] that ensures his success. The usual process of brainwashing—crisis, conversion, and cult formation [40]—is already fully in progress at the time of initial encounter between the pimp and his prospective "wife." She is not agonized by a decision to switch from one set of group solidarities to another, but rather she is alienated from the "square society" [41] and eager to barter nothing for almost anything.

Prostitution, like all other complex social behaviors, is determined by a varied set of conditions. Its four component aspects—sexual, economic, psychological, and social—each influence the kinds of people who are attracted to it, and prostitution in turn is influenced by the caliber of its practitioners. Attracting and catering to different social classes, it may more easily be understood in terms of social class behavior than as a particular type of activity. At the upper level, among the full-time call girls and part-time housewives who appear to lead economically secure, stable, arrest-free lives, there is no evidence of special pathology. At the lower levels, inhabited by streetwalkers, drug addicts, juvenile runaways, and deviants of many different stripes, the population is so prone to psychosocial pathology that it is difficult to know what part, if any, prostitution contributes to their many difficulties. There is even some evidence that prostitution may help by improving their financial condition and providing essential though minimal stabilizing relationships. The alternative to prostitution for this population could be victim-oriented crimes. It appears that prostitution is not inherently pathological, but many prostitutes do exhibit psychopathology. Furthermore, given society's restrictions on sexual behavior and willingness of a certain (sometimes disadvantaged) segment of the population to engage in sexual deviancy, it serves the social function of allowing relatively limited and therefore safe outlets which in toto preserve the social structure.

It is timely to wonder what society's attitude toward prostitutes would be if they were men and therefore were not violating a sexual taboo or, to put it another way, if the liberation movement succeeded in gaining for women the same sexual freedoms enjoyed by men. To judge from the influx of middle-class married women into the field, we would most likely see a shift toward more part-time and more socially stable practitioners who would look on their sexual activity as they would on any other job whose income furthered the interests of themselves and their families. If history is any guide, prostitution would seek its own level in the socio-economic hierarchy based on the attributes of its practitioners, the social value of its services, and the financial return it could command.

As for the present practitioners, role distinctions have been blurring in both directions between "proper" women and prostitutes. If the former are acting more like prostitutes, the prostitutes have, for the most part, modified their conduct in the direction of conventionality. The flashy and distinctive styles of dress have either disappeared altogether or have faded into the commonplace as they have been adopted as fashion by the rest of society. It is often no longer possible to distinguish the prostitute from the matrons, college girls, or debutantes who might congregate at any public gathering. This is especially true of the impeccably groomed call girls who make individual appointments with their clients and hail them with such seemingly innocent suggestions as "How about a date?" The long-haired, clean-faced amateurs from the suburbs and the "occasional" or "part-time" prostitutes making their appearance in the majority of Western countries are the vanguard of a more mobile, less regimented group of female entrepreneurs who are beginning to dominate the field. These women are less dependent on pimps and less dependent on madams and brothels than their predecessors in the 1930s, not only because women are more independent in general but also because most of them have a solid base of emotional support in the larger society.

The stages through which many of these women have passed in their metamorphosis from promiscuous housewife through amateur prostitute and then on to semiprofessional standing are at each level extensions of socially tolerated (although not quite accepted) behavior. Under a variety of euphemistic names, each one emphasizing a different aspect of exhibitionistic promiscuity, group sex has been spreading throughout the middle class. "Partying," "freaking," "scening," and "swinging," as these orgies are called, have added a new and unanticipated meaning to the designation "bedroom community" for the suburban ring surrounding urban population centers.

"It's pretty much like a party," explained a young man who lives in Connecticut and commutes to New York City each day. The man is thirty-four years old, a middle-level business executive. His wife is thirty-two, a high-school teacher. They have been "swinging" with other couples and groups for three years.

"We didn't sit down and plan it out. It was almost a surprise when we realized we were so involved. The first time happened when we were on a skiing trip to Vermont. We had taken this small lodge with two other couples. We had skied all day and were drinking and it was a really loose night. It just seemed to happen. No one discussed it, we just sort of paired off and drifted off to other rooms for the night. In the morning everyone was quiet about it. My wife and I talked about it later in the day . . . how it had been. We both enjoyed it . . . although we had also been having some problems between us, so maybe the change was good. That night it happened again, except we all discussed it and played little games to decide who would pair off with who this time.

"Back home one of the other couples brought a fourth couple to a party and we gradually expanded our circle of people. We've been to large parties now . . . one couple has them regularly now, one a month . . . where there are about two or three dozen people and it's more of what you think about with an 'orgy.' There are a lot of different degrees with this sort of thing. We like to shy away from wild group things because sometimes people open them to anyone who will pay to get in . . . you get some strange people at those. We're not really comfortable there. We mostly like to stick with couples we know well. Of course one of the things involved here is selectivity on my part. At larger things, you don't know who will be there or what will get out through the grapevine. Just a whiff of this sort of thing would have to get around in a company like mine and I'd be out on my ass. I'm very aware of that. I'm very careful for that reason."

The emotional detachment encouraged by mass group behavior effectively buffers individuals from interpersonal involvement at the same time as they are participating in the most intimate kinds of sexual transactions. Such a combination is likely to foster an atmosphere more mechanical and sterile than the most commercialized brothel. Not that this is necessarily viewed by the participants as a handicap. Quite the opposite. These are the very men and women who would most likely be involved in full-scale prostitution were it not for this communal alternative. There are at least two reasons why some people seek out such sexual experiences and are able to function better in them than in more conventional settings. First, people unable to countenance relations and relationships with the same person would be attracted to the impersonality of group sex, and if denied such opportunities might be impotent or frigid. Second, the very anonymity of the interpersonal transaction, similar to the religious confessional, the psychiatric interview, or the brothel, permits and even facilitates the expression of socially disapproved behaviors which would otherwise be repressed or suppressed.

While such group activities have cut into the market traditionally served by prostitution, they have also provided the emotional and physical experiences which have encouraged women to go into prostitution. After a girl has attended several such parties, accepting presents at first and then an occasional fee, she is in a transitional state on her way to full professional status. There is an even easier mode. The host or hostess may charge some male guests an admission fee to the party, thus making the women participants unwitting prostitutes. When the lure of easy money is added to the natural inclinations which drew these women to the parties in the first place, the pull toward prostitution, at least on a part-time basis, becomes quite strong. Many prostitutes awaiting parole revealed that they were far from dissatisfied with their lives.[42] They found hustling to be more exciting, less demanding, and better paying than most of the sales, office, and domestic jobs that would have been available to them. This was especially true of the younger women and those who had worked as call girls.

"I got to the point where I was living in a fairy tale. I was telling myself, 'Well, you just need the money and then you'll get out of this and get back to a career or something . . . you're not like the other girls who make a life out of this,' " said Miriam, a call girl who works the traveling-business-executive circuit in Philadelphia and New York.

"After about a year, I got to the stage where I was able to admit openly to myself that I liked it. I don't know, it has a style to it; a zing that I really enjoy. You're moving with really classy people. Some girls hate the marks they service. I don't. I can really get into the give-and-take of the situation. I like the sex and I like the personal contact. It's not just an assembly line with me. A couple months ago, one guy took me on a five-day trip to Puerto Rico. O.K., it was a business arrangement, but it was also great fun and we both enjoyed it.

"Of course, you do get some weirdos or kinky guys every now and then; that happens in all jobs. A lot of girls aren't able to admit how much they like it. Something inside doesn't want to let it surface. It sort of has to roll around inside you and then it breaks out and you see it and can say, 'I really do enjoy this.' "

As I have said, the relationship between prostitution and other crimes is difficult to delineate. It sometimes appears in association with drug addiction and violence, and in the past has been under the control of organized crime, but association is not causation. What birds who flock together share may not be their similar feathers but rather their similar fears of predators or their taste for similar prey. The condition of illegitimacy or stigmatization may bring together groups which have only that in common. Even if it can be established that various deviances influence each other, before we could conclude a causal relationship we would have to discount the influence which derives from proximity.

Ever since the prohibition era, when Al Capone was reputed to have headed the largest syndicate of brothels, there has been a gradual erosion of the alliance between organized crime and prostitution. This has been caused by improved law enforcement, the decentralization of prostitution with its shift toward individual operators, and the availability to organized crime of more easily controlled enterprises such as narcotics traffic or labor unions. At present, neither organized crime nor any third party, for that matter, plays an important role in prostitution.

There is less certainty about the role of drug use, which has increased greatly among prostitutes since 1939.[43] While the relationship between prostitution and drug addiction is an unsettled issue, socially the two groups appear to be drawn from the same chaotic subcultural milieu. The controversial issue is whether dependency makes economic demands on a woman which cannot be met by a legitimate job and therefore pushes her toward the more lucrative rewards of prostitution [44] or whether dependency stems from the concurrent appearance of two similarly rooted deviances in a criminal population. There is strong evidence to suggest the latter.[45] Once in "the life," the isolation and emotional deprivation of the prostitute drive her to employ the same chemical remedies as other alienated segments of society. Given prostitutes' psychosocial vulnerability, the availability of drugs in the deviant subculture within which they operate, and their capacity to pay, it would be surprising if many prostitutes resisted addiction. Of course, the populations usually studied have arrest records and are more prone to behavioral deviancy than the neurotics on the psychoanalyst's couch whose major complaints are symptoms, inhibitions, or fantasies. Study of this criminogenic segment may tell us as little about successful prostitutes as pathology does about physiology.

Although sexual promiscuity is being accepted with more tolerance and addicts are increasingly being labeled "sick" rather than "criminal," the case is quite different for violence. The aggressiveness of the prostitute has exceeded society's toleration level. It is not known whether they are more assaultive than previously or whether their assaults are being reported more readily by customers now less ashamed to confess their misadventure, but aggressive incidents are steadily increasing. "Not a night goes by," explained Daniel C. Hickey, president of the Hotel Association of New York City, "that security guards in reputable hotels are not compelled to eject numbers of prostitutes who solicit customers in its halls and public rooms." [46] And it is the experience of police officers in New York and other major cities that such "solicitations" are being accompanied by increasing levels of violence. Again in New York—the city where prostitution has made itself most visible —a policeman was stabbed to death with a switchblade by a prostitute resisting arrest. That was the first of six murders by streetwalkers reported in 1968.[47] At the level of the streetwalker, where sex is purveyed and perhaps received with little or no show of affection, hostility alternates with hard-sell seductiveness in seller-buyer negotiations. Unlike the brothel girl of the 1930s, who depended on honest service to build up a following, the streetwalker hardly ever expects to see her "john" again, and since her only dealings with him are mechanical and commercial, she often feels justified in relieving him of whatever valuables she can secure. Most prostitutes are adept at rolling a drunk, and some even resort to barbiturates or "knockout drops." Working in clusters, the streetwalkers are a formidable threat to any one male, and they are better able to avoid apprehension by warning each other of plain-clothes men.

Such women are probably typical of only the lowest operating class of prostitutes, representing the dregs, after the brighter and more refined women have, through social acceptance of promiscuity, risen to become call girls and part-timers. Prostitution is thus an interesting example of the process of behavioral diffusion. At the outset, the legitimate and the illegitimate activities tend to be polarized. Because of its illegal status, the deviant behavior is forced into locales where other forms of deviancy abound and it is socially linked to other stigmatized groups. However, as public attitudes become more tolerant, as they have toward gambling and, more and more, toward soft-drug use and prostitution, middle-class participation increases, adding middle-class values, persons, and styles to the deviancy—which is then relabeled a variation. Gradually, society extends a circle of accommodation around the previously forbidden activity, institutes social controls, and leaves an unregenerate fringe outside the pale. By acquiescing to swinger parties and failing to press arrests of call girls and amateur prostitutes, while at the same time insisting on a more vigorous pursuit of streetwalker types, society is changed by what it absorbs and prostitution is changed by the residue that is left.

In Nevada, prostitution has gone beyond social acceptance to full legalization, and in several communities "the brothel is practically an institution, like the corner drugstore and the County courthouse." [48] Nor has this change been accepted grudgingly in the places where it has been tried. If not esteemed as a source of special pride by the local inhabitants, it is at least valued as a financial asset. According to the *Los Angeles Times,* "prostitution is one of the biggest industries in rural Nevada," [49] and the more prosperous brothels even make arrangements for commuter plane service. Such elegant accommodations have been matched abroad: in Hamburg, in 1967, William Bartels developed what he called an Eros Center, or sex supermarket, based on his concept of the "rationalized brothel." A four-story apartment house completely devoted to prostitution, it contains 136 one-room apartments and even provides underground parking. At the present rate of progress, the time may not be far off when prostitutes will be accorded the same kind of limited status that accrues to attractive people, such as actors, who have restricted and circumscribed public contact. If that time comes, their services will be sufficiently routinized and legitimatized to be considered a community resource as well as a source of revenue.

In his analysis of prostitution, Kingsley Davis predicated three conditions, one or more of which would have to be present before prostitution would rise in social esteem:

1) The promiscuity is lessened by some basis of discrimination,
2) The earnings of prostitution are used for a goal considered socially desirable,
3) The prostitute combines other roles with that of sexual gratification.[50]

These conditions focus on the prostitute as the agent of change under pressure to conform to relatively fixed social standards. It is ironic that under the impetus of the female equal-rights movement, with its attendant liberalization of sexual norms, these changes have indeed occurred—but largely by compromising social standards. As coeds in mixed dorms, housewives in search of pin money, and bachelor women began to challenge the double standard, the male establishment was faced with three choices: either to retrench, which the present generation of women would not tolerate; or to renounce the discriminatory male sexual prerogatives, which the present generation of men would not tolerate; or to accept women as equal sexual beings, which was congenial to both sexes and harmonious with the spirit of the mid-twentieth century. All parties chose the latter, and in so doing perforce were required to re-evaluate prostitution not as something intrinsically bad but as an instrument which could be either good or bad, depending on how it was used. A capitalist society might withhold professional status from a purely commercial enterprise, but it could not fault a voluntary, victimless activity simply because it was profitable, especially when promiscuity is hardly considered a vice for males. Contemporary women are no longer willing to accept sexual activity as the measure of female morality. They are also less charitable toward social standards which permit a promiscuous male to be admired as a gay blade while a promiscuous female is dismissed as a woman of light and easy virtue. These changes in public attitudes have changed the kinds of people who go into prostitution and vice versa. Although the prostitute is not quite the girl next door, the call girl and semipro bear so many resemblances to her that they are, in many instances, socially and culturally indistinguishable.

Thus we find that, except for streetwalkers, who are still legally pursued although less socially despised than pitied, most prostitutes have risen in social esteem for the same reason that women in general have. Davis's three conditions have indeed been met—but chiefly by society. Let us review them: 1) Promiscuity has not lessened but increased; however, it has lost much of its stigma and is no longer considered shameful. 2) The earnings of part-timers and semiprofessional housewives contribute to familial goals. 3) The bachelor women, call girls, and housewives, each in different ways, combine other roles with prostitution. In a social reversal, prostitution is vanquishing its ignominious image in a way hardly anticipated one short generation ago.

In the progressive thrust toward equality of opportunity—as, for example, in education and medical care—there is a characteristic sequence of attitudes. What begins as a *laissez-faire* freedom succeeds to an inherent right, and under continued communal pressure becomes a social obligation. The rediscovery of sexuality in women appears to be following such a course and, as in the case of civil liberties, is benefiting men as well. Pleasurable sexual experiences are being increasingly viewed as an aspect of the total life experience for both men and women to which they feel entitled as a matter of course. To meet this need—or right, as it may soon be interpreted—"touch and feel" psychotherapies, a branch of Behavior Therapy, are becoming an accepted part of the medical procedure. Masters and Johnson, at their Reproductive Biology Research Foundation in St. Louis, have been utilizing unpaid female "partner surrogates" in the treatment of sexual inadequacies in males. If distress and disability [51] are accepted as criteria for medical illness, then sexual inadequacy qualifies as a disease and, as such, demands therapy.[52] Dr. Masters has called men with this illness social cripples and has raised the question of whether society considers them to be entitled to treatment. It is his belief that if the answer is no, it would be "discrimination of one segment of society over another." [53] If the answer is yes, how will female sexual therapists be solicited, how will they be regarded professionally, and would sexually inadequate women have access to the same form of treatment?

Extending these ideas, it does not seem farfetched to suggest that in an atmosphere of increasing sexual freedom, prostitutes may be employed as social workers specializing in problems which present themselves as sexual difficulties. Involuntary homosexuals and depressed, isolated, and impotent men, for example, might initially respond to such an approach more readily than to any other. Their role would be a transitional one which would help psychosexually afflicted men toward fuller and more satisfying relationships with others.[54] In the milieu created for and by the women's liberation movement, such proposals are no longer impractical.

Throughout the centuries, attitudes toward prostitution have ranged the spectrum from the esteem in which hetaerae were held to the contempt which greeted the medieval harlot. Characteristically these changes in attitude pivoted around feelings toward women and feelings about sex, with many interesting variations. For example, women were at times glorified but only as chaste and empty vessels; at times, sex was glorified but women were demeaned. Historically, prostitutes have been praised, tolerated, or vilified, depending on the period, and it is tempting to conclude that current changes are cyclic repetitions of the past. But this would be misleading. What has been characteristic of the past was that women in general and prostitutes in particular were primarily the objects of male attitudinal changes. What is significant about the present is that women have become the subjects as well as objects, and prostitutes are being viewed in a perspective that is broader than their mere utility to men. Like other modern women, today's prostitute is better educated, better accepted, and more independent of men. She may be a housewife, bachelor woman, or graduate student. She may even become a professional in the allied health field. Although the prostitute is not a member in good social standing, it is less because she is a promiscuous woman than because she may be an antisocial person with unsavory connections. But legalization of prostitution, along with social acceptance of female sexuality, is taking it out of the nether world of vice to which it has been traditionally consigned. The changing role of women has brought them into the mainstream of society where they can interact as principals in their own destiny. In its scope and immensity, this upward movement is freeing women of their vices as well as their virtues, and is destigmatizing sex for both sexes.

4

Minor Girls and Major Crimes

*"Keep strict watch over a headstrong daughter,
lest, when she finds liberty, she use it to her hurt."*

Ecclesiasticus, XXVI, 10

In few other fields did young women more appropriately deserve the appellation "fair" than in that of crime. In every period of history and every geographic area, their crime rate has trailed far behind that of men. The significant post–World War II increases in female delinquency, therefore, suggest that since that time unprecedented social forces have been operating to create this trend. Just who will be caught up in these forces and how they will react to them is difficult to predict, but if the annals of male delinquency are any indication, the one thing we do know is that the number of young women in crime will continue to increase and the spectrum of their offenses will surely broaden.

Since the beginning of recorded history it has been the adolescent males who have been excoriated for a variety of failings which in one form or another reflected their inveterate tendency to pursue adult prerogatives while fleeing adult responsibilities. The historical reason why girls have not been similarly criticized stems from both their characteristic docility and the limited range of expectations, personal and societal, permitted by their traditional roles. The transition from girlhood to womanhood has customarily been relatively easy because a female-dominated childhood provided omnipresent role models and, except for sexuality, the scope of female activity after puberty differed very little from the earlier one. It is in these two areas—the adequacy of early adult models for later roles and the widening of female options—that recent social changes have exerted their greatest influence on female delinquency. As a transitional developmental period, adolescence has always been fraught with turmoil and vulnerable to social deviation. But for girls of the last two decades, it is a transition within a transition. The new image of womanhood has been changing a girl's mental conception of femininity almost as rapidly as her endocrines have been molding the physical form of her femininity. This metamorphosis has been both harder and easier than it seems. Although insecurities have naturally arisen out of recent departures from established patterns, these have been partially ameliorated by the lifting of many unnatural restraints on female behavior. Freedom and insecurity are often fellow travelers on the road to social progress. Here walk our females in their fledgling roles.

The perpetuation of each civilization depends upon its possession of social mechanisms that both support stability and encourage change. This is necessary not only because the vicissitudes of the environment require periodic readjustments but also because each new generation tends to challenge tradition to justify itself. Look no further than the recent antiwar demonstrations, campus unrest, and pressures for the lowering of legal-age requirements to see these vindications in action. While stability and change are each important to social functioning, they are in some sense inimical to each other because they have different goals and because they are supported by different segments of the population. Adulthood is identified with the state of being, as adolescence is with the process of becoming. It is the ferment of adolescence and youth which periodically stimulates the establishment to progress or threatens it with disruption. In general, those civilizations which have survived have been able to navigate between the Scylla of fixity and the Charybdis of flux, but as Socrates's admonition reflects, the voyage is rarely an easy one for either the older or younger generation.

Both the denunciations of antiquity and the declarations of daily newspapers testify that juvenile delinquency is neither a newly sprung twentieth-century phenomenon nor a malady of the Western world. Places like Brooklyn's Red Hook, Manhattan's East Harlem, and Chicago's South Side, though unequal in many other respects, share a common problem of delinquency with Moscow's Lenin Hills, Tokyo's factory districts, and Amsterdam's housing projects. What is special about the current problem is that the "baby boom" of the fifties has resulted in a disproportionate increase in the population of juveniles, and the social revolution of the sixties has virilized its previously or presumably docile female segment. Furthermore, expanding technologies, shrinking frontiers, and cultural changes in industrialized nations have reduced the number of unskilled jobs while increasing the number of girls seeking employment. Never have so many young women had so much incentive to abandon traditional roles and so comparatively few opportunities within the system to find others.

High delinquency rates are found in all modern nations. Not only are rates high, but statistics from European nations, Japan, the United States, and those filtering out of Russia, China, and some of the developing countries (e.g., East African nations) suggest great increases during the sixties. Where societies place great stress on material success and upward mobility, it is unlikely that their juveniles can be easily kept within the confines of conventional behavior. Authorities throughout the world agree that the upsurge in delinquency rates is related to urbanization, industrialization, and modernization with their attendant breakdown of traditional forms of social organization.

Traditionally, the term "juvenile delinquent" has had an implicit male connotation, and with considerable justification. In the early 1900s, ratios of over fifty males to one female juvenile delinquent were quite common. However, along with the general trend toward the emancipation of women, the proportion of female offenders has increased markedly so that at present, in the United States, the ratio of males to females has shrunk to about five-to-one in favor of males. While this is a dramatic change in statistics,[1] it is likely that even these figures underreport the number of young women actually engaged in delinquent activities; the lowered figures reflect the social resistance to recognizing female criminality in general and, more specifically, female juvenile delinquencies.

Historically, the growth of the spirit of social justice in the nineteenth century was accompanied by a movement on the part of reformers to change the whole judicial process as it related to young people. Thus, consideration of juveniles as a separate entity was a relatively late development in American jurisprudence. In fact, it was not until 1899 that the first law governing juvenile delinquency was enacted.[2] The Juvenile Court Act, passed by the Illinois legislature, created the first state-wide court especially for children. At that time, the Illinois State General Assembly made initial attempts to cope with this poorly defined area between childhood innocence and adult culpability. In essence, it proscribed all behavior which is also prohibited for adults but added "protective" provisions, such as forbidding entrance into saloons and railroad engines and disobedience of parents. The chronological boundary line was set at seventeen for males and at eighteen for females. Since the writing of this statute, other state legislatures have grappled with the unique problems posed by this age group. How much freedom should they be given? How much protection do they need from their own impulses (alcohol, gambling, drugs, sex, cars) and from adults who might exploit them? Newer legislation has consistently pursued the goal of binding culpability in age as in other considerations, but such efforts have always been hampered by the inherent instability and unpredictability of the adolescent period. By 1925 there were juvenile courts in every state but two, and today there is a Juvenile Court Act in every American jurisdiction.

By legal definition, a juvenile delinquent is someone under eighteen who either commits an adult crime or transgresses into areas which society considers beyond his or her physical, mental, or moral capabilities. All state laws agree that a girl is a juvenile delinquent if she commits an act which would be a criminal offense if done by an adult. In addition, eleven state statutes include thirty-four juvenile offenses not covered by the adult criminal code, but no one state includes them all.[3] For serious or persistent antisocial behavior, most states allow the courts to exercise discretion in determining whether to handle it as a crime (adult) or delinquency (juvenile). While boys tend to be arrested for offenses involving stealing and various sorts of mischief, girls are typically charged with sex offenses which are euphemistically described as "delinquent tendencies," "incorrigibility," or "running away."[4] The sources of case referral also show a sex differential. Whereas law-enforcement agencies apprehend the majority of delinquent boys, a much higher percentage of delinquent girls are brought to court by referral from schools, social agencies, and relatives.[5] The stereotype of gender-typical offenses is self-perpetuating because girls tend to be overprosecuted for sexual misbehavior and under-prosecuted, at least in the middle class, for aggressive misbehavior.[6] This is not to say that teen-age girls are sexually less active than the record indicates, but simply that they are probably less active than boys, whose promiscuity is socially tolerated.

Paradoxically, as girls respond to the leveling of the double standard by imitating male promiscuity,[7] we can predict that they will be prosecuted less because their increased sexual activity will be matched by an increased social tolerance. The same pattern is not likely to apply to aggressive behavior, which is doubly troublesome. This behavior challenges a social stereotype, but unlike sexual transgressions it is not a victimless crime and, therefore, poses a practical threat as well. It is just because female offenses did not threaten social functioning that the entire field of female deviancy has been neglected by criminological research.[8] However good the reasons for neglecting female deviancy may have been in the past, at present we are seeing that sex roles among all classes of juveniles are more alike and thus bear equal research. In both hidden delinquency and overt deviancy, girls of all classes have departed from previously prescribed sex role behavior for the same reason that their sisters are choosing careers over domesticity or sexual experience over chastity.

Because girls were different from boys, it was assumed a generation ago that delinquent girls, like nondelinquent girls, were simpler to understand. A girl's traditional role was restricted to the family; her chief concern was her physical appearance [9] because through it she hoped to attract a proper male; and her prime but perishable claim to respectability was her virginity. Determining the rules of normalcy from the exceptions of delinquency, the conventional female teen-ager of the first third of the twentieth century moved comfortably in a two-dimensional world bounded by familial fealty and sexual abstinence. The former guaranteed her present security . . . the latter ensured her future prospects. From such a socially restricted habitat, there were only two directions in which she could transgress—disobedience and promiscuity. If she was a runaway, she might well be involved in both. Such "unadjusted" girls were considered to be somewhat amoral as well as unwise, because they frittered away the sexual capital of their irreplaceable virginity in self-defeating efforts to satisfy wishes for security, recognition, and new experiences.[10] Such efforts were often pitiful attempts by girls who lacked grace or material means to achieve respectable status.[11] This type of juvenile led some investigators to the conclusion that male delinquents tend to hurt others while female delinquents tend to hurt themselves.[12] This was not mere pious moralizing, because in the climate of the times, no matter how badly a girl fared at home, it was likely that she would fare worse in the outside world. The skillful management of her sexual behavior was the chief faculty she possessed for coping with a male-dominated society,[13] and it was unlikely that the security which chastity failed to gain for her would be achieved by promiscuity. "Nice" girls can be sexy, never sexual. In the limited confines within which women in general, and girls in particular, were allowed to operate there were very few ways in which she could be either good or bad, and most of them encompassed conformity and sex.

Very likely it is just because of the female's tendency to conform and the victimless nature of her transgressions that the study of female delinquents has been so long neglected. Deviations were primarily from the female sex-role expectation rather than from the criminal statutes.[14] The courts treated the bulk of these youngsters with paternalistic chivalry, meting out relatively mild treatment.[15] But there is another side to chivalry. If it dispenses leniency, it may with equal justification invoke control. In recommendations for institutionalization and in actual sentencing to institutions, females were often treated more harshly than their male counterparts.[16] The court's purpose, however, was less punitive than protective. The rationale is that girls gravitate to delinquent behavior as a result of poor home situations. Sexual misbehavior, so the thinking goes, is common to the distressed female because it represents her misguided efforts to compensate for affectional relationships missing from the home.[17] Therefore, institutionalization was deemed necessary to save the girl from herself or from her family.[18] Whether this was an appropriate judicial response or not, the results of self-report studies indicate that the courts have consistently erred in overestimating the sexual character of female delinquency and underestimating the number of incidents of other female delinquency. These studies suggest that if female deviant behavior were being randomly sampled by the juvenile courts, males would still predominate over females in numbers of offenses, but they would be roughly similar in the kinds of offenses.[19]

Another bias of the juvenile court is material to its treatment of females. It considers itself *parens patriae* (a role of legal parent) in relationship to the juvenile and, therefore, mandated with a special responsibility to reinforce the familial demands for morality (usually sexual) and obedience.[20] In acting as a conservative social force, it tends to uphold the double standard, thereby impinging more restrictively on the rights of female adolescents than on males. The court, like the traditional American family, has sex-differentiated expectations—obedience, dependency, and responsibility from girls, and achievement and self-reliance from boys—and concomitant sex-differentiated sanctions. The "family" court, like the family itself, views the female delinquent more from a social than a legal perspective and consequently brings a much narrower tolerance for sexual deviance to its assessment of the gravity of her offense. In its defense of the social *status quo*, the court is especially sensitive to anything the girl does to challenge the authority of the family or to undermine its sexual mores. It is because of its guardianship of these values that the juvenile court often places more emphasis on females' violations of sex-role expectations than on their violations of the law and sanctions female sexual deviancy more severely than male.

But events create the momentum for change, and the courts often follow where custom leads. By the late fifties and early sixties, a generation of female juveniles, politicized by the Indochina war, liberated by the equal-rights movement, protected by oral contraceptives, and bolstered by unprecedented numbers, was bypassing the normative positions petrified by the family court and recasting social stereotypes in its own unisexual image. The changes had a double impact because they involved two generations which synergized each other's efforts toward full equality: adult women were rediscovering sex at the same time as their fourteen-year-old daughters were heterosexually involved at the same level that their mothers had been at sixteen.[21] The crescendo of rising expectations buoyed by higher education and the opening of hitherto inaccessible jobs widened the female horizon to include the entire landscape of male prerogatives. But in spite of the mercurial pace with which these changes seemed to be progressing, the tempo was in part illusory. It owed its aura of headlong acceleration less to the process of female emancipation, which in retrospect was fairly gradual and orderly, than to the precipitous discrediting of stereotypes, suddenly refuted by events they could no longer rationalize. While the daily life of the juveniles underwent continuous changes,[22] these changes were not accurately reflected by the social institutions which were monitoring them. They suffered from the perhaps inevitable inertia of all bureaucratic structures which make them shift from under-reaction to overreaction. Furthermore, the tendency of social move-ments to be discovered only after they have already gained momen-tum gives them the impression of possessing more impetus than they may actually have acquired. In fact, a retrospective evaluation suggests that past female abstinence and conformity was overesti-mated and was probably less real than apparent. Likewise, the present acceleration of female role changes seems also to be over-estimated and is probably more apparent than real. It is our social awareness of these events rather than the events themselves which has shown the sharpest increase. Just as official statistics have overlooked the sexual delinquency of boys, so have they under-estimated that area of female delinquency considered typically male.[23] Especially in recent years and especially in the middle class, there is evidence to suggest that if law-enforcement agencies em-ployed identical criteria in making arrests of boys and girls, there would be considerably less variation in the delinquency rates be-tween the two.[24]

The increasing antipathy which teen-age girls feel toward traditional female roles could easily lead to their acquisition of even more social and antisocial male behaviors. Superficially, this new trend toward the unisexual is evidenced by the hair styles, clothing, and other items of fashion which have been adopted or rejected by today's younger females. The traditional crinoline and lace of the fifties gave way to the casual denim of the sixties, which has evolved into the overalls of the seventies.

In the words of one seventeen-year-old high-school girl: "Eye-shadow, make-up, and all of that is a real drag when you really think about it. When you stand back and look at it, the whole thing is a trap . . . set by multimillion-dollar conglomerates who want us to believe that we can only be 'whole' as human beings when we smear their prod-uct on our faces or spray it under our arms or around our vaginal areas. I want to know that I am me; that I don't need just the right smell or smear-on or bra to be me. Once you really get into yourself as a woman, a lot of the female advertising hype you see becomes absurd."

On a level somewhat deeper and far less visible, teen-age girls are receiving changing role cues from within their own family units. Both in the way parents respond to their boys and girls and in what they expect from them, there are fewer and fewer sexual distinctions.[25] Indeed, even as role models, these parents daily demonstrate the convergence of the sexes. While this has freed the middle-class girl from many restraints, it is also forcing her to compete more actively with boys as well as girls scholastically, athletically, vocationally, and criminally. The era when girls sewed dresses and boys sowed wild oats has yielded to a period when both are expected to achieve a degree of self-sufficiency. Passivity is no longer a self-evident feminine virtue, and status is not automatically conferred on the girl who is docile and chaste. Since delinquent activity, like its adult counterpart, is linked to opportunity and expectation, there is every reason to anticipate that, as egalitarian forces expand, so too will the crime rate of the female young set.

Pressures associated with role convergence make girls of today even more vulnerable than boys to delinquency. Traditionally, the biosocial difficulties surrounding pubescence were balanced by the stabilizing influence of a protective family and community. But that stability has yielded to the necessity, once exclusively male, to make one's way and to prove oneself in the world. In addition, this mandate is an ambiguous one for females because, while they are urged toward equality of education and community participation at one level, they also encounter job discrimination and are urged to reject their intellect at another level.[26] The internal and external conflicts generated by the usual disruptions of puberty plus the role change and the ambiguity of the new role create complex identity problems more intense in nature and scope than those faced by boys.[27] While all classes of female juveniles must negotiate these biosocial rites of passage, the middle-class girl, at least, often has the advantage of attractive parental models with whom she can identify in a relatively conflict-free way. The lower-class girl is less fortunate in this, as in other respects. The frequent absence of the father from the home and, in many cases, the brutal treatment of his wife when he is present [28] provide scant opportunities for healthy identification, while at the same time creating an atmosphere of emotional deprivation congenial to a delinquent subculture.

Thus the emancipation of women appears to be having a twofold influence on female juvenile crimes. Girls are involved in more drinking, stealing, gang activity, and fighting—behavior in keeping with their adoption of male roles.[29] We also find increases in the total number of female deviancies. The departure from the safety of traditional female roles and the testing of uncertain alternative roles coincide with the turmoil of adolescence creating criminogenic risk factors which are bound to create this increase. These considerations help explain the fact that between 1960 and 1972 national arrests for major crimes show a jump for boys of 82 per cent—for girls, 306 per cent.[30]

These figures reflect not only quantitative changes in female delinquency but also alterations in the kinds of deviancy which girls were finding attractive. Promiscuity, of course, is not new, but in recent years in decaying countercultural centers such as New York's East Village pubescent prostitutes, so-called teeny-hookers, have replaced the middle-class flower children of the sixties, and the transformation has been striking. Alcohol, amphetamines, and heroin have replaced marijuana and LSD; commercial sex has replaced Aquarian love; and a street-wise group of emotionally distressed, violence-prone youngsters roam the areas where idealistic flower children once trod. These youngsters are runaways, but not only in the physical sense, for they are psychologically adrift from families and social institutions which once supplied security and structure. While drug and alcohol use are on the increase [31] and are sometimes utilized by pimps in efforts to control teen-agers, they are only one segment of the many varieties of deviancies which grow in such adolescent instability.

"The greater majority of girls we see," explained one director of a California drug-rehabilitation facility, "are not drug users because they were tricked into it. They are drug users because they themselves decided to enter the drug scene—for a number of often quite complicated reasons. The girls we get here—and we are running almost fifty per cent females now—have a basic problem in recognizing who they are. The problem is essentially one of identity. They have reached the point of identity crisis, and for a number of different reasons it was too much for them. They were unable to cope with it. Instead they hoped to stay high and circumvent the problem and the decisions it necessitated.

"Their real problem is not really the chemicals they put into their bodies. It is deeper. The chemical substances are merely a symptom. These girls haven't the faintest idea who they are. What we do is attempt to take them back inside their own heads . . . back to the crisis to see the reasons they couldn't cope . . . make them recognize what drugs are . . . just an escape route."

That escape route would not be nearly so destructive if it led to viable alternatives. Characteristically, the girls who take drugs have fled from, or perhaps more accurately cut, their previous emotional ties (e.g. family, school, church) and lack the vocational or social skills to perform adequately in new nondeviant groups.[32] Historically, they have been affiliated with the male-dominated gang, either as ancillary sex-objects or as semiautonomous female auxiliary groups. They became Egyptian Cobrettes to their Egyptian Cobras and Vice Queens to their Vice Kings, but until recently they were limited to sexual and housekeeping roles and tended to avoid violent confrontations. But in the growing repertoire of female delinquencies, violence is becoming a more frequent option.

"I know it's happening, but I'll be damned if it still doesn't shock me when I see it," explained one exasperated sergeant who was slumped in the chair of a district precinct house in Washington, D.C. He was talking about the new problems which girls have created for police. "Last week, for instance, we get a call of a disturbance at the high school. A fight . . . after school. So we get down there and pull up and here is a hell of a crowd yelling and screaming at the kids in the center, who are fighting. I push my way through the crowd—they're going crazy like it is really a mean fight—and when I get to the middle . . . I liked to fell over. Here are two husky broads, and they are fighting . . . now

I don't mean any hair-pulling face-scratching kind of thing; I mean two broads squared off and ducking it out. Throwing jabs and hooking in at each other and handling themselves like a couple of goddamned pro sparring partners. I mean, I got to ask myself, What the hell is going on? What in the name of God is happening to these girls any more?"

The new aggressiveness of girls is not isolated to the sergeant's Washington precinct—or to any city, for that matter.

In New York, Gladys Polikoff has spent the last quarter of a century working with adolescent girls who have been apprehended by and are being processed through the Youth Aid Division of the police department.

"It's difficult to put a finger on exactly what is happening, but something quite drastic has taken place out there," she observed.

"Through the fifties, we'd get an occasional girl . . . for shoplifting . . . mostly it was because the girl had taken something for kicks or on a dare . . . strictly a spur-of-the-moment sort of thing. Now, of course, girl shoplifters are quite common; and they are taking specific things for resale or for their own use in a very methodical way. Girls we're seeing now are involved in a whole new range of activities . . . like extortion. A group of girls ganging up on another girl and shaking her down for money. I mean, that was simply unheard of just a few years ago. Now, you don't get the name-calling, hair-pulling that used to go between girls . . . you get vicious physical assault.

Perhaps some of the best points from which to monitor the "new" female delinquent are the prisons where the worst of her number are incarcerated.

At Muncy State Prison for Women in northwestern Pennsylvania, for instance, there has been a radical change in the inmate population.

Sue Goodwin, a prison official who has formerly worked as a probation officer in two major urban areas, feels the change in the general attitude of her charges has become glaringly apparent.

"In the first place," she explained, "there is no question that the adolescents are the hardest inmates to handle. They are the most exuberant, and the ones who rebel the most. And now we have begun to get a whole new breed of adolescent inmates . . . very violent ones. They are no longer the frightened, docile prisoners that women have traditionally been. Instead, they come in here and, within the first two weeks, they have to let everyone know that they are the 'baddest ass' in the place."

As Ms. Goodwin points out, there appears to be a certain level of imitative male machismo competitiveness developing among criminal adolescent girls, who, both in their crimes and their overall attitudes and deportment, are becoming almost indistinguishable from male inmates. In the last half of the sixties, for instance, while national attention was focused on male prisons with their riots and threats of riots, similar occurrences at female institutions went almost unnoticed. At the time, the idea of a riot in a female prison was alien to accepted notions of female behavior. But in spite of its implausibility, it became a reality for the officials at the Indiana Girls' School. There, in late 1966, two hundred adolescent girls reduced the institution to a shambles.[33] A study made during the aftermath of that outbreak revealed that the most aggressive and violent participants and, indeed, the instigators of the riots were drawn from the younger girls in the institution. These girls were the ones most frequently serving time for theft, larceny, burglary, assault, and armed robbery, rather than for the usual "soft" female offenses. Since it is this kind of economic and assaultive crime that is on the increase with the upcoming cadre of female delinquents, we can anticipate even more violence in the entire legal process from arrest through imprisonment.

Of all the forms of adolescent urban violence which have plagued our cities in recent years, none has been quite as socially threatening as that of organized gang warfare. In Philadelphia, New York, Chicago, Los Angeles, and other major urban areas, gangs have terrorized entire neighborhoods, virtually crippled school systems, and injured or killed innumerable persons. None of this is new, but a new factor has been introduced into the equation of violence—the female gang member. Her entrance was gradual and at first peripheral to the male-centered gang activity. Sex was, of course, offered and accepted, as were drugs, but her activity—it was not yet quite a role—was incidental to the main operations.

All members of a society tend to share certain perceptions, so that, ironically, even deviancy conforms to the prescribed patterns.

Consequently, we have the paradox of a counterculturally dedicated group—such as the antisocial gang—organized, regulated, and ritualized along structural lines that resemble a corporation staff—complete with specific attitudes toward women. As attitudes of the larger society have changed with regard to women, so, in parallel fashion, have the attitudes of these microsocieties. As establishment women reached for and attained positions integrated within the male power structure, so did their delinquent daughters. By the mid-sixties, police were reporting an increase in arrests of girls for being gang lookouts, carrying weapons, and generally aiding in gang warfare. By the seventies, girls had become more highly integrated in male gang activity and were moving closer to parallel but independent, violence-oriented, exclusively female groups.

In Philadelphia, where male gang violence takes a toll of as many as fifty lives a year, there are no girl gangs per se, but there are numerous aggressively disposed female "cliques." [34] They contain anywhere from a few to a few dozen girls who hang together on their own and engage in typical male mischief. At present they differ from gangs in not having the warlords, runners, and other rigid structural components found in male gang organizations.

Deborah is a fifteen-year-old who has been a member of such a group for a number of years. She comes from the 21st-and-Montgomery section of the city—a rugged area, with dilapidated housing, a high crime rate and widespread unemployment. A student at William Penn High School, she began her involvement with gangs as a hanger-on with the Valley Gang, an all-male gang from the same area. Although currently connected with a church organization seeking to break down the gangs and gang involvement, she feels no shame about her activities in the past. Her words are spoken with a hint of pride as she tells about her effectiveness on the streets and in violence-oriented gang operations.

She, along with the other girls of her group, did much street fighting, usually rivaling the other male gangs of the area. "A lotta times we'd go down to Norris Street, in enemy territory, and fight their girls. But we never shot anybody," she said, pointing out that, instead, the girls liked to confine their efforts to the use of fists and, only occasionally, pipes, clubs, and bricks as weapons. She admitted to having used a knife on special occasions. "The way it was, if any of the other girls got messed up bad, it was because they asked for it. I mean, now we might beat them up or threaten to stab them, but we weren't like the boys . . . they're mean; they use guns and all. We never used guns."

In the Bronx, more and more angry young damsels have slowly made their debuts into organized deviance. Of the 85 male gangs, almost one-third (23) have female branches, with 160 verified members and perhaps as many as 1000 unverified members. In addition, two groups, The Black Persuaders and the Sedgewick Sisters, each with a membership of 25, are exclusively female with no male affiliation.[35] As an evolutionary extension of the social course female delinquents are following, these all-girl gangs may be a harbinger of urban problems to come. Nor can this be dismissed as a problem limited to the streets of New York. In London there are some thirty gangs of "bovver birds," violence-prone girls who roam the streets in packs attacking almost any vulnerable object for no apparent reason other than the sheer thrill of it.

> . . . at night they become birds of prey. Sometimes silently, sometimes shrieking, they swoop down in groups on unsuspecting victims in dark streets, at lonely bus stops, and in deserted toilets, kicking, biting, scratching, punching, they reduce the victim—usually another female—to hysteria and then disappear, stealing perhaps only a few pence. . . . [They are] the newest and in some ways the eeriest street gangs since the Teddy boys terrorized London in the fifties.[36]

The term "bovver" is cockney for "bother," which is itself a slang expression for "fighting," and what distresses the English most is that the majority of their crimes are not perpetrated for money or other gain but are apparently committed for the intrinsic satisfaction of violence. During the past few years these female gangs have become a problem of major proportions for the British police, who blame them for the substantial increase in the rate of muggings in London. After reviewing the charges against some of the girls, a judge at Old Bailey declared, "The girls are even tougher than the boys. It was once assumed that if a man and a woman committed a crime, the woman was under the domination of the man. I think that's now rubbish from what I've seen." [37]

A London probation officer explained, "These girls seem very detached, very unmoved. Many of their attacks are for pure game, mostly done on the spur of the moment." And another police officer went on to explain why he and others were so worried about the trend toward widespread adolescent female violence. "These girls, more often than not, wear some sort of disguises when they go out . . . wigs and masks that are done quite well and which make it very hard for a victim to identify the actual attacker. The danger is, you see, the girls are much better at this sort of disguise . . . plus they don't hang about, bragging about what they've done—like a lot of boys who hang out in gangs. They're much smarter in their approach to this kind of thing . . . the problem is they may eventually become better than men, and even more numerous, as street criminals."

Another area in which young women have begun to express their aptitude for assertive behavior is political protest. In the storm of dissent which swept across the country in the late sixties, the adolescent female was an enthusiastic participant in the demonstrations and a coequal cell-mate in the jailings. Initially, during the early sixties, the movements were planned, led, and executed by males while females performed their traditional functions as office workers, coffee makers, and overseers of routine chores. But by the end of the decade, a by now familiar transformation had occurred. Neither the women themselves nor their male coworkers any longer expected that their participation would be limited to typewriters and mimeograph machines. Instead they became active, vociferous, and sometimes violent members of some of the most turbulent confrontations this country has ever experienced.

"It was something that I never really noticed, per se, as it was occurring, but there was a great change in a very short time," explained Lucy, a New Jersey woman who began her career with the peace movement as a telephone canvasser in 1966 at the age of fifteen. By the time she was seventeen she had traveled to Chicago on her own and taken part in the tumultuous Democratic Convention riots—indeed, to this day, she carries a scar on her head where a policeman's club opened a wound which required eight stitches to close. Lucy had been arrested during demonstrations in Philadelphia, New York, Chicago, and Washington, D.C., between 1968 and 1971. She has been tear-gassed, gunned down with high-pressure water hoses, and otherwise buffeted about as a front-rank member of violent demonstrations. She has—by her own account—also slugged her share of policemen and National Guards-men, as well as "trashed" storefronts and cars during protest activities.

Raised as the daughter of an affluent industrial executive in northern New Jersey, she attended private schools—mainly schools which placed a heavy emphasis on the proper deportment for a young lady of society. In the course of her experiences, Lucy has altered her image of herself as well as of the world around her. The change she has undergone, however, is typical of that experienced by numbers of girls her age.

"When I first became involved in political activity against the war," she explained, "women did have their place. Quite naturally I and the other girls were expected to do the telephone work and run the mimeo-graph machine as well as the errands and other similar things. It was the girls who did all the work, and the men who directed the show and got all the headlines. . . . I think that a great many girls began to see something of themselves in the very things they were demonstrating against. Then things began to happen . . . girls moved in and began to do more. I can remember some of the guys balking at it, but it couldn't be stopped. After Chicago and the convention, for instance, I was totally radicalized. There was no way that anyone was going to chain me to a typewriter. I wanted to be out there where the action was. I was as good as any boy out there, and I knew it."

It was girls like Lucy—with their new-found confidence—who helped to keep people like Lieutenant Al Hack of the Washington, D.C., Police Department busy through the peak years of the anti-war movement. The capital city became the focal point for much of the antiwar sentiment. From 1967 to 1971, some of the largest gatherings ever assembled in the United States descended upon Washington in the form of peace demonstrations. Although non-violent in orientation, many of them were peppered with incidents of violence from both sexes. During those convulsive years of the movement, the demonstrations took on a change in complexion which was somewhat perplexing to Lieutenant Hack and his fellow officers charged with keeping the peace.

"Well, what happened," he explained, "is that we found, all of a sudden, that we were arresting just about as many girls as boys at the demonstrations. That was quite a change from the mid-sixties, when you almost never saw girls in the actual demonstrations. By 1969, they had really changed . . . there were even cases where the front lines of demonstrations were made up of *all* females because the demonstrators knew that most of our men would be less likely to deal harshly with girls than boys. But I think even the men changed after a while . . . they had to change . . . I mean, girls were throwing bricks just as hard as boys, and their language was just as rough. They would throw the trashcans, and rock the busses and cars just like the males. No, toward the end there, we had to change our thinking, I guess. We weren't dealing with males or females . . . we had to worry about dealing effectively with just plain 'demonstrators.' "

The lieutenant's point is an important one. For Washington police handling the demonstrations, as well as for the demonstrators themselves, the gender of the lawbreakers was irrelevant. Setting aside issues of civil disobedience and *agents provocateurs,* it is clear that these were neither male nor female offenders—only offenders. Both were reacting to similar forces in similar ways. Not only in Washington but in New York, London, Moscow, and urban centers around the world, girls have shown a capacity comparable to boys for endangering lives and destroying property. With unwonted irreverence toward the traditions of their mothers, adolescent girls, products of a postwar baby boom which became a teen-age tidal wave, challenged social restrictions on many fronts, including those which limit female activity to established roles. The resulting fluidity of male and female functions often makes an anomic contribution to female delinquency by eroding the structures which have historically protected and restrained girls.

But this blurring of sex boundaries is only one of many factors which have increased the extent and altered the nature of female deviancy. Juvenile delinquency, like adult criminality, is a multiply determined phenomenon. It not only varies with social class and changing social tolerance, but it is defined differently from one jurisdiction to another, and prosecuted differently according to local customs. It can best be understood as an outgrowth of legitimate strivings which have found deviant expression.

Male predominance in delinquency has been attributed to the built-in difficulties faced by boys who are subjected to the female-dominated child-rearing practices of industrialized societies.[38] Lacking the easy access to male models available in peasant societies, boys enter puberty ill-prepared for the rapid shift they must make to the man's world of aggression and competition. The insecurity generated by this role change may result in overcompensating through aggressive delinquent behavior. Girls, on the other hand, have traditionally negotiated adolescence via clearly prescribed, relatively static behavioral structures. Like their mothers, they moved from obedience to parents to obedience to husband. They neither experienced an identity crisis nor did they rebel. If they had, they would not have gotten social reinforcement for their aggressive behavior. The modern girl, however, is passing from childhood to adulthood via a new and unchartered course. She is increasingly aware that there are diminishing restrictions inherent in her mother's role as wife and homemaker; she is partly pushed and partly impelled into fields previously closed to women, and the automobile and telephone as well as changes in social custom give her freedom with very few limitations. Clearly, the developmental difficulties which encouraged male delinquency in the past are exerting a similar influence on girls.

Modernization, industrialization, and urbanization have been invoked to account for the upsurge of female delinquency because they correlate closely with each other. As urbanization increases, traditional roles decrease; with increased mobility people lose stable, continuous personal relationships; disintegration of family life grows (the divorce rate has trebled in the last seventy years); the importance of goal attainment is emphasized at the expense of the means used to attain the goal; and society is continuously fragmented into depersonalized segments. The growing affluence hypothesis is supported by statistical data from Japan, Argentina, Sweden, the Netherlands, England, and Russia.[39] A comprehensive cross-cultural study of rebellious youth concludes that "From *avant garde* Sweden in the North, to traditional Italy in the South, the basic trend was the same: the slow superimposition upon the old bourgeois class order of the less class-ridden and more fluid affluent society. With this, as in Britain and the United States, went the economic emancipation of youth on a large scale, and with this, in turn, a spread of commercial youth culture—and a rise in delinquency figures." [40] Universally, the price of progress has been instability in the social structures which are undergoing change, and this in turn has resulted in delinquency, which further disrupts the social system. Such a social feedback mechanism appears to be synergizing the rate of role change for women and girls and accelerating the process of delinquency.

In contemporary American culture the emphasis has been placed on achievement of goals, but the importance of achieving these goals through legitimate means has not been likewise emphasized.[41] This disequilibrium tends toward a widespread anomie in those groups, such as boys of lower class and girls of all classes, who subscribe to the egalitarian goals but lack egalitarian opportunities. The futility they experience when the socially sanctioned means available to them are of little help in attaining the socially fostered goals may result in a breakdown of norms. In the past, girls were spared this conflict because they lacked both the means and the goals of the male social structure. More recently, both have become available, but to an uneven degree. As with other upwardly mobile groups, aspirations have outstripped means. The teen-age girl of today, much more than the pre–World War II teen-ager, suffers from a greater imbalance between the almost limitless ambition she is learning to nurture and the still circumscribed opportunities available to her. This condition would encourage girls, especially those who are socially disadvantaged, toward deviant means to achieve socially approved goals. However, while the blockage of legitimate access to culturally prescribed goals does indeed lead to delinquency, the specific type of resultant delinquency is determined by the illegitimate opportunities that are available.[42]

Diverse delinquent subcultures emerge from and flourish best in particular types of environmental settings. Where there are opportunities for participation in organized crime or theft, a criminal subculture results. Skill and cunning gain status. Where few opportunities are open for entrance into the rackets—as, for example, in disorganized slums—a conflict-oriented subculture results. Fists and knives gain status. For those double failures who cannot adapt to either the legitimate or illegitimate structure, a retreat is made to a group characterized by a withdrawal from conventional goals and a search for refuge in drug addiction. Up to the present, delinquent girls, charged with the traditional triad of incorrigibility, being a runaway, and promiscuity, have tended to drift toward retreatist subcultures because their opportunities in the conflict-oriented and criminal subcultures were so limited. When they rebelled against conventional society there were few other places to which they could go. But that is changing. Equal opportunity in crime is enabling those with the ability to advance from runaway to gang fighter or professional criminal rather than to gravitate to streetwalking and drug addiction. The criminal as well as the legitimate career choices which are opening up to girls will result in a less stereotyped and more wide-ranging group of female delinquents in the future.

Among some groups in our society, masculinity is reinforced by specified modes of physical aggression.[43] The importance attached to these learned behaviors may be usefully extended to the current activities of many females. The trend in the last two decades has been toward female adoption of male attitudes, traits, vocations, prerogatives, etc., as a means of raising their status also. While at the present time a female subculture of violence is still quite limited, the appearance of violent gangs, such as the Bovver Birds in London and the Sedgewick Sisters in New York, reflect changes in female orientations in the direction of the male model of status, and presages similar changes for girls in the future. If frequency, duration, and intensity of association are important factors in the transmission of criminal behavior patterns,[44] as girls continue to gain entrance into previously all-male criminal subcultures, the influence of peer pressure will shape their deviancy even further in the direction of male patterns.

Yet some societies have no notion of juvenile delinquency, because they have no traditional period of adolescence. The traditional Eskimo village, the Indian type barrio of Mexico, and the tribes of India, all folk villages, offered their young no block of time for uncertainty of goals, idleness, or freedom from supervision.[45] In those villages in transition from folk to urban patterns, however, contacts with more sophisticated cultures have transmitted new ideas to some of the young, social control by the elders begins to deteriorate, and a new stage in the life cycle—social adolescence—begins to develop with its attendant impulsive and individualized behavior. For teen-age girls in transition from folk to urban patterns, it is even more difficult. They are discarding the ways of their mothers and are not yet quite certain about how much of the ways of their fathers they will wish to or be allowed to adopt. More and more girls are hanging around the corner in psychosocial limbo with little to do, no place to go vocationally or domestically, and protected by few structural restraints from delinquency.

The youth cultural system is the product of widespread changes in the labor market and educational practices over the past half century which have kept young people in a prolonged state of idleness.[46] They are no longer absorbed into the occupational system at relatively early ages, and schools are forced to retain them whether they perform well or not. Increasing affluence and labor-saving appliances have freed middle-class girls from many of the onerous and time-consuming household chores, permitting them to act in the manner of a leisure class. Furthermore, a changed societal structure has weakened deferred gratification patterns for both sexes: whereas girls used to believe that they had to renounce pleasures of the moment, such as sexual activity and drug use, for future gains, they now consider such sacrifices inappropriate. Part of the problem stems from the clash of the opposing value systems [47] of the youth subculture with the adult establishment. A case in point is the drug problem. While adolescents recognize the illegality of drug use, they generally justify it morally by comparing it favorably to alcohol and tobacco usage among adults. The same may be said, but to a lesser degree, about teen-age sexual promiscuity. As these two cultural codes confront each other, we may anticipate an exchange of values until a compromise is reached. But until that time, teen-age girls will be arrested for activities which are considered proper only by their subculture, though they may later be sanctioned by the larger society.

Female delinquency today is a serious social problem not only because of its capacity for social disruption but because it often leads to future adult criminality. Although it is not a new problem, it is far more prevalent and has undergone ominous qualitative changes in recent years. The rapid growth of the juvenile population, the equal-rights movement, changes in laws governing females and juveniles, prolonged education, altered job opportunities, urbanization, industrialization, family fragmentation, and the perennial generation gap contribute to its rapid expansion. With the growing emphasis on competition and individual rights rather than social duties, the increasing stress on affluent goals rather than stable employment or ethical means, the growth of nonproductive leisure, longer postponements of adult responsibility, and greater dependency on peers rather than family for role models, young people have been treated and traumatized by a bewildering variety of often contradictory forces.When we add to this the current tendency for public agencies to manage minor difficulties which would formerly have been handled privately, it is not surprising that female delinquency is growing and changing. But not all the changes which are being reported result from actual alterations in behavioral patterns. Some result primarily from a different perception of behavior patterns as, for example, has occurred with sexual promiscuity. The fact that girls were incarcerated much more frequently than boys for promiscuity was more a reflection of social bias against female sexuality than a statement that delinquent females are sexually more active than delinquent males. Some of the offenses for which females were charged in the past resulted less from a violation of the legal code than a breach of social propriety. Economic factors, too, are influential. Poor people predominate at all stages in the criminal process, and poor girls are no exception. It is the lower-class urban areas with their poor housing, unemployment, school dropouts, and social disorganization which have the highest rates of female delinquency. These slum breeding grounds have been shown to maintain a high rate regardless of their racial and ethnic composition. While studies based on official records uniformly report that the lower classes are overrepresented in the criminal population, such findings may be partially misleading. There are many steps between the commission of a crime and conviction, and the weighting of the statistics toward the lower-class girl may in part reflect the difference between actual crimes committed and those which were followed by apprehension and successful prosecution. Because of the legal loopholes available to upper-class girls, the differential process of law enforcement, and the decisive importance of high-quality legal counsel, the dictum "crime does not pay" may be more a description of lower-class insolvency than upper-class morality. Certainly many high-level crimes not only pay handsomely but, when coupled with the subversion of law enforcement, confer immunity on the perpetrator. But regardless of class differences, there is general agreement that female delinquency is increasing in numbers and severity as it moves toward male patterns of deviancy.

Echoing Socrates's admonition and confirming the experience of untold generations, it must be recognized that juvenile delinquency in one form or another will always be a social problem, because it is tied to biosocial milestones of unparalleled importance —puberty and adolescence. What is different and new to juvenile delinquency in the past two decades is the female. She is pushing psychology to the limits of biology and the import of this for society will not be known for some time.

In the tumultuous years between puberty and adulthood, hormonal, social, psychological, and emotional disruptions cascade down on the awkward, ungainly girl who only yesterday was a child. She must cross the swaying bridge between childhood and adulthood many times before she is safely across, and many never do negotiate the passage. When juveniles complain that nobody understands them, they are right. They are an enigma to their parents, their teachers, their psychiatrists, their judges, and worst of all, to themselves. They are assailed by a bewildering storm of contradictory feelings—idealism, selfishness, love, hate, rebelliousness, passivity, inchoate desires, sexual drives, and a pervading confusion of who they are and what they want. The danger of the juvenile to herself and others stems from the uneven maturational upheaval which has suddenly thrust the brain of a child into the body of a woman, and the hitherto unprecedented options for male mayhem.

It will always be thus, and those societies which have experienced the fewest juvenile problems have intuitively or by design provided a flexible combination of outlets, controls, guidance, and forbearance with a large dose of faith that someday they would outgrow it.

5

Women in Wonderland: The Psychotropic Connection

Look into the pewter pot
To see the world as the world's not.
And faith, 'tis pleasant till 'tis past;
The mischief is that 'twill not last.

—A. E. Housman
"A Shropshire Lad" LXII

Of all the tyrannies which have usurped power over humanity, few have been able to enslave the mind and body as imperiously as drug addiction. For to be human is to be social; to be social is to be dependent; and to be dependent is to be vulnerable to outside sources of emotional security. That neither man nor woman can live by bread alone is demonstrated by their affinity for dependent attachments to a variety of animate and inanimate objects. These dependencies come in many forms and operate through many modes, but in the interests of simplicity they have been categorized as either physical or psychological in nature. In the former group belong the opium derivatives, synthetic narcotics such as heroin, and barbiturate-like drugs. These are distinguished by their ability to evoke chemical changes within the body which result in both physiological tolerance to their presence and physiological derangement to their withdrawal. Not only can tolerant individuals withstand far greater doses than those which would be toxic to a non-tolerant individual, but with continued use increasing amounts of the drug are required to achieve the original experience. When physiological dependence—i.e., addiction—has developed, deprivation may produce severe withdrawal symptoms. They include

111

vomiting, tremors, restlessness, mydriasis, anorexia, yawning, goose-flesh, rhinorrhea, lachrymation, fever, and perspiration. Under certain circumstances they may eventuate in physical collapse and even death.

It is little wonder that the physical and emotional distress of withdrawal in affected individuals degrades a variety of life styles to the common denominator of drug-seeking behavior. This psychosocial retreat from non–drug-related activity, this constriction of perspective and restriction of goals, becomes after a time a frenzied pursuit not of satisfaction but of survival. Much that was good and all that was noble about the individual becomes transformed by reverse alchemy into the single-minded search for one vital ingredient. Those who succeed may indeed survive, but they do not prevail.

There is, however, another kind of dependency. It does not have hard, clear-cut chemical characteristics, but it is every bit as powerful a force in shaping drug-related behavior. It is psychological dependence, often mistakenly understated as "mere psychic craving,"[1] which in its own right and as an adjunct to physical dependence comprises the total embrace of addiction. Karl Marx had intuitively and explicitly grasped this when he decried religion as "the opium of the people" and Nietzsche echoed that sentiment a generation later when he identified the "two great European narcotics, [as] alcohol and Christianity." The recognition that emotional ties can bind at least as effectively as physical dependencies is basic to an understanding of the nature of addiction.

While alcohol and marihuana are the most extensively abused substances,[2] people are getting, through both legal and illicit means, and using a great variety of psychoactive drugs, including barbiturates, amphetamines, LSD, cocaine, peyote, hashish, tranquilizers, methadone, codeine, and heroin. Although the exact scope is impossible to determine, experts generally acknowledge that it is widening [3] in response not simply to pressure from criminal elements but to deep-seated changes in American attitudes toward psychic pain and discomfort. *Angst* is no longer stoically accepted as the price of national and individual growth, nor is it appreciated as a bearable component of the maturational process; instead it is more and more being viewed as the bane of modern existence, with no redeeming social or personal value. Likewise, freedom from anxiety is coming to take its place along with freedom from want as an inherent human right. The modern prescription for pain is neither forbearance nor faith. It is neither a turning inward toward deeper resources nor a reaching outward toward communal support. Instead, it is an imperative demand for anesthesia, a retreat into a limbo where turning off and turning on are twin aspects of an effort to turn away. The quantity of ethical tranquilizers dispensed exceeds that of all other medicines asked for and received by a nation in quest of psychic panaceas. Whether our anxieties have escalated as a function of civilization or our threshold for pain has declined as a result of altered cultural values, this quest goes forward at all levels of society, each segment pursuing its own remedies through whatever channels its resources permit. Some go to the bar, some to the drugstore, and some to the drug peddler. For his part, the peddler is only one link in a chain of supply which stretches through him from the importer and wholesaler above, who are rarely addicts, to the pusher below, who is usually an addict ensuring his own supply through sales to others.

Along with alcohol and ethical drugs, the illicit drug market has experienced an unprecedented growth even in the face of equally unprecedented public-information campaigns and law-enforcement efforts designed to curb it. This would be surprising only if we view drug use and the drug user as out of phase with the predominant cultural values. They are not. Deviance expresses and reflects conventionality even in its attempts to break free from it. In social as in physical organizations the periphery is as much a part of the whole as is the center. If its distance from the spindle of social action tells little about currently fashionable modes, its proximity to the fringe of coming events tells much about future trends. This is especially true in the area of illicit drug use which, because it is primarily a youthful phenomenon, portends the shape of coming cultural changes. Such a projection is reasonable when we reflect that time will more predictably convert the status of minors to electors than it will convert their value systems. But even if we discount the effects of the aging process with its potential for a culture shift as part of a population shift, there are other reliable auguries of drug-pattern transformations that exist in currently sanctioned medical practice. Drug overuse by the many finds distorted but parallel expression in drug abuse by the few, for it must be recognized that the latter represents a different degree but not a different order of behavior. The drug subculture in America is just that—a subdivision of the predominant culture. It resonates to the same rhythms and steps to the same beat. It may chant a contrapuntal lyric of apostasy, but it pulses to the tempo of the larger society, for in spite of romantic notions to the contrary, it does not heed a different drummer. And there is no way to treat the drug problem as a pathology of the body social without a derivative physiology in the body cultural, or to deal with it as a modern malady without historical etiology.

The use of psychoactive drugs is older than recorded history and, in one form or another, will probably always be with us. It has sometimes contributed to social change but it is usually a product of social change, a narrow symptom forced upward by broader social transformations. That is why the purely punitive and *ad hoc* approaches in the past have been so unrewarding and why a fuller perspective is so important to effective management of drugs. Had we turned to history, for example, drug use and abuse by the modern woman would come as no great surprise. She is quite familiar with this escape route. She has been there, and, at times, in greater numbers than her male counterpart. Indeed, antebellum American women outdid their men in the ingestion of medicine. Starting in the 1850s, female drug addicts outnumbered male addicts by a ratio of two to one,[4] and this female predominance continued through two major wars until about 1920. The typical female addict had acquired the opium habit as easily and as innocently as modern women enter the sedative-tranquilizer world, and probably for similar reasons. For one thing, opium was legal. For another, it was more acceptable and more respectable than alcohol, both as a social lubricant and personal pacifier. Unlimited quantities were openly available either by prescription or as over-the-counter patent remedies touted under such homey labels as McMunn's Elixir. Writing in *Harper's* magazine in 1867, Fitzhugh Ludlow deplored the wide-based popularity of opium and noted the inroads it was making among alcohol users.

> The habit is gaining fearful ground among our professional men, the operatives of our mills, our weary serving women, our fagged clerks, our former liquor drunkards, our every day laborers who a generation ago took gin.[5]

In a similar vein, but with a greater appreciation of some of the causal sequences, Horace Day in 1868 ascribed the opium epidemic to the residual physical and social wounds inflicted by the Civil War:

> The number of confirmed opium-eaters in the U.S. is large, not less, judging from the testimony of the druggists in all parts of the country as well as other sources, than 80 to100,000. . . .
> The events of the last few years [Civil War] have unquestionably added greatly to their number. Maimed and shattered survivors from a hundred battlefields, diseased and disabled soldiers released from hostile prisons, anguished and hopeless wives and mothers, made so by the slaughter of those who were dearest to them, have found, many of them, temporary relief from their sufferings in opium.[6]

Twenty years later, although the physical wounds had healed, the social ills festered on. What had begun as a specific remedy to a specific malady had become, for many, a way of life, a general response to general malaise. In the biennial report of the State Board of Health of Iowa in 1885, J. M. Hull declared:

> Opium is today a greater curse than alcohol, and justly claims a large number of helpless victims, which have not come from the ranks of reckless men and fallen women, but the majority of them are to be found among the educated and most honored

and useful members of society; and as to sex, we may count out the prostitutes so much given to this vice, and still find females far ahead, so far as numbers are concerned.[7]

How far ahead was illustrated by an early survey of prominent physicians which found that two-thirds of their addict population consisted of females.[8] Ever more conformist than men, respectable women generally did not take their habit underground, into the clandestine world of the black marketeer and drug pusher, as many men did when opium became illegal and disreputable. Consequently, after 1920 opium addiction declined sharply among women, gradually among men.[9] During this period there was also a change in the choice of the addictive substances, as the oral ingestion of plain opium yielded to the inhalation and injection of derivative compounds.

Cultivated since antiquity, the opium poppy has been incorporated into a variety of drugs and beverages because of its soporific and soothing effects. In hopes of further exploiting these medically valuable properties, intense efforts were made to refine the raw product. Eventually it was learned that the active ingredient resided in the juice which may be extracted from the ripe poppy head. Dried and collected, this fluid came to be called opium, from the Greek word *opion*, meaning sap. By the early nineteenth century, the chemically distinct but clinically related components of opium were finally identified and came to be known as morphine and codeine. Ignorant of its addictive properties, unenlightened physicians and eager patients utilized opium along with its derivatives to treat a wide range of human ills. Unfortunately for rational therapeusis, the good results were uncritically accepted as a confirmation of then-current theories of disease, and many a famous physician owed his good reputation to the liberal use of opium. This is not surprising when we take into account the fact that, even today, 60 to 80 per cent of the patient load of a general practitioner is comprised of functional problems which respond well to placebos.[10] Opium was and is an outstanding drug for the kinds of hypochondriacal and psychosomatic difficulties which are the bulk of medical practice, because such patients are often best palliated by placebos. Indeed, so popular was opium that it found its way into almost every patent medicine compounded for the relief of pain and was even incorporated into confections and soothing syrups for babies. This popularity was only partially deserved because, although it was a very effective medicament, its very virtue became, Januslike, a twofold vice: it retarded the scientific search for therapeutic specifics because its dispensers sincerely believed that they were curing, not masking, disease; and it exposed many unwitting innocents to the risk of addiction. As early as the 1830s, some physicians were warning of these dangers, but throughout the nineteenth-century heyday of opium usage such forebodings were largely disregarded. In the presence of a cheap and unrestricted supply, dependency was of no practical importance. The discomforts of withdrawal were quickly alleviated by continued consumption— and they were often not even recognized as withdrawal. More often than not, they were considered simply another set of symptoms which would yield to the miraculous healing powers of opium. When, finally, the medical profession and public belatedly recognized the enemy within the Trojan horse, the opening battle had already been lost. Addiction was by then widespread, and frenzied endeavors were launched to regain lost ground.

In stratagems that have been fruitlessly repeated many times since, strenuous efforts were directed toward the task of separating the addictive from the therapeutic components of opium. Time and again synthesized derivatives, hailed as the scientific fulfillment of this promise, enjoyed their brief rocket flare of popularity, and soon took their place alongside the mother compound as one more member of the family of addictive drugs. The search goes on still, but to date it has proven easier to split the atom than to separate the euphoric from the addictive elements of the opium compound, leading to the speculation that they are perhaps one and the same. In the unsophisticated view of nineteenth-century medicine, it was erroneously assumed that the "opium appetite," as it was then conceptualized, could only develop as a result of oral ingestion of the substance. Consequently, its introduction into the body via a hypodermic needle was expected to provide the rewards of analgesia without the risks of addiction. The extensive use of injectable morphine to treat the pains of Civil War veterans exposed the futility of such an expectation. In fact, so prevalent did morphine addiction eventually become among Civil War veterans that it came to be known after a while as the "army disease." This same disappointing scenario was re-enacted in the early 1900s with heroin, a new opiate produced in Germany in 1898. As in so many instances before and since, it was heralded as a nonaddicting substitute for morphine and codeine, and on the strength of its promise given broad clinical exposure. Within several years it was revealed to be even more addictive than morphine, and now both its manufacture and importation are forbidden in the United States.

But if heroin was ill-prepared to serve in heaven, it was ideally constituted to rule in hell. Like Satan fallen from grace, heroin became the hero of the nether world. What was poison for the ethical drug market became meat for the illicit one that was established in the aftermath of laws against opium. These laws provided the necessity to mother the inventiveness which produced heroin and other synthetic derivatives. In the demimonde of black marketeers and pushers, heroin's euphoriant qualities, high potency, ease of transportation, adulterability, and potential for addiction made it first among equals, the drug of choice in the contraband trade.

Such chemical and tactical innovations, however, would have been unnecessary a century earlier. During that halcyon era of opium use, the drug was so cheap it could be eaten, so plentiful that withdrawal symptoms were practically unimportant, and so respectable that it could be enjoyed in public. DeQuincey's famous "Confessions of an English Opium-Eater," which appeared in 1821, recorded and reflected a vogue of opium ingestion for psychological effects which was becoming popular among many upper-class groups. Later in the century, "sporting circles" in San Francisco adopted the Chinese practice of smoking opium and it spread throughout the subterranean strata inhabited by prostitutes, pimps, and gamblers.

The barriers erected by local ordinances banning the importation of smoking opium were too gossamer to stem the flow which increased rapidly to exceed a hundred thousand pounds per year for every year from 1890 to 1909, when Federal legislation instituted a nation-wide prohibition.[11] Until then, attempts to discourage opium importation for nonmedicinal use relied entirely on the imposition of onerous import duties. Obeying age-old laws of economics, as legal importation became more and more expensive it diminished because smuggling then became more and more profitable.

Individual countries were unable to limit the scope of international drug traffic, and so the Hague Opium Convention was convened in 1912 to coordinate the efforts of member nations. As an outgrowth of this, the United States Congress in 1914 passed the Harrison Act designed to regulate the domestic use, sale, and transfer of opium and coca products. The Act imposed an excise tax and required extensive record-keeping and registration procedures in an attempt to expose and control the channels of drug traffic. Perhaps it was not too little, but it did come too late for more than a hundred thousand addicts, many of them highly respected members of their communities, who were already the victims of indiscriminate opium prescribing by their physicians.[12] As happens so often in politics, the excesses of one extreme rebound to the excesses of its opposite. The wave of moral indignation following the public's belated awareness of the drug problem led not to correction but overcorrection, as permissive laxity yielded almost overnight to zealous control. The medical profession was discouraged from exploring a legitimate biosocial problem. Addicts were perceived as criminals rather than as victims of an affliction. They were stigmatized as degenerates and "dope fiends," and the whole task of rehabilitation and assimilation of those unfortunates was mired in the thickets of public revulsion.

It was natural for legislators to conclude that because weak or absent regulations had allowed the drug problem to develop, stern regulations would undo it. This thesis has been expressed since the beginning of the twentieth century in a punitive and authoritarian set of drug laws which imposed ever more severe penalties on addicts and drug peddlers on the assumption that the drug-abuse problem is essentially superficial, volitional, and mediated by rational considerations. As the frustrating national experience during the Prohibition Era attested, reliance on punishment was unprofitable for alcohol problems and unpromising for drug problems. Once a behavioral pattern is firmly established it is more amenable to shaping by a combination of rewards and punishments than it is vulnerable to eradication by punishment alone. And informed experience suggests that drug abuse is less a cause of social ills than a result of social ills, and as such is best managed by finding the origin rather than treating the symptoms.

In humans, as in other animals, the pursuit of pleasure and avoidance of pain work together to achieve individual adjustment and species survival. It is both the advantage and the disadvantage of a variety of psychoactive substances ranging from alcoholic beverages and tranquilizers through euphoriants and hallucinogens that they have the chemical capacity to create effortless and almost instant happiness. This artificially contrived short-circuiting of the work-reward sequence may sometimes provide a necessary respite from life's stresses, but it may also reduce the motivational incentives which stimulate the acquisition of essential skills. For example, when electrodes are implanted into the cerebral pleasure center of laboratory rats and connected to a lever which permits them to experience intense pleasurable sensations through self-stimulation they will do so continuously to the neglect of food, water, their young, and their own vital needs.[13] Although their lives may be short and many of them may die of starvation, they apparently have the satisfaction of dying happy.

In order for large concentrations of people to live and work in socially, psychologically, and spatially circumscribed areas they must of necessity inhibit the automatic fight-flight mechanisms.

Under these circumstances, group functional stability is often purchased at the cost of considerable emotional distress to the individual. Barred, at least in peacetime, from acting out impulses to attack or flee from frustrating situations, forced to maintain sometimes intolerable interpersonal constellations in the larger interests of family and society, civilized people have earnestly sought the legendary Northwest Passage to peace of mind so accessible to the animal world of fight or flight. It is perhaps because of this that every society has institutionalized a variety of chemical and social channels for approved regressive or retreatist modes of behavior. In moderation they help sustain the capacity for continued toleration of tension; in excess they destroy it. It is little wonder, therefore, that public attitudes have shifted so frequently from abstinence to indulgence as societies grope for the delicate and precarious balance between productivity and the pursuit of pleasure.

In an earlier and simpler period of our history when the play ethic did not compete with the work ethic, when satisfactions came more from accomplishment than from leisure, and when people were not so persistently wondering if they were happy, productivity and pleasure appeared to be identical. But the technological cornucopia which spilled out an abundance of consumer products hitherto undreamed of not only dictated what we possessed but altered in the profoundest sense what we would become. Mechanization and assembly-line efficiencies separated the worker from the end product; horizontal and vertical mobility separated individuals from their roots; long periods of educational preparation for future-oriented occupations robbed the present of much of its relevance; advertising converted inclinations to wants, wants to needs, and needs to frustrations, as galloping consumerism breathlessly struggled to stay apace with the prolific, almost profligate creations of the perpetual-motion machines. Dissatisfaction with one's work and alienation from one's traditions was so widespread that it became a permanent if unwelcome inhabitant of the industrial complex. The "things" of which Emerson warned were imperiously mounted in the saddle, mindlessly riding mankind into anonymity. It was with disquieting dismay that a generation of Americans paused in their preoccupation with the expensive toys of technology to wonder in private and aloud if their gross national product of contentment was any greater than that of the aboriginal inhabitants who greeted their Pilgrim forebears at Plymouth Rock. In terms of personal happiness, the industrial revolution produced for many a litter basket full of disposable superfluities which slaked every thirst except that of the soul. Yet this need, too, found ready-made remedies in the synthetic pleasures easily available in packets and pills and injectibles. But even as the early twentieth century was garbing itself in the ready-to-wear mantle of instant euphoria, there was a burgeoning awareness of the anomic vacuousness below the fatuous façade, a reactive revulsion against the emotional nakedness beneath the magic robes.

With the passage of the Harrison Act in 1914, these counterforces gained the ascendancy and altered the demography of, if not the demand for, opium products. Several changes followed immediately from this event. Legal importations withered and illicit drug trafficking flourished. With no provision for the chronic users who were suddenly cut off from their legitimate suppliers, it could hardly have turned out otherwise. Many but not all of those unfortunates resourcefully pursued their needs into underworld channels. By and large, women, who prior to 1920 comprised two-thirds of the addict population, did not follow this course.[14] In consequence, surveys in the early 1930s revealed that their proportion among addicts had shrunk to 25 per cent.[15] Today it stands at about 20 per cent.[16]

It is beyond the scope of this book and, indeed, beyond the capacity of present-day knowledge to unravel the Gordian knot of causation, but I will attempt to trace the major factors in female addiction. Historically, we may begin with the physical dependence induced by medical treatment (iatrogenicity): Morphine is administered by a physician to alleviate a patient's pain and, if this regimen continues indefinitely, especially after the physical discomfort has subsided, withdrawal symptoms will be experienced when the drug is discontinued. Although this type of induction to drug servitude ran rampant in the years following the Civil War, it appears to be but a fractional component of today's problem. Doctors Vincent Dole and Marie Nyswander have explained the phenomenon of tolerance and addiction by postulating that heroin use produces a metabolic alteration which "impels" a continuation of drug usage.[17] Although this theory does not explain why given individuals take the initial opiate plunge, it nevertheless accounts for their continued immersion in the drug pool. Another contributing force in drug addiction, and one more relevant to nonopiates, is the culture shift which has made ours, in the view of some, a drug-dependent generation. A patient assumes that he will leave his physician's office with a prescription, and the responsive physician feels compelled to comply with these expectations, if only to utilize the extraordinary healing powers of the placebo. There are pills for all pains, physical and psychological. In 1970, over two hundred million prescriptions were filled for tranquilizing drugs.[18] Family medicine chests overflow with everything from antibiotics to antidepressants; children early learn to "take two aspirins and go to bed" at the first indication of slight discomfort; and the local drugstore advertises over-the-counter "instant relief" for pains that many of their patrons never even knew existed. Because women in the past have been more prone than men to seek the sick role, they have been more exposed to iatrogenic influences and more susceptible to the onslaught of cultural nostrums proclaiming health through ingestion or injection. Their predisposition to this was tragically evident from their pre–Harrison Act experience in the early 1900s. What is different about the current situation is the fact that females have shed much of their reluctance to pursue sources of supply into illicit channels, and they are becoming as eager as males to reach out for thrills rather than just relief.

Many psychologists and psychoanalysts perceive addiction to be a symptom of underlying psychic derangement, certain types of individuals being more vulnerable than others.[19] Accordingly, the addictive personality is thought to be characterized by strong dependency needs, pronounced feelings of inadequacy, low frustration threshold, need of immediate gratification, sexual immaturity, and a lack of internal controls. Some personality studies suggest that the greater the opiate abuse the less a given individual is able to avoid anxiety by gratification of needs through socially acceptable channels.[20]

Theories that certain types of people are predisposed to addiction have existed for over a century.[21] Recently these have been challenged because they were not supported by studies which separated the effects of the deviancy from those of the addiction.[22] Other issues being raised are: how do psychologically "sound" persons become addicted, why is there such a wide personality range within the abusing population, and what does cross-cultural variation disclose? [23]

No doubt the addiction of some persons is primarily due to severe underlying psychopathology. However, personality development is so interwoven with environmental influences that we may never ascertain with precision how much the insecurity, rebelliousness, and defensive escape through "getting high" are the result of slum child-rearing practices with their attendant frustrated emotional needs [24] or are the sequel to constitutional impairment with its attendant vulnerabilities. What we do know is that the lesser numbers of addicted females cannot be imputed to their greater psychological stability whether constitutionally or environmentally rooted. The fact that women utilize as many mental hospital beds as do males and that they account for a higher percentage of those in outpatient and private psychotherapeutic treatment leads us to search elsewhere. This search inevitably takes us outside the confines of the individual to the social bonds which connect and support the group.

Man is not only an animal with a body and a being with a brain but also a social creature who is so ineluctably interconnected with his social group that he is hardly comprehensible outside its perimeters. Of the many socioeconomic variables which influence the behavior of the addict, perhaps the most paradoxical is that of affluence. Our abundant national wealth has resulted in a contemporary America where there are more discretionary funds than have been available in any other culture at any other time. Too often the accumulation of material wealth has resulted not in the fruits of creativity but the dregs of boredom, a surfeited *noblesse* without a social *oblige*. Our rapidly expanding system of production, distribution, and consumption of goods and services has displaced most of the population from the purposeful and meaningful life of the small community to the purposeless and meaningless existence of our large cities, while concurrently it has replaced the normative standard that is supported by closely knit social groups with the anomie that is sustained by anonymity.

But if the privileged suffer from affluence, the underprivileged feel even more pain from exposure to the pervasive prosperity which can be seen but, by and large, remains unreachable. All are beckoned by the mass media to the same destination, but the itineraries are quite dissimilar. For some the route to success is a high-speed turnpike; for others it is a narrow footpath riddled with detour signs, roadblocks, and finally a dead end. There is little satisfaction and less glory in surveying the promised land which one may gaze upon but never enter. Finding the way too strenuous and prevented by internal prohibitions from taking illegal shortcuts, many give up both the destination (goals) and the legal byways (means) and escape through the secret passage offered by mood-altering drugs.[24A] Retreatists turn inward in defeat, blaming their own inadequacies rather than those of society. This may explain some flight-rather-than-fight behaviors, but it does not fully account for drug abuse among lower-class youth, many of whom have a lengthy history of deviant behavior before becoming addicted.[25] Perhaps the solution lies not in internal restraints but in external exclusions from blocked illegal passages. Not all can be integrated with the illegal "in-group" which launches them on a "stable" criminal career, and many lack the toughness and fearlessness necessary to gain respect in the conflict subculture. These "double failures," unable to find status in either the legitimate or the illegitimate hierarchy, "drop out" from both structures and seek relief in the continuous pursuit of "kicks." [25A]

In this sense, drugs are used as an anesthetic to provide relief from pain and not, as some have suggested, as a ticket to the intrigue which is inherent in their illegality.[26]

"I know why I used drugs. That ain't no great secret. My problem is to get away from it or get around it with something else," explained a twenty-one-year-old black woman who has spent the last five years using heroin regularly. She has kicked the habit six times and always gone back. Currently she is in her seventh "clean" period. She has an eighth-grade education and has lived in a ghetto in the Bronx all her life. "I shoot up for the pain, baby. It's like a medicine. You know, like people take aspirins for headache or downers for their nerves. It's like that. I shoot up because it hurts. Sometimes it hurts just to walk out in the street. It's like even the air around me hurts, you know? I got two kids, they're yelling around the place a lot and we don't have enough to pay for this or that. I mean, at times, my whole life seems to be just one endless pain I can't get away from. The only time I feel really good is when I'm on a good rush. I knew it is killing me. But I can't stop it. People need good times. Where can I get good times on the street here? What do I do, go out and steal a car for a ride into the country? Should I go out and sit in the trash on the sidewalk or walk around and look at boarded up windows . . . ? That's it, man, it's the pain. I got real pain."

But frustrated attainment of goals is certainly not the only explanation. Youthful unrest is older than recorded history and makes fertile soil for the cultivation of bizarre and unconventional behaviors to which urban adolescents are perennially vulnerable. Without the primitive *rites de passage,* young people today spend several years suspended in that nether world between the ambivalently rejected dependence of childhood and the ambivalently sought responsibilities of adulthood, a period characterized by high susceptibility to peer pressure with an unending search for status regardless of the cost. These quests often appear random and unstructured but, in reality, although the norms which guide their activities might be in conflict with those of the larger society, there *are* norms, and very definitive ones at that. Becoming an outcast is more onerous than becoming a deviant, because belonging to anything is better than belonging to nothing. Within many groups, prestige accrues from an eagerness to experiment with acts which include the element of risk or behaviors which openly defy custom and conventionality. Drug use is gaining popularity as the "nonconformity of choice," with the ability to handle various types of drugs creating a new ranking system replacing, in part, athletics, sexual prowess, and the "ability to hold your liquor." [27] Initial "shots" and "snorts" occur not under the pressures of a pusher [28] but in a group setting in which the members define as the "ultimate in 'kicks,' a practice which is generally condemned and feared." [29]

Sally is twenty. Currently, she is attending a methadone clinic and group-therapy sessions in an attempt to kick the drug habit. She enrolled in the methadone program shortly after her husband was found dead in a public restroom. He had overdosed his daily heroin shots.

"I never wanted to try drugs to begin with. . . . Can you believe that?" Sally, despite her harrowing past, is still relatively attractive-looking, although she wears long sleeves to cover the massive scars which track their way up both of her forearms. "It started back in college before I dropped out. I had met my husband and we went with this group of students. They were into drugs. My husband was involved. We'd go to parties and I'd be the only straight person there. It made me feel weird. It just happened. I started with a little and it just got more and more. Once I was into it, I couldn't stop. But I never really wanted to begin. I never even liked it all that much. The rush was O.K., but never as spectacular as everyone said *their* rush was. It was just O.K. It just got to me. I couldn't stop even though I wanted to. I mean, I didn't want to lose all my friends. I didn't have any place else to go."

That drug addiction is a norm in the criminal subculture has become increasingly apparent.[30] The patterns of behavior which characterize this offender-addict element are learned from older role models who inhabit the most deteriorated areas of the inner city either because their disadvantaged position in the marketplace allows them no alternatives or because they choose the anonymity and freedom from conventional restraints offered by these neighborhoods. Once the young recruits are caught up in the addiction web, chances are that they will continue the practice of drug abuse, for they have become entrapped in a subculture which contains their security and, in consequence, also controls their behavior.[31]

But group pressures notwithstanding, the final form that the forces of deviant satisfaction ultimately assume must necessarily be molded by such mundane considerations as opportunity, availability, and accessibility of addictive substances. Regardless of psychosocial instabilities, if there is no drug supply, there is no drug abuse. It is for this reason that the strict enforcement of even punitive laws, together with efficient police work, can exert a decisive influence on patterns of addiction. It is likely that hedonistic pressures will always be endemic to civilizations and even utopians will probably seek occasional escape from the boredom of bliss. But desire alone does not lead to deviancy, nor does it determine its shape. The amorphous pursuit of pleasure tends to conform to the cast into which it is allowed to flow. With drug addiction as with all other social behavior, necessary causes remain latent until completed by sufficient ones.

It is ironic, although not unexpected, that modern women in assuming the mantle of male power have also become vulnerable to the infirmities of male vice. The chains which women have sought so eagerly to cast off were not merely hobbles. They were also, in retrospect, affirmative anchor lines which secured them to the safety inherent in traditional roles. Without these, many women were cast adrift from safe and protected berths. Historically, the characteristic frustrations associated with the traditional female role were compensated by the satisfactions derived from fulfillment of duties as they were supposed to fulfill them. That is changing. They cannot go forward because of blocked access routes, nor can they fall back on past supports which until recently have sustained them. The days when being "a good cook" or a "dedicated mother" gave a woman status among her peers are becoming discredited and, for the lower-class female, those traditional roles are not being supplanted with social roles which supply comparable psychological need.

"I would really like to give you a whole story about how someone pushed me into using drugs—made me use drugs. Everyone has their story, you know," said Angela, a resident at a private California rehabilitation farm for drug addicts. "The truth is that I went out and actively sought to get into drugs. I was married at eighteen to a guy I really loved. I left the East Coast and came West and we lived here until he left. One day he just left. He said he didn't want to be married any longer and I never saw him again. I thought of suicide. I drank. And I went out and decided to get high all the time to forget. That was not a logical way to deal with my anxiety. I see that now. At the time I spent four days trying to get a pusher to sell me something—anything— to get off on. I finally got it and I just kept on going. At the time, I didn't have anything else to do. I had been a wife. My whole life had been spent dreaming about being a wife. That is all I ever did and then, poof!, just like that I wasn't a wife any more. I couldn't handle it."

The signals ahead are uncertain and the positions behind are eroding. More and more, the temptation is to retreat from the impasse by turning to drugs and other deviant behaviors—a recent study from the federal hospital for drug addicts at Lexington, Kentucky, attests to this. The report, which covers the period between 1961 and 1967, highlights two significant shifts in the socioeconomic status of female addicts: 1) 1967 admissions were much more likely than their 1961 counterparts to have a broken marriage, and 2) the number allegedly supporting themselves through illegal activities as their primary source of income increased from 10 per cent to 30 per cent among whites and from 36 per cent to 67 per cent among blacks.[32]

These psychosocial dislocations have affected all classes of women, including even the most affluent segment. But for this group, the frustrations are somewhat different. It is out of their ranks that the activists in the women's liberation movement are recruited and, although a considerable number of them have the confidence that comes from internalizing the edicts of the movement, vocational opportunities are still in short supply. For those who lack necessary training and skills, the climb up the economic ladder is a steep one and many lose their footing. Some, disillusioned, find their outlets by turning their rejection back onto society in the form of either passive nonconformity to its value system or aggressive political activism. These are the middle-class dropouts who lash out at the "Great Society" for its lack of flexibility, rigidity, and "uptightness" and, in defiance, challenge its norms through various deviant behaviors, drug abuse being one of the most popular. But not many become a part of that rather small subculture. Most of those in the higher socioeconomic levels who try and fail or give up without even trying are increasingly turning to tranquilizers, the middle-class counterpart of the hippie retreat to heroin.

In discussing the social forces behind drug addiction I touched on a variety of forces: limited access to goals; the alleged anonymity, purposelessness, and meaninglessness of present-day life; the lack of institutional supports; youthful unrest and rebellion; peer pressure; role models; and availability. That all of these factors are beginning to affect women at least equally and perhaps to a greater degree than men has already been shown. Suffice it to say that with the exodus of females from the security of the hearth, there is every reason to believe that the depersonalized world into which women are escaping will exact an even greater psychic toll from them because time and past experiences have not yet thickened their skin.

Even those who have been involved in deviant behaviors are having problems coping with their liberation. Prostitutes are a prime example—over half of them in large cities are addicts who prefer heroin, though some combine it with cocaine.[33] Before World War II this was atypical because the brothel prostitute was carefully watched by her madam, who was strictly against the use of any drugs. Contrasted with present-day entrepreneurs, whom we have already met, those of yesteryear had both the restraints placed on them by the head of the "house" and the support of belonging to a group, albeit an illegitimate one.

Among juveniles, too, cultural changes are having a greater impact on females. They inhabit the same teen-age limbo as adolescent boys, and although they are tormented by youthful unrest, the concept that girls require opportunities to express assertive and aggressive drives is only newly arrived on the social scene. It is a behavior whose time has precipitously come before the idea which would support it has arrived at the stage of wide social acceptance. It seems that society has always been prepared for the exuberant bursts of adolescent energy manifested by untold generations of males and has made allowances for it. The same kind of social expectancies and tolerances have not been extended to girls, and they consequently find themselves without institutionalized channels for aggressive drive discharge. Consequently, the same behavior which is charitably viewed as a normal variation for males ("boys will be boys") is often uncharitably berated as a deviancy for females.

Some insight may be gained into the kinds of problems which lead to a drug solution by examining the perspectives of two girls from different segments of the social spectrum.

The middle-class solution:

"I tend to think that the primary target of my striving for deviance is possibly the sterility and blankness of the life I had always been exposed to. . . . My parents . . . gave me a life devoid of real, deep feeling. I wanted to feel! I wanted to play in the dirt. I wanted to transgress those lily-white norms, break those rules designed to make me a good little Doris Day. And when the first transgression was followed not by the wrath of God . . . but by a feeling of being alive, and free, and different, that I had never known before, then I guess after that, all rules and norms lost their meaning and power over me. . . . I knew there was a way for me to declare my independence from the straight, conventional, and Boring! life my mother wanted me to lead. When I shotup, I felt so superior, so wicked, so unique . . . I thought I had found the ultimate rebellion, the most deviant act possible. . . . The badness of shooting heroin was precisely why I did not hesitate to do it." [34]

The lower-class solution:

"I was brought up in the Fillmore like a lot of the kids there are. I was one of seven and my homelife was pretty shitty. My father was in a lot of the operations in the Fillmore and quite often we didn't see him for weeks at a time. By the time I was eight years old my mother had started hitting the bottle. What with the kids, and the lousy school, and nothing to do and not knowing where to go, I started hanging around with some older kids. As part of my initiation into the local gang when I was eleven I was screwed.

"By this time I couldn't take school and I had begun popping pills. I took mainly 'bennies,' 'dexies,' 'reds' and 'yellows' so by the time I was twelve I was really hung up on the 'freak' scene. One of the kids started to pimp me off. . . . I first turned on to Smack when I was 14. . . . The dope doesn't get in the way, because as long as I am up I can have all the sex they can pay for and those screws wouldn't know the difference anyway. I never tried to get a job because if you are black you can't get much of a job beyond cleaning a shit-house and I can make a lot more pushing my ass." [35]

What is remarkable about these odysseys into the drug world is not that they describe teen-agers but that they describe girls. Neither as a middle-class adolescent rebelling against her established role model nor as a ghetto delinquent drifting pragmatically into the anomic expediency of the street does the gender of these troubled subjects play a prominent part in their addiction. And that is precisely the lessons we are drawing from the social upheavals which have thrust women of all ages into the positions once occupied exclusively by men. One can predict more about a person's behavior from a knowledge of his or her socioeconomic position than from knowing the gender. The closer we look at women who are making their way in a man's world, the more they look like men in their profile of physical diseases, their psychological configurations, their criminal deviancies, and their addictive patterns. That is not to say that the two sexes will eventually merge into indistinguishable forms of behavior, although that is possible, but that whatever it is that is behavioristically particular to each has not yet withstood the test of equal social exposure. Time and again, nicely fenced-in psychological prescriptions defining the presumed limits of female vices or virtues have been refuted by the inexorable logic of events. Women have risen higher and fallen lower than most historians would have dared or cared to imagine. The reasons are not hard to find. They have always been there, but until recently it never seemed important to examine them. History has traditionally been just that—*his* story. New realities and new awarenesses are now creating as well as confronting a new woman who has disdained the distaff in favor of unrestricted options. By activities more compelling than words, she is writing her own story into the annals of humanity, and as living experience brings it into sharper focus it looks more and more like his story.

6

The Link Between
Opportunity and Offense: Race

"Every soil bears not everything."
—Rabelais: *Pantagruel*, Bk. iv

No group can escape its history, and in spite of the egalitarian aspirations of our society no class deviates far from its traditional social role. In consequence, the divergent roads to liberation taken by "colored women" and "white ladies" (as they were designated by segregated lavatory signs) have negotiated different cultural obstacles and arrived at different destinations. Sheltered by the insularity of plantation life and the inertia of an agrarian economy, two stereotypes grew side by side in the rich alluvial soil of the South. The black mammy—stern, strong, superstitious, sensuous, but not sexual, and overwhelmingly maternal—contrasted sharply with the white Southern belle—delicate, pampered, beguiling, coquettish flower of the Confederacy. Even if such characterizations were atypical and exaggerated, they are the icons which express the myths which mold the social perceptions on whose vision rests the fate of all social creatures. From the beginning of her American experience, the black female was viewed by whites and eventually by herself as a kind of black rather than as a kind of woman.

The blurring of sex-role distinctions during slavery and the sex-role reversal after emancipation brought her early into the marketplace, where her job choices were limited to manual and menial tasks at minimal wages. Segregated to a world of poverty at the fringes of white prosperity, acculturated to a life style which favored physical aggression, and saddled with the familial responsibilities ordinarily assumed by white males, her propensities and opportunities would naturally lead, when criminologic influences prevailed, to crimes against persons and property. White women, by contrast, did not emerge as individuals until a hundred years later. They had been securely established in the role of homemaker (sometimes with a black domestic), protected for the most part from financial responsibilities, and, with increasing frequency, educated sufficiently to qualify for white, male positions.

In general, economic circumstances and legitimate opportunities make it less likely that a white woman will have recourse to criminal behavior. However, if she does, she will not be limited to the blue-collar crimes of vice, assault, robbery, etc. Rather, the access she enjoys to the preserves of power either in her own right as an executive or in an affiliative capacity, such as executive secretary, will enable her to engage in the most sophisticated, remunerative, and least prosecuted type of illegitimate activity—white-collar crime. Up to the present time circumstances have conspired to restrict this to white women. But times are changing. Even though black and white women have started from different points and utilized different means to achieve their legitimate and criminal goals, the differences between them are fading, the social forces which mold them are becoming identical, and their paths to liberation are converging rapidly toward each other. In order to understand the evolution of this process, let us review where the black female has been.

Throughout the ages, myths concerning women or blacks have had such infrequent and casual contact with verifiable facts that what they actually were became submerged into what they were supposed to be. Notwithstanding our twentieth-century pride in rationalism, we still subsidize a retinue of reassuring myths, not for good but for sufficient reasons: they enable us to maintain comfortable fictions in the face of discomfitting reality.

It often matters little that myths do not help us in our capacity to deal with the imminence of coming events so long as they provide temporary relief for the present. Sustained by a need not to know, they persist unchallenged so long as they are useful to the mythmakers and so long as the mythmakers remain in power. We have already seen how the misconceptions about white women were overtaken by political events before they yielded to logic. Black women have been doubly mythologized because they are doubly subordinated. Furthermore, both as objects of scorn and recipients of compassion, they have been mislabeled, misunderstood, and misguided by ill-wishers and well-wishers alike.

Addressing themselves to the black woman's social and intellectual inferiority, some have felt justified in speculating that this results from biological inferiority. Others, who want to justify equality before the law, support the position that there is no biological disparity. What is underemphasized by both groups is that fact that biological differences do indeed exist between blacks and whites, just as certainly as they exist among all the races of mankind, but the issue of inferiority-superiority is a separate one, an assigned value with no established biological criteria. Black women do exhibit behavior that is significantly different from that of white women, and criminal patterns which show more affinity for white-male than white-female deviancy. Whether or not biological factors contribute to this difference cannot be answered at this time, but even in the unlikely event that they do, their importance would still pale by comparison with the already established historical and social factors.

The historical factor most frequently implicated in the casting of the present-day mold of the black family is the antebellum institution of slavery. While some have recently disputed the long-held belief that slave families were frequently and systematically disrupted by the callous commercialism of the marketplace,[1] there is no question that this practice was a potential, if not always actual, threat to the family's integrity. Even when considerations of humaneness or enlightened self-interest motivated the slaveowner to allow familial intactness and continuity, the slaves were still ill-prepared by their communal plantation experience to shift after emancipation to the mode of the Western nuclear family. At best, they were treated by their masters as perennial children, wards of the state whose responsibility was more to their owners than to each other, and thus the growth of self-sufficient family units was inhibited. Besides such inauspicious social and economic circumstances, cultural factors also militated against the family. Not only were they unable to identify with the role model of their white master's family, but that residue of their original tribal customs which they had succeeded in preserving encouraged communal and group, rather than familial, constellations. If the best of circumstances made the creation of the family improbable, the worst made its preservation impossible. The plight of a slave husband is poignantly described in the memoirs of one Moses Grandy:

> Mr. Rogerson was with them [a group of recently sold slaves] on his horse, armed with pistols. I said to him, "For God's sake, have you bought my wife?" He said he had; when I asked him what she had done, he said she had done nothing, but that her master wanted money. He drew out a pistol and said that if I went near the wagon on which she was, he would shoot me. I asked for leave to shake hands with her which he refused, but said I might stand at a distance and talk with her. My heart was so full that I could say very little. . . . I have never seen or heard from her from that day to this. I loved her as I love my life.[2]

It was to tens of thousands of similar situations that Abraham Lincoln referred with this prescient foreboding:

> When you have put [the Negro] down and made it impossible for him to be but as the beasts of the field; when you have extinguished his soul in this world and placed him where the ray of hope is blown out as in the darkness of the damned, are you quite sure that the demon you have roused will not turn and rend you?[3]

A calm of almost a century separated these prophetic words from the storm of pent-up frustrations which ultimately exploded with the Watts, Newark, and Detroit riots of the 1960s. Quiescence was not acquiescence, nor was conformance, concurrence. But this distinction seemed irrelevant so long as blacks lacked the means and the spirit to lash out at the white community, so long as they dissipated their anger in shiftless passivity, alcoholism, and futile fratricide. In words dripping with sorrow and hatred, James Baldwin described the plight of the black male:

> Rope, fire, torture, castration, infanticide, rape; death and humiliation; fear by day and night, fear as deep as the marrow of the bone; doubt that he was worthy of life, since everyone around him denied it; sorrow for his women, for his kinfolk, for his children, who needed his protection, and whom he could not protect; rage, hatred and murder, hatred for white men so deep that it often turned against him and his own, and made all love, all trust, all joy, impossible.[4]

Underrepresentation in the work force, overrepresentation in the ranks of those convicted of violent crimes, and institutional impediments blocking male access to legitimate methods of achieving power, money, or security were only some of the consequences of the slave era. Role reversal was another, because the most accessible, often the only, route to legitimate economic opportunities led from the black ghetto to the white kitchen. The mantle of black power—such as it was in a group socially, politically, and financially debilitated—fell on the reluctant but sturdy shoulders of the black female.

In one of history's frequent reversals, the black male, whose strength made him the preferred worker in an agrarian slave setting, became obsolescent in a machine-oriented industrial society. It was not that he lacked the ability to be trained to skilled tasks but that society lacked the motivation to train him. The situation was much different for the black female. There was and is a constant demand for cheap labor to do domestic housework. White fears of black sexuality did not permit black males into this area, so ironically the weaker member of the team became the most employable. With employment came control of the family's meager financial resources, and with this, dominance in the communal hierarchy. Some black males turned to violence against themselves, their group, and ultimately the larger society. Many gravitated into retreatist patterns of alcohol, then drug abuse, seeking to solve the insoluble or, failing that, to salve the irremediable despair. But in the center of this cultural chaos, assailed by the demands of economically castrated consorts, burdened by unwanted, unruly, and unmanageable children, impoverished and uneducated, stood the black female, the chief bulwark against the social and financial catastrophies constantly threatening to engulf her family. In a role which history and economics had thrust upon her, and with a strength born of necessity—a strength, incidentally, which her white sisters would later emulate—she sallied uncertainly into the white man's world. When survival is at stake, the legitimacy of its attainment is not ordinarily a primary consideration. Necessity knows no law and black women were neither in the mood nor the position to have their struggles hobbled by legalities.

Bankrupt by fortune and with no reputation to lose, the black woman became well-versed in deviant methods. Anyone who has spent even a brief time in any of the country's prisons, courts, police stations, or jails needs no subtleties of statistical analyses to be impressed with the racial imbalance among female offenders. The unequal percentage of black women who are arrested and processed through this system is immediately apparent to the most casual observer. While we have no national data broken down by sex and race, there are individual studies which reveal that, statistically, black female criminality parallels the criminality of black males more closely than the criminality of white women does that of white men. A Philadelphia homicide study reports,

> Among female homicides, whether victims or offenders, or both, a Negro was much more likely to be involved than a white. Proportionately, Negro females were twice as frequent as white females among victims, and about six times as frequent among offenders.[5]

Another urban investigation revealed that the community's population ratio of approximately three whites to one black was reversed for the crime count of the offender population: 73 per cent of the offenses were committed by blacks, 27 per cent by whites.[6] On the national level blacks account for 11 per cent of the population, but 53 per cent of all urban arrests for prostitution.[7] In Los Angeles 33 per cent of the prostitutes arrested are blacks, although they comprise only 9 per cent of the population.[8] And so the story goes in one study after another.

In her criminal behavior, the black female is ahead of the white female statistically and, to the extent that she represents a trend, perhaps chronologically. The reasons for this are not clear. It may be that the racial imbalance in arrests accurately reflects a racial imbalance in crimes, but there is a possibility that it is a distorted result of prejudicial arrests. If this is the case, the bias against the black female vis-à-vis the white female is more blatant than it is for males, because the figures nation-wide illustrate unequivocally that the black female's criminality exceeds that of the white female by a much greater margin than black males over white males. However, the color balance of female offenders has begun to shift in recent years. Increasing numbers of white women are entering the criminal-justice system for the first time, and there is reason to believe that this trend will continue with a resultant racial homogenization of defendants in the future.

Historically, black women have occupied a peculiar position in the sociological order, a position in the shadowy middle ground between the strict male and female role designations. It has been asserted that

> the extent to which the [crime] rates for males exceed the rates for females varies with the social position of the sexes in different groups within a nation. In the United States the sex ratio is less extreme among Negroes than it is among whites, and it is probable that Negro males and females more closely resemble each other in social standing than do white males and females.[9]

This blurring of social boundaries among blacks and its influence in making black females statistically more equal partners in crime with black males has interesting and important criminogenic implications for white women. As discussed earlier, in their education, vocation, personal habits and life style, white women are drawing ever closer to their male counterparts. In consequence of this, there is every likelihood that the criminal propensities already exhibited by black women will be matched in the near future by those white women who have crossed the sexual barrier and are inclined to cross the legal barrier. But as we shall see later in our discussion of white-collar crime, the different opportunities available to white women will stamp a distinctive brand on their deviancy.

In a grimly sardonic sense, the black female has been "liberated" for over a century. Expediency not aspiration, necessity not preference thrust this upon her many years ago when circumstances coerced her out of the traditional American female role of submissiveness and compelled her into the masculine role of dominance. It was not a position she sought, but one she accepted. She needed no liberation movement to gain the right to head a single-parent household, to be free within her home from masculine authority, to find a job outside of the home, and to have parity with or superiority over black men. But therein lay the rub. She reached for the moon but grasped only its darker side. She attained pseudo liberation, not real liberation. Her emancipation extended to the ragged fringes of the black world, but hardly beyond. She was no more free than animals in a zoo who are transferred from a cage to a compound. True, she had extended her range of movement within a confined area, but the borders were narrow, strictly defined, and hemmed all about by the white world.

Even so, her less-than-enviable position represents a significant sociolegal milestone, considering the starting point of her long night's journey into day.

> I am anxious to buy a small healthy negro girl—ten or twelve years old, and would like to know if you could let me have one —I will pay you cash in State money—and you allowing the

percentage on it—I will take her on trial of a few weeks—please
let me hear from you as soon as possible (—I would like a dark
Mulatto)—address Mrs. B. L. Blankenship . . . Nottoway Co.
House Va.[10]

With this brief note another black girl was cut adrift from the traditional American value system which enshrined individual liberty.
Through such notes the concept of blackness stood revealed as more
significant than the concept of gender because when black combined with female she was transformed into a chattel with no more
rights than any other commodity—mule, grain, or cotton. Black
women on the plantations were clearly not men, but operationally,
neither were they women. After slavery they had few role models
or social structures around which to build a cohesive grouping.

Unaided by institutional supports, the black female had to
pick up the pieces of the fractured family and provide, through her
own capacity for bonding, the mortar which might hold it together.
This she did by coalescing around herself a family structure which
came to be referred to in the literature as a "female-based" household. By definition, this is a nuclear unit in which a male parent
has either deserted the home completely or, when present, provides
only minimal financial and social support to the children. The unit
is comprised of one or more women and their offspring and frequently includes two or more generations, matrilinearly related by
marriage or blood.[11] The tragedy of this situation is painfully re-
counted by a mother:

> They tell us we are "neglectful"; we don't take proper care of
> the children. But that's a lie, because we do, until we can't any
> longer, because the time has come for the street to claim them,
> to take them away and teach them what a poor nigger's life is
> like. I don't care what anyone says: I take the best care of my
> children. I scream the ten commandments at them every day,
> until one by one they learn them by heart—and believe me they
> don't forget them. (You can ask my minister if I'm not telling
> the truth.) It's when they leave for school, and start seeing the
> streets and everything, that's when there's the change; and by
> the time they're ten or so, it's all I can do to say anything,
> because I don't even believe my own words, to be honest. I tell

them, please to be good; but I know it's no use, not when they can't get a fair break, and there are the sheriffs down South and up here the policemen, ready to kick you for so much as breathing your feelings. So I turn my eyes on the little children, and keep on praying that one of them will grow up at the right second, when the schoolteachers will have time to say hello and give him the lessons he needs, and when they get rid of the building here and let us have a place you can breathe in and not get bitten all the time, and when the men can find work—because *they* can't have children, and so they have to drink or get on drugs to find some happy moments, and some hope about things.[12]

While the wider sociological effects of this matriarchal influence go far beyond the question of black female criminality, it is important to note that it is in harmony with black culture, which does not consider it either unusual or unreasonable to expect a female to support and run a family singlehandedly. This situation does not seem strange to many of the women who find themselves in it because they have been raised in and around other families in which the female was the dominant figure. The fact that the family centers on the mother plus the likelihood that blacks will have more children than white slum families means that the mother has a more difficult job to do with fewer resources.[13] Although clinical psychologists and sociologists have investigated the impact a female-based household has on the family members, there is virtually no information to date on how the matriarch herself is affected.

Aggressiveness, toughness, and a certain street-wise self-sufficiency were just a few of the characteristics necessary for the black woman to shepherd her beleaguered flock of children, siblings, and consorts through the wastelands of educational, social, financial, and cultural deprivations. Lacking socially sanctioned role models and the sustaining strength of institutions, she had to manufacture her own image. In the words of Toni Morrison, black novelist and feminist, she "had nothing to fall back on: not maleness, not whiteness, not ladyhood, not anything, period, and out of that profound desolation of her reality, she may very well have invented herself." [14] It should not have been surprising that this unconventional inventiveness and resourceful expediency would sometimes spill over the boundaries of legitimacy into crime. It is unnecessary to invoke an explanation based on inherent tendencies, for the early influence of inner-city ways is sufficient.

"I don't feel much about money because I was always poor. But I wanted some things like a car and I always had to get things for myself. So when I was sixteen I went out of school and started going to clean with my mother where she works. But they only gave me eight dollars a day because I was just helpen and I couldn't buy no car on that. So at night I started getten some money from men. One night me and my girl friend ran into a cop and we both got probation. I got a job washen dishes but I had to be there at this bar all night and I couldn't take those hours. I started liven with this guy Link and then I got a job cleanen offices three nights a week. One night me and my girl friend heard Link talken to his boys about getten some cars and we thought it sounded easy so we went and stole a car. But we ran out of luck. We was caught that night. There just ain't no way I can get a car."

The survival of the black girl often depends more on her own resources than on those of her family. This too precocious self-sufficiency, this too isolated unfolding of potentials leads to early closure of developmental possibilities, the foreclosure of educational, vocational, and social options, and increases the susceptibility to criminality.

In the criminal-justice system, as elsewhere, the black woman is viewed differently and responded to differently by everyone from the arresting officer to the probation officer. At every juncture stand processes and processors whose programs and attitudes reflect not current truths but ancient myths which have dogged her steps up every rung of the social ladder.

Long before black gained any semblance of beauty or power it was ineluctably and irredeemably bad. Through tortuous hair-straightening sessions and dubious skin-lightening lotions, the black woman labored to bleach out the blackness and the badness in poignant efforts to pass into the thin-lipped, blue-eyed, straight-haired world of white power. She suffered not only from an ambiguity of gender role but also a crisis of personal identity, which was to afflict her until she could extract her own separate and equal liberation from the larger movement. Not until the sixties, when black education and black politics and the specter of black violence evoked a recognition of black power, did black become beautiful. Early models of such beauty, like Lena Horne and Dorothy Dandridge with their finely chiseled, even, Caucasian features, were hardly distinguishable from white women. Liberated advertisements portrayed sleekly coiffed, hot-combed Peck & Peck tan girls standing beside their Chevrolets with Ivy League, Belafonte boy friends. But the Miriam Makeba and Angela Davis Afros are appearing with increasing frequency in magazine pictures. The era of "black stay back, brown hang around" is being replaced by a new pride in black identity, itself part of a country-wide ethnic revitalization movement. As a people, we have ventured into the melting pot and returned with a renewed regard for our national origins and minority differences. The effects of this shift, together with the broadening scope of legitimate opportunities for blacks, may harness black rage into socially useful black respect and ameliorate one of the chronic sources of black crime as it exists today. But it may also accelerate the entrance of blacks, especially black women who are in the economic vanguard of their race, into white-collar crime. Such is the irony of progress.

A significant factor in the battle for black power was the effort to mobilize the black electorate to work within the system. Voter-registration drives were organized and civil-rights leaders exhorted blacks to shift the arena of contention from the streets to the ballot box:

> the vote is . . . the Negro's most important weapon in his struggle for full citizenship.[15]

> the age of the ballot is upon the black man. It is the tool of survival.[16]

> the biggest step the blacks can take is in the "direction of the voting booth."[17]

As with other civil liberties, blacks were late to acquire the right to suffrage. Although black male Americans had voted from time to time since colonial days, it was not until 1870 that the Fifteenth Amendment granted them the right to vote nation-wide. By 1877, "although there was still some question whether blacks could vote in the North, the Southern black electorate reached its greatest heights and placed black public officials in hundreds of political posts at the state and national levels." [18] This development, however, was so distasteful to the Southern whites that they succeeded in arranging the Compromise of 1877, which withdrew federal protection of the voting booths. Then they contrived a variety of methods, ranging from blatant violence to the destruction of ballots, to abridge the rights of black voters. Despite efforts by determined blacks to void their disfranchisements by the Southern states after 1890, and despite pockets of voting activity in various states, it was not until 1944 that the *Smith v. Alwright* decision permitting whites to help blacks register to vote gave the movement the additional judicial support it required. The years that followed for the civil-rights movement were, depending on the perspective, either the fulfillment of a dream or the realization of a nightmare.

The early period of the movement bore the imprint of the conservative and cautious approach of the National Association for the Advancement of Colored People. Their gains over the years were modest but substantive, and theirs was the only voice of consequence representing American blacks. But a younger, more vociferous, less patient generation of blacks, a generation less accustomed to bondage and often unwilling to acknowledge the debt that their aspirations owed to the quiet fortitude of their elders, began to chafe at the deliberate pace of legislation and to clamor for immediate entrance into the promised land of equality. At first their approach wedded the conservatism and nonviolence of their NAACP heritage with the intrusiveness and activism of the younger, more impetuous elements. From this confluence issued the "freedom riders," the Southern Christian Leadership Conference, and the Student Nonviolent Coordinating Committee. But while the movement was Gandhian in its cool outer response to frustration, it drew its vigor from the passionate impetuousness of a youth which would be served—and not just at lunch counters. This momentum for freedom *now* soon shifted the ideological stance from reconciliation and brotherhood to power and defensive separatism, and with it the balance of power swung to militants like Rap Brown and Stokely Carmichael. The change was epitomized by SNCC's dropping its "nonviolent" designation and proclaiming itself the SCC. Many important liberal white adherents were alienated, financial support dried up, and the more notorious leaders were jailed for their new militancy. In spite of, perhaps because of, the injection of this more assertive thrust, the Voting Rights Act of 1965 was passed and with it a new phase in the revitalization of the black masses was brought to fruition. The election of many black officials, including the mayors of several large cities, promises to accelerate the incorporation of blacks into the American mainstream.

While they were climbing upward politically, blacks were also moving geographically. In the last fifty years the migration of rural blacks to urban centers has transformed both the blacks and the cities. Unskilled, uneducated, impoverished, and stigmatized for their color, their moves often brought them not the hoped-for relief, but new forms of disappointment, disillusionment, and frustration. Added to their plight was the futility of abandoned hope. " 'For where does one run to when he's already in the promised land?' " [19] Into the behavioral sink of the Northern urban slums, already brimming with white discontent, these Southern black migrants poured. Here was no melting-pot amalgamation of diverse cultures. Instead, black and white coagulated into immiscible masses, unwilling or unable to dissolve their differences. The resultant mixture was often a brew of pure vitriol. As racism catapulted so also did police brutality, economic exploitation, and social disintegration. These rural refugees had arrived with no opportunity save that which the ballot might open. However, quickly realizing that voting rights were not sufficient to accomplish change, they sought other means: many went on welfare; others opened their own small business dealing in drugs, numbers, untaxed whisky, sexual favors, or gambling; and still others turned to pursuing their goals through violence.[20]

Out of the maelstrom of forlorn hope, political impotence, confused social roles, unemployment, endemic alcoholism, and frustrated rage emerged the black female, leader by default, the great black hope of her race. Those who have not experiencd the debilitating emptiness of utter hardship may extol its virtues. Disraeli philosophized that there is no education like adversity. From this perspective, the black female suffered from an embarrassment of advantages because she usually had a surfeit of both—adversity and "no education." But the insulation, not to say the insolence, of some well-trained scholars allows them to overlook the fact that adversity is most useful to the most highly educated—not to ghetto women. However, what she learned from the streets was probably, considering her circumstances, what she most needed to know.

With hardly any encouragement and few opportunities, she achieved only little in the way of regular schooling.[21] But even that was no mean accomplishment, considering the obstacles.

> [In Natchez, Louisiana, there were] two schools taught by colored teachers. One of these was a slave woman who had taught a midnight school for a year. It opened at eleven or twelve o'clock at night, and closed at two o'clock a.m. . . . Milla Granson, the teacher, learned to read and write from the children of her indulgent master in her old Kentucky home. Her number of scholars was twelve at the time, and when she had taught these to read and write she dismissed them, and again took her apostolic number and brought them up to the extent of her ability, until she had graduated hundreds. A number of them wrote their own passes and started for Canada. . . .
>
> At length her night school project leaked out, and was for a time suspended; but it was not known that seven of the twelve years subsequent to leaving Kentucky had been spent in this work.[22]

In the devastated South of the post–Civil War era there was a dearth of money, books, teachers, and schools. The only thing in plentiful supply was four million newly freed slaves, many of whom were as eager to acquire an education as they were to till their own land. Unhappily, this brought them into direct competition with white farmers and laborers embittered by the war and in no mood to yield much more than could be taken from them by force. Onto this soil of white resentment, fear, and projected anger were strewn the seeds of hatred by rabble-rousing demagogues. They cultivated such violence-prone organizations as the Ku Klux Klan, dedicated to suppressing black strivings for equality. Chief among their targets was a suppression of black educational aspirations. The extent of their opposition to black schools is illustrated by an excerpt of the testimony of a thirty-four-year-old black female at a Congressional investigation in 1871:

> QUESTION: Why did they not want you to have schools?
> ANSWER: They would not let us have schools. They went to a colored man there, whose son had been teaching school, and they took every book they had and threw them into the fire; and they said they would dare any other nigger to have a book in his house. We allowed last fall that we would have a schoolhouse in every district; and the colored men started them. But the Ku-Klux said they would whip every man who sent a scholar there. There is a schoolhouse there, but no scholars.[23]

While times have changed dramatically and many black women are attaining college degrees, the average black female still ends her education in junior high school. Since there is a correlation between the amount of education a woman receives and the amount of income she will earn, black women who head families are likely to earn substantially less than their white counterparts. The median income of the nation's white women who headed households and worked at full-time year-round jobs was $5749 in 1971, while in that same year black women in the same situation averaged $5181.[24] Almost 45 per cent of all households headed by black females had incomes running well below the Labor Department's "low income level," and this picture of unemployability and poor salaries is similarly bleak for black women in general. Because of the lack of education, because of racial bias in hiring, because of other culturally erected barriers directly related to their ethnic background, all black women tend to earn substantially less than white working women. In 1972, 56 per cent of those black women who were working held positions categorized by the Labor Department as low-pay industrial operatives and household service workers.[25] Only 35 per cent of white women held such positions. As a result of these low-level, low-priority jobs, black women are also more likely to lose their jobs in times of industrial economic crises. In 1971, the unemployment rate of working-force black women was 10 per cent, while white women averaged only 6 per cent.[26]

Even for those black women who marry, conditions are much more unstable. In 1970, 19 per cent of all black women who had at one time been married were either divorced or separated, in contrast to 6 per cent of their white counterparts.[27] In urban areas where blacks are now heavily concentrated, one finds that the government has unwittingly involved itself in the financial support of these ghetto-based black matriarchies. In many ways, the much-criticized "welfare state" is no more than the fusion of black matriarchy and governmental bureaucracy. Currently, it is not unusual to find a welfare home which contains as many as three generations of welfare mothers, together with their children, who have never had a single live-in husband or father among them. A black woman who is out of marriage, out of work, out of money, and out of luck does not contemplate the theoretical niceties of her socioeconomic profile. She deals pragmatically with the reality of her situation, and is wont to take what she can when she can get it.

In many ways, black females are a unique group whose socioeconomic characteristics fall somewhere between white males and white females. Occupationally, they are outdistancing black males in the pursuit of American cultural goals. Although black males outnumber black females in the general work force by a ratio of four to one, in the white-collar occupations black females take the lead. Whereas black males comprise only 1 per cent of all males in white-collar jobs, black females make up 3 per cent of the total female white-collar labor force.[28] From the performance of black teen-agers, it appears that, at least for the next generation, black females will continue to move more quickly than their brothers into positions of leadership. Of all applications for the National Achievement Scholarship Program, financed by the Ford Foundation for outstanding black high-school graduates, roughly 70 per cent are girls even though high-school principals have made special efforts to submit the names of boys.[29]

In increasing numbers, black women are following that "tortuous road which has led from Montgomery to Oslo . . . over which millions of Negroes are traveling to find a new sense of dignity." As these words suggest, Martin Luther King, Jr., was convinced that this road would be widened into a "super-highway of justice." But even though legal and social barriers are crumbling, there are those who are unwilling to make the slow, arduous journey along this route. Other pathways beckon to those who lack the incentive, the community support, and the financial resources to scale the educational-vocational ladder to success. For this significant minority, the track leads away from legitimate but generally frustrating efforts toward an increasing proclivity to utilize illegitimate but often more immediately satisfying expedients.

"Turning tricks is a little more boring than my old job as a waitress —one guy looks like all the rest . . . but it's good money."
—Doris

Because the black woman is burdened with the problems adherent to the family provider, because she must meet these financial obligations under conditions which afford her little access to conventional means, and because she lives in a time frame of impulsive immediacy, she is more likely than a white woman to turn to the lucrative forms of deviant behavior. Vice offenses, although not special to a particular racial group, are special to particular socio-economic situations because they provide ready access to easy money. Because there are too few other places to which she can turn for money, she turns tricks.

". . . at first some of them [johns] scare me and I remember I felt real bad but now I know the business and they don't scare me no more."

—Evelyn

Once she is caught in the web of justice, the criminality scale of the black female becomes even more unbalanced. If she is tainted with an arrest record—whether it is a product of her wilful transgressions, an unfortunate sequel to environmental pressures, or simply the result of intensive police patrols in ghetto areas—a black female acquires an additional stigma. As a woman who previously was handicapped in the job market by her race and sex, she is further disadvantaged by an offense record and often additionally impaired by confinement in a correctional institution. The cycle of recidivism accelerates with each escapade and each confinement, because it compounds a socially lethal mixture of increased bitterness and increased contact with criminal elements. After several excursions between the jail and the ghetto, prison may become a graduate school for crime acculturation and the outside world an arena for fieldwork in the profession of last resort.

The experience of Sally, the oldest of nine children, is typical:
"My mom was the boss in our family. I was thirteen years old when she started to hit the bottle real bad. I had to fix the meals and I wanted to get out of that house. I started hanging around with some older kids and they gave me some 'bennies' and 'reds' and 'yellows' so I was freaked out when I was fourteen. I made some money off of some tricks and then I turned on to Smack. I got busted and got ninety days. Then I got busted a few more times. I was in the House of Detention but then I had to go to _____ and there they don't treat you no way but like a prisoner. That was the worst place in the world. All day I washed windows and I got up at five in the morning. That's the time I used to get home. Well, anyway I got involved with girls. My best friend there was in for armed robbery, but she was real mad . . . and she didn't even have no gun. But we spent a whole lot of time figuring out this job on a jewelry store. This friend said she could get her friend who cleans the place to come in on the job. This friend who works there messed up and didn't have it set up right and we got caught two blocks away and we didn't even get no jewelry. After I got out of prison that time I was so messed up I just started shootin' again and now I don't know what's goin' to happen."

For women like Sally, the frequency of court visits as well as the level of violence and types of deviant behaviors may well have blunted the chivalry that police and courts routinely accord to women. They have forced the law-enforcement system to deal with the criminal act rather than the gender of its perpetrator.

Black women have been "liberated" as criminals for many years. In the century that has elapsed since the era of slavery, black women have freed themselves from the fetters of male domination while, ironically, white women are still fighting to loosen the socio-economic chains that have kept them in psychological bondage to their husbands. Today black women generally shy away from or even openly scorn the women's liberation movement. Liberation—in the sense of living on their own, being the breadwinner for large families, existing free from male control—has been theirs for years. They did not have to fight for it; it is liberation without options and, in consequence, it is often a cruel mockery of liberation. The black woman is the head of the family but the family is in disarray; she may work at any job she can get but there are few good ones for which she is qualified; she has freedom of movement but there is no place to go. Her visions of fulfillment were, after all, a mirage, for in leaving the old world to conquer the new, she has ended up with the worst of both.

In contrast, the white woman has generally spent her hours sequestered in kitchen or bedroom, unmotivated and untempted toward criminal activity because she could count on a relatively protected environment. Outside of a sporadic bit of shoplifting, or secretly selling sexual favors, she had few needs or opportunities to involve herself in criminal behavior. Her more secure financial position, her domestic confinement, her cultural proscriptions, and her institutional supports have shielded her from involvement in the more aggressive and lucrative forms of criminality. All of this is changing because many white women no longer want to be protected and supported if the price is submission. They are opting for the promises and problems of emancipation. Black females have always been referred to as "women." Now white females are fighting for that label in place of the term "lady," which encompasses helplessness, modesty, and dependence. There is no "ladies' liberation"—only "women's liberation."

But the accession to power of a previously subordinate group rarely occurs without the use or at least the potential to use force. It took a Civil War and belligerent militancy by an army of men in 1865 to release the black woman from physical bondage. One hundred years later a civil-rights movement and an army of politically militant women succeeded in redefining emancipation to include social, vocational, and psychological equality—not just with their husbands but with all men. Superficially, many of the demands for which the women's liberation movement has been fighting resemble those which were thrust on the black female: single-parent families, self-support, cohabitation without marriage, and social and economic equality with their men. The significant difference is that for black women these were onerous responsibilities rather than esteemed rights. It is no great privilege to share an equality of denigration and squalor. The game under such circumstances was not worth the proverbial candle, and, in consequence, fewer and fewer women, white or black, are willing to play it. Nor has the prospect of serving in a male heaven retained its attractiveness as a sought-after advancement. Neither in ruling the weak nor in waiting upon the strong are women seeking their proper niche, but in the freedom to elect either or neither as her wishes and circumstances determine.

Just as the white female is moving toward the blurring of sex-role distinctions which have already occurred for black women, so also is she moving in the direction of her higher criminality rates. This new trend underscores the fact that the criminality of the black woman had little if any connection to biological make-up, but was rather related to her role in society. Well over a century ago she was forced to tap into inner strengths which have just begun to be discovered by white women. It is not that the black woman has forever outdistanced the white woman as a criminal, but rather that cultural conditions forced her to run earlier, faster, and farther before white women entered the race. Now that white women are on the track, they are running with considerable speed. They are becoming more involved in crime every year. It does not seem unrealistic to speculate that if one looks at where black women are as criminals today, one can appreciate where white women are headed as liberated criminals in the coming years. But the parallel is not exact because the differences in their socioeconomic positions will result in crimes which are perceived, executed, prosecuted, and corrected differently. This is inevitable because of the nature of the criminal-justice system. The distinctions of which we are understandably proud between the rule of men and the rule of law in fact-disappear when we reflect that it is the men who rule that make the laws.

7

The Link Between Opportunity and Offense: Class

"Tis more by fortune, lady, than my merit."

—Shakespeare

Pericles 2.03

If one would discern the centers of dominance in any society, one need only look to its definitions of "virtue" and "vice" or "legal" and "criminal," for in the strength to set standards resides the strength to maintain control. No power group with the potency to do otherwise is likely to disenfranchise itself by espousing a value system uncongenial to its own interests. That virtue is its own reward or that crime does not pay are not idealistic homilies but self-evident socioeconomic truths because they are pragmatic dictums expressing the operational codes of every society. Stripped of ethical rationalizations and philosophical pretentions, a crime is anything that a group in power chooses to prohibit. Thus when the definitions of crime are extended beyond those deviancies practiced by the lower class to include activities previously countenanced by the upper class, we are witnessing not a discovery of new crimes but the ascension of newly strengthened social segments.

In the last quarter century the concept that criminal behavior is limited to directly and often violently antisocial behavior (murder, assault, robbery, etc.) has yielded to egalitarian influences which are seeking to apply the same ethical standards to bank embezzlers as to bank robbers. In the shorthand by which we concretize our abstractions into graphic descriptions this affluential form of misbehavior is designated "white-collar crime." In the mode of its practice and in the class of its practitioners it contrasts sharply with traditional blue-collar crime, and its investigation exposes to legal accountability a group whose position had hitherto made them immune to public scrutiny.

To pursue these opulent offenders one must travel horizontally or vertically from the grimy ghettos whose climate nourishes blue-collar crime but is inimical to the white-collar variety. One must ride the network of commuter trunk lines which fan out from the congested urban blight, separating it by thirty minutes and untold light-years from the manicured lawns of the fashionable suburbs. One must board an elevator and depart from the ground-level arena of street crime and violence to seek the heady high-rise prosperity of top-drawer offenses. For the quarry in question are not societal outcasts, denizens of the deep pockets of poverty, but those who are securely sequestered in society's lap—the inhabitants of the upper echelons of the American economic system who thrive in the rarefied atmosphere of high finance, high living, and, alas, high skullduggery. Business theft, consumer fraud, embezzlement, anti-trust violations, and malfeasance or misfeasance of office are not crimes within the reach of the average citizen—or average criminal, for that matter. They can be perpetrated only by people occupying prestigious and protected positions in the ranks of industry, government, and the various professions. Edwin Sutherland's foresighted recognition that the kind of crime committed depended more on different opportunities than on stereotyped criminal propensities [1] provided the theoretical framework while political changes provided the impetus to prosecute this long neglected but, by no means, rare genre of crime which Al Capone referred to—in combined envy and contempt—as "the legitimate rackets."

That this type of behavior was so long tolerated in Western civilization, or that it was extended such a protracted grace period of benign neglect by law-enforcement authorities even after it was identified as antithetical to our system of justice, is due to both historical and practical considerations. Historically, the rigidity of closed class structures coupled with the social insensitivity of authoritarian political systems quite naturally favored the property rights of the upper classes. Typical was a thirteenth-century English court declaration that there should be "no remedy for the man who to his damage had trusted the word of a liar." [2] And five hundred years of jurisprudence did not mitigate the principle. In the eighteenth century, a British chief justice asked, "When A got money from B by pretending that C had sent for it, shall we indict one man for making a fool of another?" [3] The sanctity of private property was uniformly upheld over public trust and the passage of commercial fraud laws met persistent and consistent opposition. Avarice was masked by a self-serving ideology which transferred the divine right of kings to the unchallenged right of ownership. Language itself reflects the identity of property with propriety. Even while the American Constitution championed the cause of individual liberty, it was formulated by men of significant material substance—property owners whose appreciation of the importance of property rights became indelibly impressed into the laws of the land. Chief Justice Stone, in his attack on the concept of laws dealing with fraud, admonished that "any interference with the operation of the natural laws of greed [was] subversive of liberty." [4]

Although embezzlement was made illegal in the eighteenth century, other commercial deceptions—false advertising, sale of fraudulent securities, restraint of trade—were not similarly proscribed until the nineteenth century. The philosophy of *caveat emptor* grudgingly yielded to *caveat vendor,* but only after the shift from an agricultural to an industrial economy, accumulation of great fortunes by a select few, and a transfer of property from the private to the corporate sphere impelled the state to protect consumers by intruding on the dictum of *laissez faire* with legislative mandates.

By 1940, attention was being drawn to those whom Albert Morris termed "criminals of the upperworld"—"that numerous but never clearly identified group of criminals whose social position, intelligence, and criminal technique permit them to move among their fellow citizens virtually immune to recognition and persecution as criminals." [5] In the wake of burgeoning public alarm, federal regulatory agencies proliferated, the mass media headlined scandalous stories of white-collar crime, and politicians, like cuckolded husbands, outdid each other in decrying the inequities of a deceitful segment of the business community that society had loved not wisely but too well. From pulpit and podium, by rhetoric and legislation, the declaration of consumer rights was proclaimed and an era of commercial responsibility ushered in. As revolutions go, its pace was halting and irregular, its innovations quiet and orderly, but its impact was momentous because it overturned the privilege of property and redefined the ethos of business morality.

From the start, the concept of white-collar crime has had many diverse meanings. Its original definition contains five components: 1) it is a crime; 2) often a violation of trust; 3) perpetrated by a respectable member of the community who enjoys a 4) high socioeconomic status; 5) and is in some way related to his occupation.[6] By targeting on a heterogeneous range of crimes committed under widely varying motivations and by centering attention on the societal position of the offender rather than on the offender himself, the original conceptualization may well have left a monumental task for those who go on to study it. There have been advances and retreats but this perimeter endures and the effort to organize a wide range of disparate data into one classification of deviant behavior continues.

In attempting to categorize such a diverse gamut of crimes as those called "white-collar" some degree of ambiguity is unavoidable. Merged together are offenses committed by contractors who substitute inferior materials for those specified; political grafters who accept payment for illegitimate favors; loansharks who charge illegal interest rates; stockbrokers who take money for securities they do not buy; advertisers who disseminate deceptive offers; theater operators who permit youngsters to watch X-rated films; lawyers who misappropriate funds in receivership, "chase ambulances," or secure perjured testimonies; and doctors who dispense illegal prescriptions or write fraudulent accident reports. Also falling within the scope of white-collar crimes are the kind of shabby quasi-legal, commercial practices exposed by the McCone Committee during investigations of urban ghetto conditions: sales of tainted food, high interest rates for time payments, the marketing of poor-quality goods at exorbitant prices, and exploitations by insurance companies.

Frequent impediments to justice arise from the reluctance of an unaccustomed public to entertain the idea that its respected citizens are engaging in illegal activities or to finally label them "criminals." For example, it took almost ten years for the biggest criminal case in the history of antitrust legislation to wind its way into the courtroom. This 1961 case, referred to as the "incredible electrical conspiracy," [7] for the first time placed high-ranking American businessmen in prison for violations of the Sherman Act of 1890. The facts, indeed, are astonishing:

> Forty-five executives of the leading electrical companies met for a period of many years in plush resorts and motor hotels to eliminate competition among them, to split up the electrical equipment business in proportion to the size of each company, to eliminate "outsiders," to engage in contrived and fictitious "bidding" and to maintain price. To avoid detection, they used public telephones rather than their office equipment. They used only blank stationery and omitted names . . . they used code numbers to refer to the members of the team. They never gathered together in public dining rooms or hotel lobbies. . . . Expense accounts were often altered to hide the location of the meetings.[8]

And Richard Austin Smith, writing in *Fortune* magazine at the time of the case, commented:

> The conspiracies had their own lingo and their own standard operating procedure. The attendance list was known as the "Christmas-card list," meetings as "choir practices." . . . At the hotel meeting it was S.O.P. . . . not to have breakfast with fellow conspirators in the dining room.[9]

What is incredible about this is not its scope—there have been larger crimes—but the fact that it took almost ten years to reach indictment. In the threads of continuity which bind the traditional attitudes toward commerce of our Western heritage with the current practices of our Establishment we may find the answer. There are many ways in which the ethos of ancient Carthage differed from that of the American founding fathers, but in one respect—the sanctity of the profit motive—their views were congenial. The Carthaginian Creed, as stated by Polybius, that "at Carthage, nothing which results in profit is regarded as disgraceful," found sympathetic echoes in Franklin's declaration "that the business of America is business," and in a later pithy, self-righteous dictum that "what is good for General Motors is good for the country." The capitalist system of free enterprise, the inviolability of the free marketplace, enlightened self-interest, rugged individualism, taming the wilderness, manifest destiny, and many similar phrases were not merely catchy slogans broadcast by enthusiastic orators. They were the embodiment of American faith in unfettered industry, the litany of American worship of success and the shrine of prosperity to which morality itself paid homage. Until recently, and even still, it is considered irreverent and perhaps ungrateful to challenge the practices of a large employer who pays taxes and declares dividends. In addition to a visceral aversion to tampering with a commercial cornucopia whose prodigious productivity has made us heir to the highest standard of living on earth, there is also an ingrained reluctance to challenge the integrity of socially respectable people. In the electrical conspiracy of the sixties and again in the Watergate scandal of the seventies every effort was made to avoid undermining the pillars of communal probity not merely because they had earned social deference nor necessarily because they deserved special forbearance, but because the public needed them to be what they should have been.

But lest the spectacular nature of such transactions mislead with regard to the incidence or scope of white-collar crime, it should be borne in mind that when we include such widespread and ordinary practices as unnecessary repairs, unreported income, watering down milk, padding expense accounts, etc., many citizens who consider themselves respectable and law-abiding fall under the shadow of this crime. Although accurate statistics are unavailable because most of the evidence is hidden in official reports of major investigations, or disguised in the complexities of the transaction, or diverted to the records of agencies other than the criminal courts, the actual financial costs of white-collar crime are many times greater than the cost of the traditional crimes that are generally referred to as "our crime problem." Just a glimpse of the massive drain on the economic system is found in the report of the President's Commission on Law Enforcement and the Administration of Justice which reveals that undeclared income ranges as high as forty billion dollars a year and embezzlement losses for all organizations costs approximately two hundred million dollars per year.[10] In spite of this sizable financial drain, our system of ethics is still ambiguous with regard to the principles governing the relationship between large organizations and individuals. Perhaps it is because we are only a century removed from the small, static, personal communities where transactions involved neighbors, family, and friends, and behaviors were strictly enforced by mutually validated norms. In the interim, while governmental agencies have struggled with the development of regulatory legislation which clashes with the American ethos of *laissez faire,* business has informally generated its own code which is uncomfortably suggestive of the one proposed by Dickens: " 'Do other men for they would do you.' That's the true business precept." From the Robber Barons of the 1800s to the electrical conspirators of the present we hear echoes of these sentiments:

> A. B. Stickney, a railroad president, said to sixteen other railroad presidents in the home of J. P. Morgan in 1890, "I have the utmost respect for you gentlemen, individually, but as railroad presidents I wouldn't trust you with my watch out of my sight." [11]

> Colonel Vanderbilt asked, "You don't suppose you can run a railroad in accordance with the statutes, do you?" [12]

And seventy years later:

> There was old, portly Fred F. Loock, president of Allen-Bradley Co., who found conspiring with competitors quite to his taste

("It is the only way a business can be run. It is free enterprise.").[13]

And in politics, we find a counterpart as exemplified

> by the St. Louis boodler, who after accepting to vote against a
> certain franchise was offered a larger sum to vote for it. He did
> so, but returned the first bribe. He was asked on the witness
> stand why he had returned it. "Because it wasn't mine!" he
> exclaimed, flushing with anger. "I hadn't earned it." [14]

In principle, white-collar crime may be understood to be that
antisocial deviancy which is native to upper-class modes of behavior
in the same way that blatant robbery and physical assault are extensions of lower-class modes. From this perspective they are separated only by means, not goals. Each group functions within its
own range, generally limited in its deviancy as in its normalcy to
the confines of its *modus operandi*. It is for this reason that when
the fortunes of an ethnic, racial, or sexual group rise, it is likely
that their offenses will be snatched from the ignominy of physical
crimes and elevated to the status of white-collar lawlessness. One
would be understandably surprised if an accountant held up a
grocery store with a gun. His special skills and opportunities would
allow him to accomplish more with less risk by using a pencil on
ledger books. When, therefore, we find women being convicted of
embezzling large sums it is a certain sign that they have become
not only more important criminals but also more important people.
In this regard, white women are far ahead of their black sisters.
But they have not yet reached her destination. Perhaps symbolic
of the distance females must span to reach full equality in a world
of crime is their conspicuous absence from Watergate events. Like
understudies, they have been waiting in the wings, not of their own
volition but because men have all the parts. And they do still have
the leads. But women have performed so well that now they are
being offered more and more roles and they are accepting all of
them, even the criminal ones.

· Alberta, a black woman convicted of embezzling a substantial sum of money through the welfare agency office she headed in a large city: "You're damned right I took it. And I spent it and I enjoyed it. People had been stealing from me all my life. I got a job where I could get a little, and I went for it. City Hall in this city—or any other major city—runs on money. That is what politics is really about. Money. I was caught because I was on the wrong side of the political fence this year. It wasn't that I was being dishonest. The main reason was because I was butting into someone else's action. That's how it all works."

It was in the same year that women gained the constitutional right to vote (1920) that the Women's Bureau of the United States Department of Labor was created "to formulate standards and policies which shall promote the welfare of wage-earning women, improve their working conditions, increase their efficiency, and advance their opportunities for profitable employment." [15] At that time, 23 per cent of all working-age women were in the labor force. Each decade since then has witnessed kaleidoscopic changes both in numbers and in the nature of employment. The economic seed planted in the twenties sprouted with the manpower needs of the forties and came to full fruition with the equal-opportunity legislation of the sixties. As shown in the following list, the percentage of women in the labor force has more than doubled in this century. [16]

Year	Women as percentage of total labor force
1900	18.1
1910	20.9
1920	20.4
1930	22.0
1940	24.3
1945	29.6
1950	28.8
1955	30.2
1960	32.3
1965	34.0
1970	36.7
1972	37.4

The variety of opportunities that have opened for women in the last decade have multiplied their access to a whole new range of illicit behaviors. It is not that women have replaced one deviant behavior with another; they have merely added new ones to their repertoire. This is particularly true in the area of acquisitive offenses whereby a whole spectrum of white-collar crimes have supplemented shoplifting, the traditional female property offense.

Shoplifting is an ancient art of females, one in which the goods have changed, but not the techniques of stealing them. Generations of women have participated, no matter how small the gain or how great the risk:

In 1726, Jane Holms was found guilty of stealing

> some twenty yards of straw-ground brocaded silks value 10 [pounds] . . . on the first of June 1726, of stealing . . . forty yards of pink-coloured mantua silk, value 10 [pounds], on the first of May, in the same year, of stealing in company with Mary Robinson, a silver cup of the value of 5 pounds . . . on the seventh January; of stealing in company of Mary Robinson afore-said, eighty yards of cherry-coloured mantua silk value 5 [pounds] . . . on the twenty-fourth of December.[17]

She was executed.

Most shoplifters are petty pilferers rather than professionals. They engage in this type of behavior over many years, usually have no prior record, are respectable employees or housewives, exhibit no consistent psychoneurosis or psychotic patterns, typically steal merchandise valued under fifteen dollars, have no knowledge of arrest procedures, and, although they have thought about being caught, they have never thought about being arrested.[18] The composite picture of the pilferer portrays a woman who

> comes into the store usually equipped with a large handbag, briefcase, shopping bag, "bad bag," or sometimes even booster bloomers or a booster bag in which to carry off merchandise. She may have scissors or a razor blade to snip off price tags. She deliberately directs the sales clerk's attention elsewhere and slips various items into her bag when she believes herself unobserved. She may even bring with her a shopping list of items she

wants to steal. . . . Having acquired a portion of her loot, she
may go to a store rest room and flush price tags and other in-
criminating evidence down the toilet. She will wear as much as
is possible of her recently stolen merchandise in order to lighten
her load and then proceed to stash away the rest. Her loot at
the end of the day may range from one to thirty pieces of merchandise.[19]

But this portrait of the traditional female property offender is fading and is likely to become almost as uncommon as the male shoplifter. Until recently, a woman who wanted to acquire property
illegally had very few options open to her because her traditional
role as homemaker shackled her to the domicile from which she
departed only for her occasional routine excursions to the department store or supermarket. It was only a short jump from woman
shopper to woman shoplifter. The woman bookkeeper or woman
executive would be no more likely than a similarly placed man to
stoop to such petty theft nor to settle for such a petty return for her
efforts.

Grace is a middle-aged woman who, until 1972, was an assistant
purchasing agent at a large equipment supply firm not far from Chicago.
In July of that year, she was arrested and charged with embezzling
some $122,000 in a complicated scheme which involved phony bank
accounts, nonexisting vendor companies and never-made deliveries.
Her case was ultimately dismissed as the result of a legal technicality.
When she was employed, she earned a salary of $16,000 a year. Today,
she drives a brand-new Lincoln Mark V and runs a small public-
relations agency.

"I'm speculating to your question. I'm certainly not implying that
there was any merit to the particular case against me. However, I was
in a position to get a good feel of the general problems that face female
executives in industry. They are passed over, underestimated and
grossly underpaid. It is not unusual to find women making a full one-
third less then men doing exactly the same work. It is easy for a woman
to begin to feel patronized. Many women have needs, like men. They
are not immune to temptation. I know companies where male executives
buy their yachts and finance their mistress's apartments with the kick-
backs they write into their delivery contracts.

"The same men will underpay and mistreat their female colleagues
and feel safe that they will never dip into the till . . . that, for some
reason, women are more inherently honest in the way that they are

supposedly inherently weaker. They aren't weaker and they are not any more honest. They just haven't had as many opportunities to be near large amounts of money as men."

As opportunities open up, the new woman moves in—and she makes her entrance at all economic levels. There are now women exterminators, jockeys, crane operators, rabbis, ministers, pipe fitters, morticians, bellhops, generals, admirals, United States Government commission members, and so on. Like fledgling birds, women are rapidly learning how to press power into their new wings. Higher-quality and more accessible education, continuing technological advances resulting in more spare time, increasing demands in certain fields for the skills of women, higher salaries, and more equality of opportunity have all combined to substantially increase their numbers in the labor force. While the adult female noninstitutionalized population increased by 40 per cent, the female labor force doubled between 1947 and 1951,[20] indicating that the number of working women is increasing at a pace greatly exceeding the rate which would have been anticipated on the basis of population growth alone. And there are other significant statistics:

> while the percent of noninstitutionalized population 16 years and over in the total labor force went from 87 percent to 80 percent for males, it rose from 32 percent to 55 percent for females between 1947 and 1972.[21]

> for those married, spouse present, the percentage of the population in the labor force decreased from 93 percent to 86 percent for males, but increased from 20 percent to 42 percent for females between 1947 and 1972—and this increase in work participation of married women has been particularly pronounced among women with small children.[22]

> more than 3,000 women gathered in Chicago in late March 1974 to form the Coalition of Labor Union Women which resolved to organize more of the 34 million female workers . . . and to elect more female officials of AFL-CIO.[23]

> while the number of white-collar workers 16 years and over rose from 15 million to 20 million for men, it increased from 11 million to 19 million for females between 1958 and 1972.[24]

In 1971 women were granted 44 percent of all bachelor's degrees, 40 percent of the master's degrees and 14 percent of the doctorates.[25]

15 percent of the 600 students attending Graduate School of Business at Stanford are now female while a decade ago the school had only one woman.[26]

labor force projections for females, assuming the two-child family average, yield a 70 percent increase in the size of the potential female labor force from 25 to 34 years of age during the 1970's alone compared to a 48 percent increase for men of the same age.[27]

These figures clearly demonstrate where women have been and, if Labor Department predictions are correct, where they are going. But it has not been an easy journey. Since the Equal Opportunity Commission received enforcement powers in March 1972 it has filed 73 lawsuits alleging sex discrimination.[28] The American Telephone and Telegraph Company consented to allocating thirty-eight million dollars in back pay and increases to its women and minority male personnel. In the year ending June 30, 1973, the Commission received 24,300 sex discrimination complaints, had a backlog of 65,000 cases from 1973, and expected to reach 80,000 in 1974. Major companies are demonstrating by their hiring practices that they believe the federal government means to enforce Title 7 of the 1964 Civil Rights Act. Across the nation women in industry are no longer token females or window dressing but are instead filling upper-echelon jobs; they are gradually moving into those managerial positions that feed into the "pipeline" (business jargon for the key jobs from which incumbents are chosen to run companies); and they are outdistancing blacks in certain traditionally all-white, all-male areas, such as brokerage and banking.[29]

Legally and socially the economic barriers are falling and women are slowly climbing up the business ladder. But just as social liberation increased the options in the traditional crime structure, corresponding vocational liberation opened opportunities for white-collar criminality—a heretofore "for men only" deviancy. As more and more women achieve competence, they ascend to occupations which carry the burdens and opportunities of trust along with the chance to violate it.

A Sunday school teacher described as a quiet woman was arrested by the Federal Bureau of Investigation . . . on charges of embezzling nearly a half-million dollars. . . .
Mrs. Storer, an employee of the bank since 1948, was the institution's head bookkeeper.[30]

Mrs. Irene Lutz, a former tax collector . . . was sentenced to four years in prison and four years' probation . . . for embezzling $165,000 from township and school tax revenues. . . .
Judge Smillie said that imposing the prison sentence on the mother of four children was "probably the most unpleasant task I've had.
"But," he said, "there must be a red flag that says to public officials: if you steal from the public, you will go to jail." [31]

A woman [bookkeeper] described by her lawyer as a "lady Santa Claus" who embezzled money to give to the needy started psychiatric tests. . . .[32]

A married couple were indicted—on charges of stealing $250,000 from the wife's employer, a sum that she allegedly had tried to conceal by depositing $20 million worth of forged promissory notes in a bank. . . .
Assistant District Attorney Leonard Newman [said] that the bulk of the stolen money had been spent in an effort to develop a spark plug that would last the life of a car.[33]

. . . a 26 year-old secretary (who was given the authority to sign checks) bought a bed for $3600 . . . and jewelry for $41,000 and rode to work in a chauffered limousine . . .
Her employer, a real estate investor who rode to work every morning on a subway train, never noticed until one day last August . . .[34]

So frequent have such revelations of "unladylike" behavior become that they are replacing romantic gossip as the scandal of choice for newspaper reportage. They are so frequent, in fact, that they no longer shock and soon they will hardly surprise the public. But this is only the beginning, the first, faint ascendancy of a trend which will arch its way upward for at least another generation and shatter the stereotypes of both women and criminals before it levels off. In this development we are witnessing the decline of femininity as we knew it, or thought we knew it, and the rise of a type of woman whose lack of traditional role models makes her as unfamiliar to her parents as she is to herself, a social experiment in unisexual modes of normalcy and deviancy. If she is black she may deviate within the scope of blue-collar crime. If she is white she may have the additional option of white-collar crime because she lives and works closer to the axis of business and industry. We are discovering that neither black women nor white women are as reluctant as men always tried to make them believe they were to exercise their criminal options or to take advantage of their situation. While their past is full of contrasts, it is their similarities which emerge with time.

Black women have known leadership for generations but they are just now learning the feel of power. White women have had neither but are acquiring both in one short generation. As befitted their respective opportunities black women have led the way into blue-collar crime, white women into white-collar crime. Both have tapped the sources of wealth and power and status and have shown a not surprising affinity for its uses and abuses. In the future a greater proportion of this wealth and power will pass through feminine hands, and almost all of it will be wielded responsibly. But it would be an unrealistic reversion to quixotic chivalry to believe that, for better or worse, women will be any more honest than men.

8

New Crimes and Old Corrections

The laws of God, the laws of man,
He may keep that will and can;
Not I: let God and man decree
Laws for themselves and not for me.

—A. E. Housman
"Last Poems" XII

That man is a creature who needs order yet yearns for change is the creative contradiction at the heart of the laws which structure his conformity and define his deviancy. It has fathered and flawed all his efforts toward government since he first substituted a group campfire for the reliable genetic code that regulated the behavior of his forebears. Like all contracts, the social contract was written in jaundiced contemplation of its breach, and consequently tells as much about what man fears he is as what he hopes he can be. The problem of the group's need for acquiescence and the individual's need for expression, as well as the social contribution made by divarication (divergence), is one confronted by all societies, human and subhuman alike. The solutions have been as diverse as the constitution and the goals of those societies. While the regimented regularity of insect societies and the hierarchical stability of higher social animals are in some ways enviable, they are paragons only of efficiency, for they have bartered the dynamic for the static, and change itself is in bondage to the genes.

Since group cohesion and adherence to group codes of behavior are decisive for the survival of social animals, there is always a mechanism for controlling the deviant. The stranger is as much a threat to mice as men. However, subhuman groups provide very little rehabilitation to the deviant, and the environment offers no forgiveness. The correction is conclusively genetic because the genes perish with the offender. But death is a useful remedy only for genetically programmed animals where the method for modifying the program requires destroying the carrier. *Homo sapiens,* the social animal with culture, has, by contrast, almost unlimited options for change. To this end he has erected a legal structure to codify his interpersonal transactions and a set of rewards and punishments to shape them. Interestingly, we differ less in form than in content from our subhuman predecessors because the criteria for tolerance are still basically rooted in the survival of the social organization. Ethical systems are often moral rationalizations to serve this essential evolutionary goal. There is hardly any deviancy, no matter how reprehensible in one context, which is not extolled as a virtue in another. There are no natural crimes, only legal ones. Furthermore, even those aberrations which are proscribed within the context of a cultural system may be widely tolerated within that system either because they are condoned as a necessary regression or because deviance per se is intuitively appreciated as a vital leavening influence which serves the larger purpose of social growth.

There are few qualities which are evenly distributed throughout mankind, and in that sense we are all deviants hoping our differences will bring us acceptance and fearing they will make us outcasts. The declaration that the poor will always be with us is less an economic forecast than a statistical and philosophical recognition that the deviant is the exception that proves—i.e., defines—the rule and, in consequence, is as integral to the social structure as the conforming majority. Because dissension is both an instrument for social disruption and a vehicle for social change, it is a problem which every group must resolve by finding its own path between repression and permissiveness. The twin needs for growth and stability will direct that path toward the long-term goals which each society values. At best, the utopian dream of equality has always hovered between the nightmare of tyranny and the insomnia of anarchy, and the moral climate of a society may be judged by what it labels deviancy and what pressures it exerts for conformity.

Characteristically, the fate of a deviancy depends on its potential for social debilitation and the remedies available within the complicated social and psychological system.[1] For example, that deviancy which results in distress and disability due to physical or mental causes is labeled sick and carries with it a therapeutic imperative; that which results in distress and disability due to law-breaking and apprehension is labeled a crime and carries with it a more ambiguous set of imperatives. Victimless crimes, like drug abuse and alcoholism, vacillate between the two.[2] The decision on whether to confine the person is based on social tolerance as well as individual need. The physically ill are hospitalized, the mentally ill are institutionalized, and the criminally deviant are imprisoned. Once the decision to incarcerate has been made, the options for correction lie among punishment, deterrence, and rehabilitation, the choice being dictated as much by value orientations as by efficacy. Here, as elsewhere, women offenders must negotiate a more complicated prison course because they are twofold deviants: not only have they deviated from the general male standards of conduct by reason of being female, but they have deviated from male standards of female conduct. This chapter will look at the tortuous course of women in our prisons in an effort to describe how their changing social and criminal patterns are interacting with a correctional system run primarily by, for, and with men.

While the biblical version of Eve's creation from Adam's rib as an afterthought did not hold up under embryologic investigations, this model does accurately depict the excision of a truncated female corrections system from the body of male corrections. Women prisoners have until recently been a correctional afterthought, for several operational as well as emotional considerations. Practically, their numbers were always small, their "moral offenses" did not materially threaten social harmony, and, as we have seen, prostitution often contributed to the stability of the family and, by extension, society by providing self-limited outlets for potentially disruptive drives. Furthermore, once they were incarcerated, women's docility brought little attention or concern to themselves.[3] At a deeper level of social response, their deviancy made people uncomfortable in a way that male deviancy did not, so there was no ready perceptual niche to which they could be easily consigned. The criminal activities of these nonmales were unexpected behaviors, which relegated them to the status of nonpersons in a noncorrectional system.

Correctional programs appropriate to females have been deficient and inadequate throughout the history of penology. In colonial times the county jails and workhouses accommodated women and children, as well as men, in a setting of integrated indifference, although later, probably out of concern for sexual promiscuity, women were provided with separate apartments even before children were segregated from adult offenders. Not until 1873, however, was there a separate female prison, the Indiana Reform Institute for Women, created at the urging of the Annual Meeting of Friends in that state in 1866.[4] The innovation of this single-sex prison was hailed as a reform, and in the context of the times it was, but only in terms of more humane custodial care. It did nothing to encourage the inmates to greater self-sufficiency. On the contrary, the efforts here, as in the other single-sex prisons which rode in on the wave of reform, were directed toward reindoctrination of passive, docile, female role expectations, and the guards were so preoccupied with stamping out the rampant lesbianism that they had little time for anything else. Unfortunately, the zeal to protect women from the moral depravity of homosexuality also protected them only too well from the essential human need for companionship. Congregation was discouraged by architectural design and prohibited by regulations, achieving isolation within the prison as well as from society at large.[5] Tragically, a well-meaning but misguided endeavor had succeeded in throwing out the baby with the bath water. The reform movement which attempted to protect women from men and from each other by erecting separate prisons or segregating them into separate sections of male penitentiaries fell prey to other problems. Because of their smaller numbers and the requirement of separate facilities, the per capita allotment of funds could not be utilized as efficiently as it was for males.[6] In consequence, their quarters were more cramped, women of all ages and crime types were thrown together, there was little provision for work or exercise, understaffing was thought to necessitate more rigid rules, visiting privileges were restricted, and job training was inadequate. There was little they could do besides sleep, talk, play table games, or sew.[7] In addition to these internal impediments to socialization and self-fulfillment, the distance between the prison and the closest population center made visiting difficult, and access to contact with prospective employers almost impossible.[8] By default, if not by design, such a system of social and vocational deficiency would be likely to produce a perennial problem.

It would be a mistake to conclude that the deprivations of prison life for either men or women result in the extinction of previously conditioned behavior. On the contrary, the frustration of efforts toward self-sufficiency, the paucity of opportunities to learn ways of channeling drives acceptable to society at large, and the isolation from that larger society to which it is hoped they may someday return create a milieu which generates a perverse subculture. "The vilest deeds like poison-weeds/Bloom well in prison-air," reminisced Oscar Wilde. "It is only what is good in Man/ That wastes and withers there." The loss of previous social supports, unmitigated by the meager offerings of the correctional system, creates a psychosocial vacuum into which pour the regressive dregs of each person's potential. Under the stress of deprivation, individuals tend to drift downward to narcissistic and antisocial levels of functioning which tap into the more primitive mechanisms necessary for sheer survival. Groups do the same, but because their viability requires some minimal consensus, they unite against the prison authorities and the society they blame for their plight. The result is often an antisocietal prison subculture which is not asocial but a kind of culture in pure form, distilled from the lowest common denominators accumulated during development in the larger culture. The behavior patterns which emerge, or, more properly, survive, form a social configuration which is part mimicry but mostly a caricature of those patterns which flourish outside the walls.

Since people can only regress to the levels at which they had previously functioned, males and females traditionally retrace different developmental courses and finally gravitate to distinctive sex-differentiated modes of adaptation to prison life. Male prisoners, for example, long ago developed an unwritten but explicit code designed to alleviate their frustrations, provide substitute satisfactions for their deprivations, and reassert their masculinity. The specific deprivations were those enjoyed naturally by the men before incarceration—namely, liberty, goods and services, heterosexual relationships, autonomy, and security. As a compensatory structure, this inmate code was designed to mitigate the pains of imprisonment. Its maxims have been summarized as 1) don't interfere with inmate interests, 2) don't lose your head, 3) don't exploit inmates, 4) don't weaken, and 5) don't be a sucker.[9] In addition to its functional value regarding conduct, the code also provided a male prisoner-role expectation that was both attainable under the circumstances and sufficient to maintain the self-respect associated with virility. While this construct provides a useful rationale for the observed data, there are more economical explanations for the necessity and utility of this code.[10] All humans require for their security the approved behavioral patterns, supportive rituals, and interpersonal satisfactions provided by a group, as well as a system for understanding their surroundings. Incarceration separates the individual from his previous sustaining group and the changed realities of confinement demand a change in his *Weltanschauung*. Thus, what the prisoner is deprived of that he needs most is his group-system, and unless he withdraws into isolation, depression, or psychosis, he will inevitably improvise a new group-system covering the skeleton of the old one with the new materials at hand. While some codes are more adaptive than others, it is not *the* code but *a* code that the prisoner craves. The enthusiasm with which black prisoners joined the Black Muslim movement and the benefits they derived from it seems to support this point. It is inaccurate to declare that there is no honor—i.e., a code of behavior and system of values—among thieves, or any other group of human beings, for that matter. It is just that "honor" is subculturally redefined to meet the particular needs of the group. For example, in juvenile institutions, toughness and manipulative competence are accorded prestige, while the overlapping traits of violence, psychopathy, and dominant homosexuality earn high status for their older brothers.[11] But the constant in all these situations is that there will be a code and that its value will be beneficial for its adherents.

Some investigators contend that the male inmate code is an *ad hoc* modification of his preincarceration group code designed to satisfy security and utilitarian needs.[12] For similar reasons, females have fashioned their group code from their behavioral patterns before incarceration. Because they start at different points and confront different circumstances of imprisonment, they expectably result in a different end product, but, as we shall see, this is changing. Investigations in the early sixties found a lack of support among women prisoners for the inmate code which served males so well, and this was attributed to its lack of relevance to the deprivations which imprisoned females suffer.[13] Unlike their male counterparts, they have been generally acculturated to the roles of dependent wives or nurturing mothers who relate to their dominant male supporters as sex-objects. Thus the pains of female imprisonment, like female motivations in general, were considered to be primarily emotional—the deprivation of dependency needs and the loss of affectional relationships. Building on such special female needs, it was concluded that need satisfaction should come from the establishment of a social organization based on homosexual liaisons.[14]

Conventional wisdom about the traditional female prisoner and her social organization as it existed through the early 1960s does not reflect the changing role of women in American society and the new genre of female offenders it has created. Customarily it has been accepted that men responded to stress with fight reactions and women with flight reactions, that men defied and women complied, that men sought status through occupation and women through marriage, that men acted and women merely talked, that imprisoned men were dangerous but imprisoned women were docile, and that imprisoned men needed to learn a trade whereas imprisoned women would be content with busy work. While this may still be characteristic of the general prison population, it becomes less so each year with the influx of a new type of female offender. The women in and out of prison who no longer subscribe to the established role distinctions are challenging both society and the corrections system to deal with them on sexually equal terms, and the challenge is not limited to words.

The events, in September 1971, which catapulted Attica from anonymity to anathema and transformed it from a name to an emotion sundered the complacent notion that forgotten men are willing to remain forgotten. With forty-three people killed and eighty injured, these men had gained a claim to public attention which would otherwise have seemed unwarranted. The public attitude toward their unknown citizenry had long been described by W. H. Auden: "had anything been wrong, we should certainly have heard." What the public finally heard, after years of benign neglect, was not simply the protest of pent-up fury over past grievances but an impassioned demand for a correctional promissory note by men whose negotiable collateral was their willingness to stake their lives because they had nothing to lose. There were also many women who had nothing to lose. When the Official New York State Commission stated, "Attica is every prison, every prison is Attica" [15] there was as much prophecy as description in their declaration. Women had been matching men in jobs and crimes at an accelerating rate. It could not be very long before they would begin to match them in mob violence. On September 21, 1971, one hundred and thirty women at Alderson prison staged a sympathy riot which raged through four days and could be contained only by extreme force. They were not only calling attention to their deprivations, they were calling attention to the fact that they were experimenting with new ways of compensating for their deprivations, that they were reformulating the old female inmate code, and that they had added another mode of behavior to their increasingly masculinized repertoire. There is every reason to believe that this is more likely the beginning than the end of such female protests and that they herald as fundamental a change in female prison society as has occurred in female civilian life. While one major theory holds that the inmate code corrects for specific deprivations [16] and another claims that it is an extension of societal sex roles,[17] both agree on one point. As the social roles and social activities of women in general approach those of men, they will experience similar deprivations of imprisonment, project similar social roles into the prison system, and arrive at a similar structure of inmate codes. Given the present trends, tomorrow's female inmate will bear a very close resemblance to her male counterpart of today.

Although almost unnoticed by the public, women are less and less willing than their predecessors to accept their lot in prison, and for good reason. Because women inmates are, for the most part, a judicial and correctional annex to a system designed for processing and holding men, their existence is even more hopeless than that of incarcerated males. They are liable to serve longer sentences for the same crimes.[18] They are systematically denied access to even the inadequate and minimal level of training and educational services available to males, and they are restricted in their movements and in their access to recreational facilities. They are frequently isolated within confines so limited that they would be described as solitary confinement in male prisons.[19]

Like their male counterparts, female inmates have rioted, destroyed buildings, set fires, and attacked guards and matrons. They have made their escapes, delivered their demands, and gone on hunger strikes. Even among those who have not participated in any overt, physical violence against the institutions which hold them, there has been a perceptible change in attitude. The change is one which has many officials puzzled as well as wary. In many cases, they are heading institutions built decades ago to hold passive, docile females who were sent to jail for victimless sexual and moral "crimes." Today these low-security, overcrowded, understaffed facilities are finding themselves confronted with increasing numbers of women convicted of aggressive crimes against persons and property; women who are highly politicized and not at all hesitant about making a point with a loud voice or a balled fist. It is not at all inconceivable that a female Attica could occur at any one of a number of institutions and upset the traditional applecart of benign neglect which has ruled the field of female corrections in the past.

The road to the Alderson Federal Reformatory for Women snakes its way for hours through the rugged mountains of West Virginia, until its travelers finally reach a small, dusty town deep in the heart of the Appalachian poverty belt. The road takes one final half-mile curve along an ancient railroad and opens to a broad expanse of red-brick buildings bounded on all sides by mountains. The first, and perhaps the most lasting, impression of Alderson is that of its absolute isolation.

That isolation must be understood in the context of the philosophy of female corrections. It was purposely planned and it demonstrates a good deal about the traditional thinking behind the ineffective prison system that we know today. The traditionalists were plainly out to punish people for their crimes, and isolation suited such a goal well. As with Devil's Island, Alcatraz, and Siberia, the physical distance which was routinely put between prisons and population centers was a measure of the social distance which society wished to maintain from its criminals.

For the most part, that traditional school of thinking has passed, but its stone handiwork remains. Now, wardens at institutions such as Alderson must spend a good deal of their time struggling with the vocational and rehabilitative impediments that such isolation causes. For one thing, Alderson's out-of-the-way location virtually ensures that the husbands, children, and other relatives of an inmate will have a difficult, if not impossible, time getting to the prison for a visit. It helps little that the institution itself sprawls across five hundred rolling acres of woodland, or that its buildings are generously spaced and the areas between them well carpeted with close-clipped lawns and clusters of park benches. The over-all architectural atmosphere is that of a small college and, like its location, even its design reflects the traditional philosophy which once guided female penal institutions.

In the past, women were sent to prison for moral crimes which were considered to be more of an embarrassment than a danger to society. The design specifications for institutions such as Alderson reflect the same paternal graciousness which so characterized the treatment of women in other areas of law enforcement. Women inmates live in cottages, are free to roam the grounds, and are restrained only by the most feeble security measures. Functionally, it is a place built to house people who meekly agreed to be housed; people who were never expected to question the propriety of their institutionalization; people who would never take any overt action against that institutionalization.

With five hundred and fifty women, Alderson is overcrowded and has come a long way since those days when its bricks were put together with equal amounts of mortar and male chauvinism. Just how far became apparent on September 21, 1971, when a mob of rock-hurling, window-smashing women took over one of the campus buildings. The incident, overshadowed by the Attica events which were still reverberating in the public consciousness, was one that deserved more scrutiny than it received. No one was killed at Alderson, but the uprising was a clear indication that the correctional system, like the criminal-offense system, had a new type of woman to deal with, a sort of woman it did not want to believe existed, but one who now plainly poses ever-increasing problems to a system designed to hold only docile, cream-puff prisoners.

The Alderson incident was stopped short of serious violence largely because of the open atmosphere which has been fostered at the facility by its outspoken warden, Mrs. Virginia McLaughlin, an unusually candid person who believes the current system of corrections is like "trying to stop cancer with a Band-Aid." She is painfully aware of the new aggressiveness and militancy being displayed by female offenders.

"I think there is a different sort of woman now coming into the whole justice system. It is only a natural extension of what is happening through the society in general," explained the fifty-seven-year-old warden. "In the closed community of the institution, social changes and kinks tend to be brought into intense focus. Here, open aggression is on the increase among the women. We're getting more and more women who are actually involved in robberies and other similar 'hard' crimes.

"One of the areas where it is most obvious is among black women—who account for most of the people in this place. You find blacks on all levels of society no longer willing to sit back and say 'yes, sir,' 'no, sir.' Black women are very verbal and assertive. That is probably one of the hardest things for the general middle-aged staff members at an institution like this to deal with.

"Alderson certainly isn't unique in this respect. It's happening in women's facilities everywhere. These places were set up with lax security and very loose structure. The Bureau of Prisons is in a bad way right now for funds. There is a population explosion going on throughout the system. And we continue to get an increasing number of hardcore cases. We've got way too many now. I'm not really sure where it is all going, but I know that you cannot pack a place like this with hardnosed, highly aggressive, potentially violent women and have nothing happen. Something will have to give. I'm not sure what the future holds."

Throughout the correctional system on all levels, there is a similar trend toward increasing aggressiveness and militancy in female prisons. In Chicago, at the new Cook County jail facility for women, 80 per cent of the inmates are in for homicide.

"The change here has been very obvious for anyone who has been in the system for a few years," explained Mrs. Claudia McCormick, director of the women's facility. "Now while most of of our women are in here for murder, it is not stranger-to-stranger murder. In a large number of cases, it was the husband, boy friend, or child whom they killed. I've heard it said, 'Well, that's how it always has been.' That really isn't so. Not many years ago, we'd get an awful lot of women who had *hurt* their child or husband and only a very few who had actually killed them. There was something that stopped the women short of actually murdering. Whatever that 'something' was is gone. They murder pretty easy now. Then in the other twenty per cent of our population you'll find an unusually high number of women in for armed robbery. Now you never saw that before at all.

"At the same time, it's hard to really put your finger on, but there is a new attitude among these women. Like, you'll hear them talking of their *first* murder, saying, 'Well, you know, the first one gets to you, but afterward, it just don't touch you.' It's become a status symbol in their peer group to murder. Now, no matter how you cut it, that is a drastic change from the way things used to be with females here."

In upstate Pennsylvania, at Muncy, the only state female facility, a similar increase in the level of aggressiveness has been noticed.

"The change has become pretty apparent," explained one thirty-one-year-old counselor and former parole officer. "Females are getting into more and more crimes of violence. I'm not speaking of the old-timers we get who are chronic alcoholics and get violent as a result of mental deterioration in their later years . . . I'm talking about the large number of young women that we're seeing now who have walked into a bank or a gas station and said, 'Give me your money or I'll kill you,' and meant it.

"This is particularly true among the young black women who are coming through here. It used to be that women came to prison with feelings of inadequacy. They had a lousy concept of themselves and they were very confused as to what they should be as mothers or wives or lovers. That is no longer true. We have a whole new breed. They are no longer the frightened people women prisoners are 'supposed' to be."

At the lower end of the state, a few hundred miles from Muncy, the reality of this new female aggressiveness took Philadelphia by surprise. There, on February 18, 1973, fifty women went on a rioting rampage through the Philadelphia House of Corrections. Armed with kitchen utensils, broomsticks, and clubs made from sections of wrecked furniture, they attacked and injured four male guards and a female matron. They took over the dispensary, looted other sections, and successfully held off armed correctional officers for over an hour before order was restored.

Philadelphia's was the latest in a series of violent outbreaks in female facilities across the country that were no less devastating than those staged by males in their own institutions. One of the worst occurred at the Indiana Correctional Institution for Girls in June 1966. There, three-quarters of the two hundred female juvenile inmates overran their facility.[20] They attacked correctional personnel, destroyed furniture, sacked offices, and crashed their way through minimal security enclosures to escape en masse. Perhaps more than other similar riots, this one should have been recognized as a harbinger of things to come, given the fact that none of the girls was over eighteen.

In Connecticut, in May 1972, four women inmates of Niantic Women's Prison escaped after taking a prison official hostage at knifepoint. After walking out of the prison, the women stole a car and started west across the state with a large contingent of state and local police in chase. Traveling at speeds as high as 120 miles an hour, the women eluded police and finally careened their stolen vehicle off the roadway. The auto was demolished, but the women were not seriously injured. They promptly flagged down a passing motorist, abducted him at knifepoint, and continued their flight. Confronted with a state police roadblock on the turnpike, the women accelerated to crash the barrier of men and vehicles, leaving squads of male officers and newsmen aghast. Finally, after a few more hours, and with police vehicles from two states on their trail, the women were overtaken and forced off the road. In addition to the vehicular wreckage strewn in their wake, they left behind them an equal amount of fractured myth about the nonviolent nature of females. Had males been driving that escape car, no more than routine interest would have been stirred. But the fact that women were involved made the incident a grand escapade which simultaneously shocked and entertained the police and public.

Outbreak of violence among males is an accepted phenomenon. It is assumed to be natural for men who are confined and confronted with the frustrations of incarceration. It is also assumed that incarcerated females either do not experience such intense frustration or that constitutionally they do not express their discontent in such intrepid ways. Outbreaks of violence at female institutions—such as Muncy, or Alderson, or Philadelphia, or Niantic—

always seem to draw from the press and general public a reaction which is more surprised than fearful, an expression of the widely held disbelief that women could "do such a thing."

Overall, the frustrations of incarcerated women may be significantly greater than those of males. Aside from their characteristically pleasant architecture, institutions such as Alderson and Muncy offer little else. They are nicer to look at than most of the concrete bunkers which house males, but they receive fewer funds, have a lower priority, and offer less in the way of educational and recreational facilities. As a result of the sexist philosophy which still influences the design and programming of female institutions, they are even less likely than the male prisons to effect a true rehabilitation of the criminally prone person.

Women's institutions in the past have received treatment under what can be described as the "four-per-cent plan." Estimates of recent data show that the approximately fifteen thousand females who are incarcerated on any one day in America constitute only four per cent of the total prison population of the country.[21] That is a figure which is often put forth in prison circles when female offenders and their problems are being discussed. Under the aegis of this four-per-cent mode of thinking, women in the system have been assigned an extremely low priority justified by the "numerical reality" of the situation—which, in practical terms, means the cost effectiveness of limited funds available to the prison system. Money spent for educational, self-enrichment, work-release, job-training, or counseling programs for women has the potential of reaching only four per cent of the total prison population. The same money can be spent more efficiently in the densely populated male facilities to purchase more goods and services. While this is true and is an economically defensible position, it is also part of an institutionalized devaluation of women's needs which has downgraded the quality as well as the quantity of what the system is willing to offer them.

Even the little money that is allocated to female institutions is channeled into programs which are based on sexist stereotypes that are no longer valid. For instance, in Cedar Knoll, a Washington, D.C., facility housing four hundred juveniles, males are offered their choice of training in the fields of printing, painting, gardening, auto mechanics, furniture repair, upholstery, shoe repair, building-trade skills, and electronics. Females at the same institution are offered one trade: data processing. They may take it or leave it, or choose to take noncredit courses in such things as sewing, cooking, and cosmetology. The story is the same at institution after institution. Those that have any training programs at all train participants in "women's jobs." These low-paying, low-skill jobs ensure that she will return to the mold of the preliberated woman, bound to one of the traditional female job ghettos in the outside world.

"The problem is one of real therapy versus Betty Crocker counseling," said Alderson's Virginia McLaughlin. "We are trying desperately to enlarge our training facilities from something other than just a garment sewing factory. We have just put in data-processing. We need a lot more, but the problem is you only have this little bit of money and you have to weigh what you do with it against the total numerical picture."

Even the Department of Labor, which has been carrying on an impressive ten-year program aimed at upgrading prison retraining programs and increasing the probability of vocational success among released inmates, has chosen to ignore women. In its 112-page book on the decade-long Manpower projects in the correctional field, the Department gave females one paragraph. There it apologized for the omission of women by explaining that, among other things, "female adults comprise a small fraction of the incarcerated offenders" and "the female offender who is a mother will be receiving financial assistance in the form of welfare payments." The Department went on to suggest that the problems of the female offender "be explored." [22]

While women in the female institutions of the state and federal governments get little help, the thousands of others [23] who are kept in the thirty-six hundred county and municipal jails across the country get even less. There, in what are mostly overcrowded male facilities to begin with, females are kept in lodgings that amount to a jail within a jail. Because of the obvious threat of rape, women are confined to a single cell or a single area within the prison that can be readily isolated from male inmates. Women are routinely excluded from even the minimal program selection that exists for the males. Their quarters are merely an afterthought within the institution, and their isolation is justified as a matter of "financial reality" or logistical expediency.[24]

In Chicago's Cook County Prison, the women lived under such conditions for years until the new women's facility was finished in late 1973. Prior to that, the eighty or so women in the 115-year-old jail were crammed into cells and small compounds which were secure from males. Their life was one of almost total isolation.

"It really was intolerable," explained Mrs. McCormick, "but it wasn't unusual. It's done this way all over the country. You scatter the women wherever you find a spot for them. They weren't allowed access to recreational facilities except for one very small day room. They weren't allowed to move around at all unless they had a guard with them. They had no training. They had nothing. They just sat all day. That was their program. Obviously, that sort of thing didn't do a lot to help their state of mind or their general attitude."

In its new prison, Cook County has taken a new approach to women and provided them with facilities that are almost comparable to those being provided for males in the county jail system. At least, conceptually, the county has recognized that women inmates have needs and abilities similar to males. The new approach attempts to deal with female inmates as troubled people rather than just troublesome women. The new training opportunities for women include high-school educational services and traditional programs such as cosmetology and secretarial job training; they may also select training as laboratory technicians, dental assistants, paramedics, and small-engine and appliance repair workers; and 80 per cent of the women choose to participate in educational programs to improve their reading ability and other fundamental skills.

However, most of them belong to minority groups, and most of them will be returning to the same urban areas and to the same job market which, even when they could find employment, kept their income below the poverty level.

For whatever reasons—socioeconomic, judicial, or cultural—today's female offender differs from her predecessors of the first third of the century not only in attitude and aspirations but in basic intelligence. Whereas earlier investigators in the thirties [25] found that females in the prison population exhibited inferior intelligence, recent Labor Department figures indicate that approximately two-thirds of the women incarcerated in federal institutions score above average on I.Q. tests.[26] Whether this brighter-than-average group will be returned to society as better citizens or better criminals will be largely determined by their experience in the correctional system. Vocational training becomes a particularly important factor in the prognosis for rehabilitation when we recall that the sharpest increase in female offenses has resulted from anti-social efforts to improve their economic position. Whether for biological or cultural reasons, women are still less prone to violence than men and still less exposed to violent subcultural influences, so they may require less counseling in this regard. But the fact that more and more of them are the chief or only supporters of their households underscores the impact which vocational training may have on their future. They may be less likely than men to employ violent means to economic ends, but the difference is no longer so great that it would not be overridden by necessity.

Enlightened programs are striving to equip women for finding legitimate routes to the financial and emotional success they are now demanding. Unless this occurs, we shall have to continue living with the alternative—a chronic recidivism which each year returns almost as many people as it discharges to prisons that daily grow bigger, more crowded, and less able to benefit their inmates. This chronic recidivism, which is as much a part of our current prison system as barbed wires and bars, is the result of an approach oriented toward locking people away and offering them little or no meaningful training, education, or counseling. Aside from any moral considerations, this approach is important purely on financial grounds. If offenders who were imprisoned never returned to society again, there might be some economic (although not humane) justification for withholding help. But, in fact, most of them do return, and if their conditions on re-entry are no better and perhaps even worse, the costs to society increase with each excursion.

"You have to remember that we are attacking a fundamentally illogical situation," explained Harry Trauig, superintendent of the Maryland Correctional Institution for Women. "That is, you take an individual who is not adjusting with the community and you say, 'because you are not adjusting, we are going to place you with other individuals who failed to adjust, then we'll teach you how to adjust with the community.'"

In Trauig's Maryland institution, as well as in other female institutions in the nation, it is well recognized that prisons prepare a woman only to live in prison. The routines and programs really have little, if anything, to do with the problems which are at the root of the inmate's criminality. In recent years, a number of experiments have been aimed at making prison life a more therapeutic experience. Some innovations have been minor, such as a change of uniform style and color. But there have also been major programs, like Niantic prison's "Operation Rebound," in which female inmates are taken for days into the mountains and woods of New England and taught to survive off the land. Aside from the refreshing change of pace and new life experiences it provides for the women, the program has also aided greatly in instilling new levels of self-confidence in the participants.

The experiments large and small and the studies currently in progress about the effectiveness of present penal programs underscore the fact that few people believe the system works at all. There simply are not many workable alternatives at this time. The issue is no longer whether the system should be changed, but rather how it might be changed and what the mechanics of the change should be. Aside from the problems of securing an adequate budget, and a societal commitment to rehabilitation, the issue of how best to influence the behavior of inmates is the most difficult because it is the least understood. A review of the conflicting theories and unsettled issues in the fields of psychiatry and psychology, fields which specialize in human behavioral change, justifies the kind of bafflement Chaucer expressed when he asked, "If gold ruste, what shal iren do?" The fact that such issues are even being debated among specialists in corrections, however, represents progress, because until relatively recent times there was an unchallenged assumption that punishment was both necessary and sufficient—and, at any rate, all that was deserved.

In general, there are two opinions about the treatment of prisoners. One is traditional and supports an approach which may best be described as a "sanitized" version of the old prison system. It emphasizes punishment as the primary purpose of imprisonment and aims to avoid "coddling" prisoners. The traditionalists continue to rely heavily on isolation from the community, fortress architecture, and ponderous security measures. In this camp, one finds several officials in the Federal Bureau of Prisons, the police establishment, the courts, and a large section of the general public.

On the innovative side are those organizations and governmental officials who are exerting increasing pressure for a radical "humanization" of the prison system. Generally speaking, their program calls for the virtual abolition of the prison system as we know it today. In its stead, they propose that criminals be handled through a nation-wide network of community treatment centers and social services which would address itself to individual offenders' personal problems rather than their criminal history.

Among traditionalists in the prison system and in the law-enforcement establishment, one finds a recurring duality between what is routinely said about the problems of prisons and what is actually done about those problems. Most of the prison officials interviewed enthusiastically called for "new and progressive" ways of handling corrections. At the same time, these officials spend the better part of their total time and energy tending to the logistical reinforcement of the old, ineffective, and self-defeating methods they verbally decried. Perhaps the traditional system's basic philosophy is best summed up in a financial statement reported by the Federal Department of Labor: of all the hundreds of millions of dollars appropriated each year for corrections in America, less than 15 per cent actually are channeled into rehabilitative programs; 85 per cent goes strictly for the old-time, hard-line administrative and security measures which have become the hallmark of the prison business.[27]

Connie Springman, an official with the Bureau of Prisons in Washington, points out that community-based treatment centers are "probably what the future has in store for the corrections system." Like others in the Bureau, she explains that the time has come to rethink the idea of what prisons are and how they ought to work. The Bureau has six halfway houses in the country as an experiment in prison alternatives. However, they take only people with six months or less to do on their regular sentences. Ms. Springman said the Bureau feels that longer periods of time would be "unrealistic. That really is as long as we feel they can make it without getting into trouble.

"We've got women throughout the system who, frankly, couldn't make it in a community treatment center. You're always going to have that group of persons who require security conditions. In Alderson, for instance, there are a large number of women inmates who cannot be out in community-based programs. That's the way it is and will be."

Officially, the Bureau supports the idea of new thinking for prisons, but logistically it appears to be anticipating a continuation of the *status quo*. Despite the agreement in principle to "new methods," the Bureau has undertaken a ten-year, seven-hundred-million-dollar construction program which will see sixty-six new, old-style facilities built across the country. It is just this sort of philosophical and fiscal investment—seven hundred million dollars worth of buildings designed to service a penal approach which is known to be ineffective—that has been criticized by a number of experts.[28]

A 636-page report issued by the National Advisory Commission on Criminal Justice Standards and Goals in 1973 calls for a moratorium on all prison building. The two-year study cost almost two million dollars and called for a pause in all building and planning of prisons, pending a new evaluation of the factors which contribute to an effective correctional system. The report concurred with the conclusions reached by a number of other agencies and independent groups in the recent past: "incarceration is not an effective answer for most criminal offenders. The failure of major institutions to reduce crime is incontestable. Recidivism rates are notoriously high. Institutions do succeed in punishing, but they do not deter." [29]

Similar views have been expressed by officials of the federal Law Enforcement Assistance Administration, an agency legislated into existence in the Johnson Administration and expanded in response to bipartisan commitments to law and order under the Nixon Administration. In only five years, LEAA's budget for funding various aid and research projects for the nation's police, courts, and prisons has risen from sixty-three million dollars in 1969 to eight hundred million in 1974. One of the strongest stands taken at the LEAA concerns basic penal philosophy.

Ken Carpenter, who heads the Corrections section of LEAA, explained why that agency feels that the current methods of institutionalization should get a very low funding priority. "Institutionalization doesn't work. It's that simple. We know that it does not work or accomplish that which it is meant to accomplish. If you look at recidivism rates, they go as high as eighty per cent and more in the current system. Those people we put into institutions only get out and go back to institutions. Obviously something else is needed.

"We're not that sure that community-based treatment will work either," said Carpenter. "But, you see, the important thing is that we *know* what does not work. Why go on with it? In building security facilities, the costs today are as much as twenty-five thousand dollars per bed. That's a terrible price to pay for something that doesn't work. On the other hand, costs for community-based facilities go about one thousand dollars a bed or so

"LEAA doesn't have the answer, but the idea is that a number of other alternatives need to be tried. This ought to be a time of experimentation, not dogged construction of old-style facilities."

Among the innovators are a number of organizations working toward the total elimination of prison institutions. One of the first and best known of these is the Pennsylvania Program for Women and Girl Offenders, in Philadelphia. Since 1970, the organization has been working to get all the women within the correctional system in Pennsylvania out of the institutions and into community treatment centers. Those centers, which form the core of the new corrections approach, would house up to twenty-five women each and serve as residential units located in various parts of every major city. Rather than go to county or municipal courts, for instance, women who are awaiting trial or who have been sentenced would be sent to the community center. There, they would enjoy a small, family-like group and would have access to and continuing contact with a number of community resources. Such resources would include schools, churches, jobs, job training, and so on. Each center would be run not by the usual custodial staff but, rather, by people from the immediate community.

The Pennsylvania Program for Women and Girl Offenders has established nine satellite agencies in various ghetto sections of Philadelphia, where they hope to prove that a high level of community involvement can be achieved.

"We know that in prisons nothing constructive happens, either from the point of view of the public or the women offenders themselves. We have to begin there . . . knowing that the system we have now is useless," explained Margery L. Velimesis, director of the project.

In such a program, women would have close contact with their families, especially their children. They would, theoretically, have access to schools and jobs. Although gaining in popularity, such a program has its problems. The first and perhaps the most important problem is locating sites. Halfway houses and similar projects have fared badly in terms of public acceptance in almost every community in which they have been tried—in Philadelphia, Chicago, Washington, New York, Los Angeles, and other major cities, residents have consistently refused to allow such facilities anywhere but in the most undesirable neighborhoods.

"One of the problems with the halfway, community-based approach is that you can't find a place to start," said Claudia McCormick. Cook

County, where she directs the women's facility, has recently attempted to get Project Support rolling as a halfway house for Chicago inmates.

"The community-based thing looks great on paper. I think it might work well, but when you get down to the actual mechanics of implementation you get a whole new picture. I know. The city of Chicago knows. We decided to start a community-based project and had the funds and were ready to go. We went to middle-class black and middle-class white neighborhoods. We went to the poor whites and the poor blacks. We looked at sites in every kind of neighborhood the city has to offer. You find that the same people who support the theory of 'community-based correction' change their tune when you come to their neighborhood with it. In every neighborhood, the residents rose up and rejected the idea."

In the end, Project Support was put into effect in the downtown YMCA, the only location which did not generate severe political repercussions. The YMCA, which is only open to men and has limited room and facilities, is, unfortunately, a far cry from what is needed if a community-based program is to fulfill the hopes of its planners.

The lack of public acceptance which required Cook County to alter its community-based project plans is not peculiar to Chicago. The same scene has been played out hundreds of times in every major American city which has ever attempted to set up a halfway house for alcoholics, wayward children, drug addicts, or other socially disadvantaged groups, such as ex-felons. The American community is not at present willing to accept or peacefully accommodate to halfway houses. This public resistance, together with the accompanying political resistance, raises serious questions about the feasibility of opening or maintaining a nation-wide or state-wide system of community treatment centers for felons. Given the political, sociological, and financial realities of the corrections situation, it appears that a compromise between the traditionalists and the innovators may be possible. At least one institution in America has taken a new approach to the problem and forged what might be that workable compromise. It represents an experiment in penology which has gone further than any other toward true humanization of the system.

The Purdy Treatment Center for Women is located just outside Tacoma, Washington, and 1973 marked its third year of operation. Those first three years the center maintained a low profile for fear that widespread publicity might upset the delicate political balance required to obtain funding and approval. Purdy is now the only state facility in Washington for female offenders. Its way of handling these women incorporates a number of new ideas which are quite likely palatable to both sides of the corrections controversy.

On one level, it is still an institution, a place to which judges can sentence people. As such, it is traditional enough for the general population or the politicians who demand that criminals be "put away." On another level, Purdy is a uniquely human facility, staffed by persons completely opposed to the traditional "prison life" concepts. In terms of both its architecture and its staff, the institution enjoys an atmosphere of community warmth which is without parallel in other female prisons. For all intents and purposes, it is its own halfway house. Extremely little emphasis is given to physical security measures, while a great deal of effort is expended to strengthen interpersonal bonds through attention paid to the individual dignity and problems of the residents.

Visually, Purdy makes a strong impression on visitors—it is almost lush in its design and landscaping. Set in a heavily wooded area of Pierce County, it is surrounded by the scenic waterways and rolling hills which abound with recreational facilities around the Tacoma–Seattle area. The buildings are quietly modern, low-slung forms in red brick and pre-cast concrete. The grounds between them are heavily landscaped with greens and colorful flower gardens. The center of the campus-like layout is connected via a multilevel garden mall. There are no guards, barbed wire, or uniforms. Inmates and counselors dress alike and stroll the areas in casual clusters.

"Purdy did not just happen, it was carefully planned to be totally different from anything else that was being done in corrections," explained Mrs. Edna Goodrich, who is superintendent of the facility as well as one of the guiding hands behind its planning and ultimate development. "A full two years before the actual funding of the project we formed a committee and included not only corrections people but people from the community nearby. The main emphasis was on developing the kind of structure and programs which would allow residents to develop self-responsibility. One of the main faults we saw with the way things were being done in traditional corrections was that people were locked up and taken care of to such an extent that they never learned to take on responsibilities or make adequate decisions. There was no room for mistakes. Mistakes were not tolerated at all. Make one mistake and you were punished. That cannot work. It was unrealistic. People learn through their mistakes. They fall down and pick themselves up.

"The first emphasis was put on the architecture. Our architects spent a great deal of time traveling around the country looking at other facilities for ideas. The first design they drew up was a cliché of the old prison theories: there were high walls and guard towers and the other things we've all come to associate with correctional institutions.

"That is where we started: with that traditional model. Then we began to tear down everything from there. In every way we could, we were designing a place that didn't have all those barriers which prevented people from making their own decisions and developing their own sense of responsibility."

The site which was selected for Purdy was far enough away from nearby Tacoma to be quietly private, yet close enough that the inmates ("clients") have no trouble getting back and forth to the city for the many educational and job-training programs they attend daily. Prior to actual construction, the Purdy committee consulted with local politicians and community leaders to make them part of the project. They brought in bankers and businessmen and authorities of the school system for seminars on what Purdy was going to be and how it could be helped.

During the last few years of its operation, Purdy has benefited greatly from its initial cooperation with community and business interests. A number of businesses now help with on-campus training programs and then phase the women inmate workers from training programs into daily jobs on work-release programs to solid jobs when they are released. Banks have set up a system of checking accounts so that, unlike other prisons, where inmates are forbidden to have money, Purdy inmates are encouraged to handle their own financial affairs, and develop a better understanding and working knowledge of banking and other financial transactions.

"The architecture was very important to us, but it was just the beginning," said Mrs. Goodrich. "It wouldn't have been anything without the proper staff and programs to create an atmosphere of dignity. We watched the small things . . . like clothes. We felt it was vitally important for a resident of an institution to know who she is. Clothes, and the choice of those clothes, are a large part of a person's basic identity. Why make them dress like robots? Then they think like robots—or don't think, like robots, is more accurate.

"We found just this one thing made a dramatic difference in the way the women acted. We had been with them in the old facility, where it was cells and uniforms and the whole traditional 'lock-up' way of doing things. Here, the transition was amazing. It didn't have to do with only the cloth they were putting over their bodies, but with the entire way in which they perceived themselves. They became people again. They began to care more about how they looked, and just generally changed in their reactions to themselves and to one another.

"It was the same with the elimination of the fortress-type concrete structure. At Walla Walla we had women in there for years who had sat around and made the 'problem' in their lives the hideous structure which held them. Their total focus was against the structure, rather than at any part of themselves. They spent their days concentrating on how to beat the structure. Here it's almost a pleasant place to be. The resident knows that with very little effort, she can walk away and get out. But what is she running from? Where is she running to? These are the real questions which an atmosphere like this causes women to ask."

It is no problem at all to get out of Purdy. The almost total lack of traditional security measures is surprising at first. The facility's population is not "soft" or specially picked for a minimum-security arrangement. As the only state facility for women, its inmates are there for everything from first-degree murder to passing bad checks.

"Our philosophy is that security does not come from structure," explained Mrs. Goodrich. "Security comes from programs. If you have the programs you should have, and you get the people really involved with their life and the direction their life is taking, then that will hold the person. We've proven that. Even when one of the residents does escape that must be understood in the context of the behavior change you're trying to make in the individual. When you're trying to get a person to look at and deal with her strengths and weaknesses, a lot of women will run from that. That is the way they've dealt with problems all their lives. You don't break a person's life habits in a day. It takes time.

"We've even seen what we call therapeutic escapes . . . I'm sure that this kind of discussion can be misinterpreted, but let me explain. We've had women come in and just goof along, unable to get a grip on themselves and just go along in sort of a daze. Finally, they walk off and go home, only to find that what they really thought was there isn't. They don't know really what they were looking for. They'll come back here and really get into the programs and become deeply involved.

"Now I'm not saying you ought to let them run off when they feel like it, but it must be understood that escape is more than a mere movement over a fence. Escape is just one of the many mistakes a woman will make while she's trying to put herself together."

There are no block logistics inside Purdy; the women live individual lives. For instance, they do not have to get up at a certain hour in the morning, nor are they compelled to attend meals. Each woman is issued an alarm clock. She is expected to get up and attend the classes, sessions, or programs she has scheduled for that day or explain on her own why she did not. It is totally her responsibility.

Perhaps the most important feature at Purdy—and one which probably makes more difference than the architecture or the flowers —is the staff. Those people in this group are hired for their high levels of education and tend to be young individuals who become deeply involved with the women to whom they are assigned. The committee went out of its way to ensure that the staff atmosphere at Purdy would be like that of no other institution. Hence, few of the staffers have ever worked in corrections before.

"We were trying to create a philosophy, an atmosphere here," said Mrs. Goodrich. "One of the things that really concerned us about staff problems was that there were thirteen matrons from the old facility at Walla Walla who had a right to jobs here. Twelve of them came here, and I was worried about them. At Walla Walla, they had been typical matrons; their only job was to keep people locked up. I learned something from those women. We brought them here and put them in an atmosphere that was totally alien to them. Not only did they shift from the heavy-handed authoritarian approach they were used to, but they have since gone on to become some of the best and most sensitive counselors we have here today.

"There is a lesson to be learned in that. The traditional prisons have quite a problem with staff who are brutal or apathetic. People tend to assume what stance is called for by taking clues from the atmosphere around them. I think when you change that atmosphere you can significantly change the person. I think that despite the architectural handicaps that exist in the other traditional prisons today, a substantial change could be made if serious efforts were made to effect a change in the over-all atmosphere."

One of the wholesome changes the Purdy officials have made concerns the children of the residents. In Purdy, as in the other female institutions of the country, a majority of the women have children. The Labor Department estimates that in the federal prison system 80 per cent of the women are now or have been married and 75 per cent or more have children. In the past, as a rule of thumb, children have been prohibited from seeing their mothers in institutions. Many institutions still strictly enforce those prohibitions. Others provide that a mother may have contact with her children only through glass walls or over a telephone line. It was major news in April 1973 when the Bedford Hills Correctional Facility in New York State had a "children's day" for its inmates. Newspapers and television crews covered the event in which female inmates were allowed the "unique" privilege of touching and playing with their own children.

At Purdy, residents are encouraged and aided in relocating their children to foster homes close by the institution. Children are urged to visit frequently and may stay for the weekend. Well-stocked toyboxes are provided around the facility. They enjoy free run of the campus and frequently bring their pets with them—indeed, it is not unusual on any given day to see a small kitten being chased by a young toddler through the administrative offices.

"I could never understand what sort of minds came up with the idea that it was somehow beneficial or desirable to keep a woman separated from her child," said Mrs. Goodrich. "I think women in prison have a much harder burden to bear than men because of their children. If they're going to be helped, if we're really going to help her get a grip on herself and her problems, then we have to see that she and her family are inseparable. Their problems are her problems and vice versa. We want children here and we want them here as often as possible. Children are comfortable here; this is not a threatening place, and most children react here just like they do in a shopping mall or a school campus. It's quite comfortable for them.

"It is too early to officially say or statistically prove," said Mrs. Goodrich, "but the gut feeling here is that it *is* working. Our residents are leaving here with concrete plans and jobs that they find fulfilling. They are leaving with a level of accomplishment and personal satisfaction which I never saw before in my years at traditional institutions. Perhaps that is all they ever really needed: to be treated lke human beings."

Over the last three years, Purdy has a recidivism rate of only 3 per cent. While this experience is too limited and the time period too short to justify unqualified optimism, the prognosis is probably good because this approach has been working well in a related field. For several years preceding such innovations in the prison system, another group of social deviants, mental patients, were being introduced to similar changes in their therapeutic management. First in Europe and then in America, there was a movement to decentralize and deinstitutionalize mental treatment. To this end, large state hospitals are being dismantled and their occupants distributed throughout a network of neighborhood community mental-health centers. This was made possible in part because of the effectiveness of new drugs. But it owed its success chiefly to the use of milieu therapy in the setting of a therapeutic community, a term originated by Maxwell Jones [30] in the early 1950s to describe the use of the hospital community staff and patients alike to direct and maximize therapeutic influences. The effectiveness of this influence is based on the transcendental power for change inherent in the interpersonal bond. Indigenous self-help groups, such as Alcoholics Anonymous, have long utilized these bonds to rehabilitate otherwise hopeless addicts.

The interpersonal ties that bind us to each other and to our community outside the prison walls are being revitalized at institutions like Purdy after years of their systematic destruction in traditional prisons. The fragmented lives of these women are finally coalescing under the influence of a caring community which not only provides a stronger security from escape than stone walls but may even provide enough security for them to escape from their former lives. The classical tradition of social theory has long recognized that the well-being of individuals was dependent on their full membership in the community. Philip Rieff typified such ideas when he wrote that "to cure a man one need only return him to his community or construct a new one." [31] If such prisoner communities reforge the social links for women, they will undoubtedly do the same for men. It is satisfying to reflect that the social revolution of changed sex roles is freeing both the slave and the master from the bondage of dehumanization, that what women have taken from men in power they are restoring to him in liberty, and that the gain of freedom for each is a gain of freedom for both because neither men nor women are islands complete unto themselves alone.

9

Ladies and the Law

The life of the law has not been logic: it has been experience.

—Oliver Wendell Holmes, Jr.
"The Common Law," 1881

Woman throughout the ages has been mistress to the law, as man has been its master. Sometimes pampered, sometimes reviled, usually disrespected, and always misunderstood, she has been the object rather than the subject of legal decisions. Monologue, not dialogue, has characterized the law's discourse with her. The controversy between rule of law and rule of men was never relevant to women—because, along with juveniles, imbeciles, and other classes of legal nonpersons, they had no access to law except through men. The democratic interchange of public opinion, legislative act, and judicial interpretation that ensured the viability and responsiveness of the law for men was totally silent for women. They had no public opinion of record, no voice in the legislature, and no standing in court. Barred socially and legally from opportunities for effecting change and discouraged emotionally and psychologically from pursuing change, they were consigned to a legal limbo with little say and less control over the regulations which governed their lives. Helpless they were in the eyes of the law, and helpless they remained in their own. Public image and self-image, public perception and self-perception merged in a devalued self-concept which separated womanhood from the full range of human aspirations. Like self-

203

fulfilling social prophecies, women actually became what they only seemed to be, childlike, timid, inept, and passive, an illustrative foil to highlight the luster of manhood.

Consequently, as we survey her historical experiences for a composite picture of womanhood, we can only glimpse her through the glass of culture, darkly, but never face to face. What emerges is a series of images which reflect hardly at all what she was or might have been, but rather what each age required her to be. The legal system and the social system, after all, could only project a vision distorted by their own refractive errors. The picture of femininity thus represented by each cultural period tells us much more about men of the time than about women, because woman was an expedient stereotype designed to satisfy particular masculine needs. How it happened that she came to bear this psychological burden for men and why she willingly conceded her birthright to male domination is embedded in the prehistory of a race whose penchant for exploitation is well documented. In more recent historical periods, the crystallization of habits into social custom and the reification of custom into common law perpetuated a practice which common sense and common decency should have expunged. The social history of these trends, the judicial evolution of the laws which reflected them, and the current animus of change which is convulsing the legal system to its roots will be explored in this chapter.

Social History of Trends

Systematic and sanctioned discriminatory treatment of women was not created by Genesis, which simply recorded practices already extant, but deplorably the Bible did bestow on such practices an undeserved aura of piety. In the ensuing centuries, these early values persisted partly because of the hallowed status of the Bible and partly because they were so congenial to men's view of themselves. If the Devil himself could cite scripture for his own purposes, he was only one member of a large and growing fraternity. Proponents of female discrimination found it convenient to quote God frequently in support of their position. The biologic doctrine of special creation had an explicit male bias, for women were created not only separate but unequal.

The paramount destiny and mission of woman are to fulfill the noble and benign offices of wife and mother. This is the law of the Creator. And the rules of civil society must be adapted to the general constitution of things, and cannot be based upon exceptional cases.[1]

But if the law restricted with one hand, it protected with the other, binding capability to culpability for females as it had for juveniles, with whom they were often identified. The doctrine of presumed coercion—which William Blackstone, writing in the eighteenth century, declared was already a thousand years old [2]— turned female incompetence into innocence and held women who were accomplices of their husbands guiltless because it was presumed that a wife was merely obeying her husband's commands.[3] This was a curious defense. It did not pretend that the woman did not commit the criminal act, but simply contended that she was legally incapable of having done so on her own. While this doctrine created a "powerful shield in [their] defense," [4] it was also erected at incalculable cost to the female psyche. Also in common law was a feudal practice which suspended many of the legal rights of a single woman once she was married. This doctrine of coverture, rooted in biblical concepts of the unity of flesh of husband and wife, served as yet another mechanism for supporting the "natural" dominance of the male. The wife's legal personality was submerged within that of her husband and her emotional personality could not fare much better.

Male sexual privileges have been similarly protected. Throughout recorded history in Babylonia, Egypt, and Greece, as well as in Europe and America, the social burden and guilt for adultery has fallen most heavily, if not exclusively, on the woman, and the legal penalties have been more harsh for her.[5] The explanation for this lies largely in men's reluctance to accept responsibility for their own sexual drives and the consequent tendency to blame women.

The Fall of man refers to the sexual corruption of the human race —men and women alike; the fallen woman, by contrast, represents the corruption of only her own gender. In exhorting Adam to taste the apple, Eve epitomizes all the seductresses who have tempted guileless men from the paths of virtue down "the primrose way to the everlasting bonfire." [6] With regard to both her virtue and her vice, each heavily laden with sexual meaning, women have rarely been portrayed for what they are—a gender variant of human— but rather they have been represented as a disembodied symbol of qualities which men wished to extol or castigate.

Building a system of ethics based on wishes rather than facts, men first tried to deny that woman had a sexual drive and then that she could or should derive any personal satisfaction out of sex other than that associated with pleasing her husband. Reflecting such views, Byron declared, "Man's love is of man's life a thing apart;/'Tis woman's whole existence." That women could lust or be casually commercial about sex as, of course, men have been was more than just distressing to men; it was antithetical to the system of morality they had constructed around the female. [7]

In spite of the fact that the number of women in America has consistently matched or exceeded that of men, legislative progress has been slow. It was not until the latter half of the nineteenth century that the Married Women's Property Acts throughout the United States granted them a measure of contractual and property rights; not until 1920 that women won the constitutional right to vote; not until the Civil Rights Act of 1964 that sex-discrimination in employment was banned; and not until 1968 that discriminatory sentencing practices were declared unconstitutional.

> Our cases hold that people who stand in the same relationship to their government cannot be treated differently by that government. To do so . . . would be to treat them as if they were, somehow, less than people. [8]

Even jury service was an area restricted from women. In 1880 the Supreme Court supported the position that "the state" might limit jury duty to men.[9] It was not until 1898, in Utah, that women were first permitted to serve.[10] But throughout the early 1900s the trend was moving unmistakably in the direction of women's rights. By 1928, women in twenty-one states were allowed to serve on juries.[11] Today, women in all fifty states may do so.

The road to the full equality envisioned in the Equal Rights Amendment has been a tortuous one. Discrimination in age of attaining majority, voting rights, jury service, capacity to enter into binding agreements and to sue and be sued, right to a separate domicile, change in citizenship upon marriage to an alien, and change of name upon marriage are only a few of the sex-based legal inequities it was designed to correct. Since 1923, resolutions proposing an Equal Rights Amendment have been introduced in every Congress, and it has passed the Senate twice, in 1950 and 1953,[12] but thus far it still has not been ratified by the necessary thirty-eight states.

Long-thwarted desires are rarely sated by tokenism. On the contrary, concessions often accelerate the momentum of aspiration and demands frequently multiply beyond the power of appeasement to gratify. As the goal of equality moved from improbable to possible to likely, as each gain spiraled into the vortex of rising expectations, and as yesteryear's utopian proposals became today's minimal demands, the wonder grew that women had so long acquiesced to a dominance their organized efforts could have long ago deposed.

The reasons offered for women's age-old tolerance of male domination generally fall into two categories. Some have contended that in a world where size and strength were power, women reluctantly accepted their subordinate status as a *fait accompli* and resigned themselves to powerlessness;[13] others, that the satisfactions of protection from competitive stress, in addition to all the accoutrements of chivalry, were sufficient inducements to perpetuate the double legal standard.[14] There is ample evidence to support both explanations, which are in any event more complementary than contradictory. Let us explore each of them separately, even though they operate in tandem and recent changes in social customs have caused both positions to converge toward activism and egalitarianism.

To begin with the female resignation to her own powerlessness, behavioral scientists are familiar from animal studies with the phenomenon of being conditioned to helplessness.[15] This may be produced experimentally by a procedure in which a chemically paralyzed animal is exposed to stress of a type which would ordinarily result in fight-or-flight reactions. Since neither is possible under the experimental conditions, the animal learns at an experiential level that activity or attempts at activity are useless. Later, in the absence of any chemical inhibitors, when the animal is re-exposed to stress, it endures it passively without utilizing the opportunities for attack or escape which are now available to it. Natural examples of this may be found in the training of dogs, cattle herding, bronco busting, etc. This may also shed light on the otherwise inexplicable submissiveness of demoralized groups of humans—prisoners of war, concentration-camp inmates, perhaps even disciplined combat troops—who, once "broken," are unwilling-unable to fight their way out of a mold of conformity inimical to their interests. Conversely, it has been a characteristic and heartening aspect of the American experience that downtrodden groups of immigrants transplanted to the open atmosphere of the United States have exhibited a degree of assertiveness and creativity unmatched in their lands of origin.

In insidious, subtle, and pervasive ways, females have been conditioned from infancy not to fight, not even to be assertive—especially with boys. Other options such as tearfulness, submission, or resignation were encouraged, and hypochondria and the sick role were charitably although contemptuously tolerated. The penalty of social disapproval was usually reserved for those few girls who were "inappropriately" aggressive. Regardless of the possible existence of any sex-differentiated genetic tendency toward passivity, the pressures to conform to docile female social roles would have been sufficient to account for such a yielding attitude. Up until very recent times, the male musculo-skeletal balance of power was the decisive factor in the equation of dominance. As the evolution of the legal system shifted the arena of battle from physical combat to judicial dispute first for men and then for women; as male life insurance and female longevity shifted wealth into the hands of women; and as myriad manifestations of changed social consciousness permeated cultural institutions, succeeding generations of girls could dare to hope, and in so doing begin to shed the guise of the willing victim. Confining conditions can often be tolerated indefinitely without rancor and without frustration so long as the possibility of improvement is remote. As a matter of fact, frustration, the subjective feeling of being blocked, is more in evidence when restrictions can be expected to be mitigated than when they are perceived as inevitable. Frustration is the stuff of revolutions, social as well as political and military. Thus it was the widespread frustration and discontent among women, after centuries of resignation, which signaled that in daring to complain about their social condition they were coming of age, that they had breached the emotional barriers which inhibited their strivings for equality. They felt hampered, not because they were more restrained than their mothers but because they expected to be as unrestrained as their fathers. The legal changes which followed in the wake of these psychological changes were important to their fulfillment but they were the rear guard of the liberation movement, not its harbinger. It was a triumph of unrivaled social, political, and psychological significance that large numbers of women were aspiring not just to be the obedient partner but the coequal partner of men. In their contentment, women were necessarily defeated; in their dissatisfaction they were already tasting the first fruits of victory.

The second major reason explaining the female's long sufferance of the legal double standard is simply that many women felt that they benefited from it; what they gave up in control they recovered in deferential treatment. In short, so the argument went, they had struck a good bargain. Examples included the protective labor laws which limited the hours to be worked and the weights to be lifted by women, the judicial preference for awarding custody of minor children to the mother rather than the father in divorce cases, the general rule which holds the husband rather than the wife responsible for financial support of the family, the extension of that rule to issues of alimony, child support, and property distributions following divorce, and the exclusion of women from military conscription. All of this was true, but as stated in a recent Supreme Court decision it was only a partial truth.

> There can be no doubt that our nation has had a long and unfortunate history of sex discrimination. Traditionally, such discrimination was rationalized by an attitude of "romantic paternalism" which, in practical effect, put women not on a pedestal, but in a cage.[16]

In many ways women were treated as perpetual juveniles, albeit by a male legal establishment which prided itself on being at worst benignly despotic. The normal need and desire of children to grow up—i.e., to exercise their own options and, within the limits of the social order, to control their own destinies—was systematically denied women. It has been argued that this was done for their own good, but such arguments would win few adherents if they were applied to justify discriminatory treatment of smaller, weaker men. It has been argued that the equal-rights movement will hasten the death of chivalry, but there is an authentic question as to whether chivalry ever really lived in a system that dispensed courtesies and denied rights. Finally, it has been argued that discriminatory laws merely protect the natural roles of the woman as wife and mother. But if this were so natural, restrictive laws would be unnecessary and in any event women should be as free as men to decide what their natural inclinations are. In practice, what the law regards as the natural role is at best the traditional role. Furthermore, cultural anthropologists long ago established that a great variety of overlapping social roles are natural to both sexes.[17] The needs of social stability require that current social-role expectations be accorded special standing in the courts, but to suggest that such standing is based on divine injunction or biologic determinism rather than social custom is to perpetually deprive disadvantaged groups of the opportunity to improve their position.

Judicial Evolution

If laws are to remain responsive to evolving social needs, they must accommodate changing social customs. Historically, social custom and legal practice have maintained a peculiarly disingenuous relationship. At one level they have purported to reflect one another's ideal images; at another they have engaged in efforts at mutual conversion. Each has attempted to take the lead while pretending to merely keep abreast. The only way to appreciate the reciprocal relationship between legal norms and social norms is to see them operate in a dynamic equilibrium. While consistency and fairness are essential to respect for the law, and while the ethos of a rule of law rather than a rule of men has been a special source of judicial pride, these bulwarks of justice have been tacitly recognized as being too insensible to the complexity of the human condition to be considered any more than guidelines. Judicial interpretations, especially those addressed to the spirit as opposed to the letter of the law, have provided the elastic couplings which attach abstract codes to vital social processes. Although this way of living with the law is necessary to the maintenance of the body politic, in the past it has served to subvert equal protection under the law for women, because it tied them to the male establishment's inaccurate and self-serving concepts of female roles. The most important implications of this were extralegal because they influenced the social norms governing the male-female relationship in all its economic, social, and psychological aspects. But because legal norms and social norms are always in a fluid relationship with each other, the trend toward female equality which has been gaining momentum in recent years has been slowly prompting many legal changes.

However, the law's responsiveness to social influence has been neither universally recognized nor universally approved. In 1948,

Justice Frankfurter wrote in an opinion for the majority in the Goesart Case:

> The fact that women may now have achieved the virtues that men have long claimed as their prerogatives and now indulge in vices that men have long practiced does not preclude the states from drawing a sharp line between the sexes, certainly in such matters as the regulation of the liquor traffic. . . . The Constitution does not require legislatures to reflect sociological insight, or shifting social standards, any more than it requires them to keep abreast of the latest scientific standards.[18]

Such judicial support for legislative conservatism may have been meant to shield the legal system from social fads and scientific fancies, but it also risked preserving the chaff with the wheat. In practice, state legislatures, as well as the Constitution itself, already do reflect social insight and embody normative social standards, but they are those of a much earlier day. As such, they are usually appropriate for their period of origin, but unless one is willing to deify the past, an attitude alien to the American reverence for progress, current values deserve their own opportunities for expression. Otherwise, inequities, once established, no matter how meritorious they may have been at their point of origin, are in danger of becoming venerated irrelevancies.

The sex-differentiated age for marriage is a pertinent example. Most states have permitted and social custom has encouraged women to marry earlier than men. In recognition of the likelihood that early marriage with its attendant responsibilities impedes the acquisition of educational and other cultural skills related to extra-family activities, society has ruled that males must be older before they can marry. This delay was designed to ensure that, as the main financial resource of the family, men would not be prematurely diverted from the task of preparing themselves for their future occupations. Women, on the other hand, were not expected to participate in any but domestic activities, and the sooner the care of their moral virtues was transferred from the protection of their fathers to that of their husbands, the better for both. Whether the burɒen of such a rule falls most heavily on men or women is not at issue, but what is exemplified here is the increasingly inappropriate social attitude that the ruling reflects.

Discriminatory prosecution of prostitutes is another example of how male-oriented social values have influenced law enforcement. Men have been consistently exonerated for the same sexual activity for which the prostitute was charged on the rationale that their importance to the community was so vital that society would be disrupted by their imprisonment. Given that the clients outnumber the prostitutes in geometric proportion and that the commercial nature of the transaction makes it likely that the clients are gainfully employed, this reasoning may have been correct. But correctness aside, it is one of many instances which illustrates the fact that the legal system does not, nor could it, avoid reflecting particular social values. In the past the values have generally been those which favored males.

Not surprisingly, it is in the area of sexual conduct that the American legal system intrudes most inequitably into the lives of women, but not to the extent it once did. The statutes which had the practical effect of permitting adultery for husbands but not for wives have all but disappeared—surviving only in Kentucky.[19] Similarly, declining expectations of chastity are reflected in the requirement that female marriage-license applicants, previously exempted, must now furnish proof that they are free of venereal disease—except in the State of Washington.[20] Nation-wide, sexual regulations associated with seduction, enticement, and statutory rape prescribe different standards of conduct for males and females. Another set of regulations, the criminal abortion laws, while not intended to harm women, have had the effect of exposing them to the risk of injury or death at the hands of unskilled practitioners. The partisan procedures associated with prostitution and the "unwritten law" defense available to married men but not to married women furnish additional evidence of the different standards of behavior imposed by the law.

In all the varieties of interaction between the sexes, the one which evokes the most visceral distaste is the crime of rape. In its primitive exploitativeness, in its selfish utilization of the woman as an object, it distills all that is bad out of what could be good about the man-woman relationship and crystallizes woman's deepest distrust of man. Unfortunately, the mechanisms which have evolved for handling the crime of rape are nearly as cruel to women victims as the crime itself. Essentially, those mechanisms are a direct reflection of the traditional male bias and dominance evidenced throughout the criminal justice system. The antiquated laws, procedures, and *ad hoc* police practices in this area tend to be offensive, demeaning, and mentally debilitating to the woman involved.

"If I had it to do again, I would never have gone through with the prosecution. I wouldn't even have reported it," said one twenty-seven-year-old woman who suffered through months of legal proceedings and publicity only to see her rapist found innocent because she was unable to prove that she did not consent to the act. Despite extensive body bruises and a wound in her forehead that took six stitches to close, the defense attorney argued that "vigorous love play" did not necessarily indicate nonconsent and, in fact, could even indicate enthusiastic approval and passionate involvement in the act.

"From the beginning I had this feeling that I was the one who was on trial rather than the guy they picked up and charged," said the woman, raped by an intruder who entered her apartment through a window, from an adjacent rooftop. She was at the time sleeping in the nude . . . a fact that is frequently alleged in rape cases to prove "willingness to have intercourse."

"Right after it happened . . . I mean here I was lying on the floor, my face was streaming with blood, I was damned near hysterical when I called the police. They arrived and the very first question this one guy asked me was, 'Did you enjoy it? Did you *really* try to resist the guy?'

"Then the questions really started. I couldn't believe what they asked me. About five officers were crowded into my bedroom. They said things to me like 'Lay on the bed exactly as you were when the guy came in. Why did you spread your legs if you didn't want to be raped? Did you see his penis? Describe it. Did you touch his penis? Did you put it in your mouth? Did you have an orgasm?'

"Then there was the hospital they took me to. There were maybe three dozen people sitting around in this large ward. This one guy in a white coat takes my name and he yells down the ward, at the top of his lungs, 'Hey, Pete, I got a rape case here. Check her out, will you?' It was just incredible. The guy checking me out left me sitting on this table for like an hour. One of his questions was, 'Did you give the guy a blow job or what?'

"Later at the police station. They caught the guy from my description. He was sitting there and one of the cops went out to get him a cup of coffee and gave him a cigarette. They told me, 'Sit over there, lady, we'll get to you in a minute.'

"Over and over again, the police, the district attorney, the defense attorneys, even my own goddamned private lawyer asked me the same thing: 'Are you sure you really resisted? Did you *really* want to get raped subconsciously?"

"In the end the guy who did it got off. They even brought in this one boy—a man now—that I knew in high school. That was ten years ago. He testified he had intercourse with me, after a prom. The defense attorney said, 'She was pretty easy, wasn't she?' The guy just grinned and shook his head.

"I learned. I still live alone, but now I have a gun. I have a permit and everything like that for it. I keep it right on the night table, loaded. If someone ever comes in my apartment again, I'll kill them. If I don't kill them with the first shot, I'll keep shooting until they are dead. I also keep a knife right below the headboard of my bed. No one is ever going to put me through that again."

It is little wonder that rape is one of the least reported crimes. Perhaps it is the only crime in which the victim becomes the accused and, in reality, it is she who must prove her good reputation, her mental soundness, and her impeccable propriety. While the letter of the law treats the victim equitably, in reality, the spirit of its application is one of innuendo and suggestion about "sick women" who may want to "trap" men with "fabricated stories" supported by "vivid imagination." In the adversary process prejudicial questions become sinister suggestions as cooperation, consent, and chastity are contested; past encounters determine present credibility as the victim struggles to establish her sexual purity. Merely because she consents to intercourse on some prior occasion, has she forever forfeited her right to choose sexual partners?

Not unexpectedly, women's liberation proponents have taken an avid interest in this issue and their growing involvement will have an understandable impact on the crime as well as its prosecution. The more open sexual attitudes associated with the movement will affect the crime of rape in at least three major ways. There will be an actual increase in the incidence because men will habitually expect sexual intercourse and be less willing to accept refusals based on moral prohibitions; there will be an apparent increase because changes in the criminal-justice system will make women less reluctant to report rape; and there will be a partially spurious increase because women will broaden the definition of rape to include the ambiguous area of coercive seduction. The tendency to reinterpret established patterns is but one aspect of a trend toward reappraising the entire heterosexual relationship with an emphasis on female control of outcomes. The Rape Crisis Center begun in June 1972 in Washington, D.C., to provide lessons in self-defense is an example of the new activist attitude which has pervaded women's thinking about themselves in a man's world.

In the past, the law has been utilized to stifle such activism; more recently, the law has encouraged it. Of special importance in this regard is Title VII of the Civil Rights Act of 1964. By prohibiting sexual discrimination in employment, it permitted women in large numbers to reassess their place in society for the first time and to view themselves as potential career people rather than simply as domestic partners. And for the first time, also, it provided many unmarried women with financial independence and security outside the bonds of matrimony. The momentum associated with this movement toward equality was felt by every segment of the female population and, because the status of juveniles and women have so frequently coincided, it touched the young with a special impact.

Addressing themselves not only to the philosophical issue of civil rights for juveniles but also to the very practical problems created by the 18-per-cent rise in illegitimacy rates for teen-age girls,[21] many state legislatures have passed medical-emancipation statutes. These allow a girl to obtain care and treatment for pregnancy and "pregnancy-related conditions" without the necessity of obtaining parental consent and with the protection of a confidential

doctor-patient relationship. Because the care and treatment re
to in the statute have been construed to include contraceptiv..
therapeutic abortion, it has created a legal paradox—viz., adolescent girls who have not reached the age of consent for sexual intercourse are nevertheless permitted to consent to medical procedures
encompassing contraception, pregnancy, and abortion. It appears
that by countenancing this judicial inconsistency, the law was ac-
knowledging that altered social patterns have increased the likelihood that a minor girl may become pregnant without official or
parental sanction. Having confronted the unthinkable with the
liable, it has attempted to provide legitimate opportunities for
avoidance or correction. Since teen-agers already possess the where-
withal to become pregnant, it seemed reasonable to give them the
supplementary power to mitigate errors of judgment. Furthermore,
by freeing the female half of the partnership from the burdens of
pregnancy which she alone had to bear, it put the sexes on a more
equal footing. However, though this aspect of the equal-rights movement has been generally underemphasized, males have also been
the beneficiaries of its influence. A 1972 Circuit Court decision [22]
overturned an Oklahoma statute which allowed female offenders
aged eighteen and under to be processed as juveniles, while only
males aged sixteen and under could be similarly processed. The
court considered it an "invidious discrimination against males" and
could find no "logical constitutional justification for the discrimination inherent in the classification." [23]

This process of interpretation, as it shuttles back and forth
across the judicial matrix at the state level and binds it to the network of federal courts, is constantly embroidering the system of
law with strands from the social fabric, thus making each an integral
part of the other. Such interweaving of social values with judicial
regulations assures mutual responsiveness by lacing the law with
threads of living experience. In the words of a 1966 decision:

> The Constitution of the United States must be read as embody-
> ing general principles meant to govern society and the institu-
> tions of government as they evolve through time. It is therefore

this Court's function to apply the Constitution as a living document to the legal cases and controversies of contemporary society.[24]

By thus defining and redefining established principles such as "equal protection" and "due process" in the light of changed contemporary perceptions of women, the courts have been able to improve the legal position of women even before new legislation was enacted. While this traditional practice of interpretive molding of the law to accommodate to social customs used to discriminate against women in the past, it is now working in their favor and providing a judicial impetus to their efforts.

But there is another avenue for change and expression which is not dependent on legal appeals or interpretations, or even litigation: the clandestine pursuit of remedies in the arena of public opinion, which is ultimately as important as the law of the land for the present dispensation of justice and the future shape of legislation. From these unorganized beginnings are formed the social system of institutionalized evasions which has evolved in response to the fact that while laws may be uniform, the society which they regulate is not. Differing social attitudes and differing needs of the various segments of a pluralistic society, while not sufficiently strong to foist their views on the majority, nevertheless still enjoy a wide enough base of public support to command acceptance, if not respectability, for deviant modes. This process, which sanctioned the status of such victimless crimes as prostitution and gambling, has also ameliorated the predicament of those women in the vanguard of role change whose behavior was tolerated by only a small minority. A set of evasive methods was developed to close the gap between the legal and generally acceptable rules and the quasi-legal and narrowly acceptable behavior of these women. If a woman was dominant at home, she had to either pretend subordination to her husband or downgrade the importance of her domestic function. In employment, if she was doing a man's job, ruses had to be utilized to conceal this. Many regulations which discriminated against women were circumvented in practice long before the Civil

Rights Act of 1964, because public attitudes were changing, and to have done otherwise would have precipitated a confrontation from burgeoning feminist groups. During such an interim period when the positions of social and legal norms are approaching each other but do not yet coincide, a pattern of institutionalized evasions evolves whereby the rules are still regarded as nominally in force, but stratagems for defying them develop. This condition prevailed for women's rights from the early 1940s up until 1964. The current and final stage in the evolution from deviancy to normal variation and from illegal but socially legitimatized to full legal approbation spans the period from 1964 to the present and will be defined by the enactment of the Equal Rights Amendment. Its passage will mark the transfer of power from the antifeminists to the feminists, and with it the mantle of respectability will shift to the previous outcasts and evaders. But that succession, borne on the shoulders of public opinion, has not yet arrived. When it does it is uncertain whether it will enter through the courts or the legislature. Both offer possibilities of success, and each route is being vigorously explored, sometimes exclusively but usually in tandem with the other. When progress becomes stymied in the courts, the effort is shifted to the legislature as part of a continuous effort to exploit the positions gained by breakthroughs in either.

Current Changes

In its 1963 report the Committee on Civil and Political Rights of the President's Commission on the Status of Women [25] urged interested groups to "give high priority to uncovering and challenging by court action discriminatory laws and practices." [26] The impetus generated by this exhortation from the highest levels of the executive branch sparked many constitutional challenges of laws that discriminated on the grounds of sex alone, and the initial results were encouraging. In general, those cases which were decided before 1963 had sustained sex-based discrimination. In spite of legal objections that invoked the equal-protection clause, the privileges-and-immunities clause, and the due-process clause of the United States Constitution. Since 1963, however, challenges based on these clauses have met with sufficient success to justify my belief that given continuous pressure sex-discriminatory laws will increasingly become constitutionally invalidated.

The Fourteenth Amendment to the United States Constitution, with its Equal Protection Clause, is indeed the driving force. It provides that no state shall "deprive any person of life, liberty, or property without due process of law, nor deny to any person within its jurisdiction the equal protection of the laws." In spite of these guarantees, women in the past have generally been unsuccessful in their attempts to obtain judicial relief from sexually biased laws. However, in the recently changed social and judicial climate, constitutional questions of "due process" and "equal protection" have been raised with increasing frequency and accorded a more sympathetic hearing.

Prostitution

It would be inaccurate, however, to conclude that the challenges to discrimination derive from only two specific constitutional areas. In fact, sex discrimination is thought to be vulnerable because it infringes on several individual rights. The First Amendment guarantees of free speech have been invoked against statutes that restrict the language permissible in the presence of women, and rights to privacy have been used to attack the constitutionality of prostitution laws.[27] No matter how judicially neutral the wording of state prostitution statutes has been, it is recognized as a sex-defined crime which in practice is applied only against females. Depending upon the particular statute, the equal-protection attack involves two aspects of discriminatory legal treatment. The first challenges the law to allow female prostitutes the same immunity from prosecution as that enjoyed by male prostitutes; the second challenges it to be as lenient to the prostitute as it is to her male patron.[28] Pursuing an entirely different tack, the privacy argument focuses on the right of the individual to control his or her bodily functions without unreasonable interference from the state and contends that making prostitution illegal is an invasion of that right.[29]

Aside from the belief that women have a less legitimate need for a faithful partner than men, there is a notion that, in or out of marriage, women are less entitled to exercise their sexual proclivities. When they do, they are more heavily penalized than their male partners. And this involves some peculiar mythical legerdemain. To suppress female sexuality and limit it to cases of male demands and female acquiescence, society has subscribed to the supposition that sex is something men do *to* women and women do *for* men. However, regardless of the public and private support for this curious idea, it is officially waived for the prostitute who is, by virtue of an *ad hoc* reversal of the sexual convention, regularly charged with doing something *to* rather than *for* her customers. The prostitute's forgiveness of her clients is debatable, but it is certain that in most jurisdictions she is tried for their sins. In fact, the very definition of criminal prostitution is usually limited only to the conduct of the woman. Even when laws in some jurisdictions make it possible to punish men also, interpretations by sympathetic police officials and district attorneys have eased their liability and diverted it to the female. Even when customers are arrested it is usually only to induce them to aid in the prosecution of the prostitute. And even when males are charged, it is usually only for a "violation" punishable by a small fine. At no time is the sexual innocence of men more righteously defended than when they voluntarily pay a female to be relieved of it!

By comparison, the legal apparatus associated with the arrest, prosecution, and sentencing of prostitutes is a morass of contradictions within contradictions. It is a Gordian knot of procedural ruses and legalistic subterfuges contrived to harmonize that which authorities do not wish to carry out with that which they cannot afford to ignore. The result is often a ceremonial ritual dance performed by the police and the courts, each stepping to the mandatory measures of the law but improvising sufficiently to express their concepts of justice. The police discriminate in enforcing prostitution statutes, when they do, by arresting only the woman. The courts respond by compensating for this unadmitted injustice not through encouraging the prosecution of the male but by dismissing charges against the female. There is also sometimes a light fine or overnight incarceration of the prostitute to justify the efforts of the arresting officer and to acknowledge a measure of judicial concern. The present system of revolving-door justice is not exclusive to prostitution but is characteristic of the status of other victimless crimes toward which private attitudes are more permissive than public laws. But in neither sphere is there sufficient consistency nor conviction to pursue avowed principles to legal conclusions. In this milieu of sociolegal ambivalence, the courts, the police, and the prostitutes drift uncertainly, awaiting decisive direction from any quarter. The confusion may be illustrated by the fact that the prostitution statutes in several jurisdictions specifically indicate that they apply only to female prostitutes. Their validity has been challenged. While the statutes in most jurisdictions are sexually neutral in language, in practice only women are arrested.[30] However, out of 3047 arrests in one New York City precinct in a six-month period, only 75 resulted in formal prosecution.[31] In 1971, the San Francisco Commission on Crime found that only 15 per cent of those arrested for prostitution were ever jailed.[32] It was concluded that "neither the district attorney's office nor the judge take this kind of arrest seriously unless there is a previous conviction." [33] A frequently heard judicial viewpoint was presented by Judge Budd G. Goodman of New York City:

> Unless a prostitute is involved in crimes of violence, most judges do not feel her crime merits jail—not when they're constantly faced with far more serious crimes like robbery and murder.[34]

This reflects current values which differ markedly from those of fifty years ago. Whereas in 1920, 75 per cent of all those arraigned were convicted, in 1967 the figure was 25 per cent. Whereas in 1920 of all those convicted, 34 per cent received probation, 77 per cent were institutionalized, and none were fined, in

1967, the comparable figures were 55 per cent, 9 per cent, and 23 per cent.[35] The drop in conviction and institutionalization rates, together with the rise in probation rates, demonstrates the half-century attitudinal shift from illegal and disapproved to illegal and tolerated.

In the heady self-righteousness of the early twentieth century, when sexual virtue was taken neither lightly nor easily, there was no equivocation about the moral rectitude of prostitution. In 1919, the American Social Health Association drafted a model vice-repression act which over the next few years stamped itself into the legislation of nineteen states.[36] Prostitution was defined as "the giving or receiving of the body in sexual intercourse for hire," and the customer as well as the prostitute was penalized. Since then, laws prohibiting the establishment or maintenance of houses of prostitution have been enacted in every state. But the antiprostitution movement, like the later temperance movement, was not sufficiently strong to extend the fervor of passage to a zeal for enforcement, and the ensuing public apathy tended to neutralize both movements. Consequently, the decade of the 1930s produced no significant antiprostitution laws. Instead, geographical isolation—segregation into red-light districts—came to be relied upon by most urban centers as a device for satisfying the otherwise irreconcilable demands of the socially repressive and socially permissive community forces. But this was not a stable solution because sentiment was too evenly divided between conscience and drives to allow either to hold undisputed sway. Since the fifties, suppressive legislation has become increasingly stringent and was aimed at the abolition of large-scale, organized prostitution. The targeted institutions were indeed broken up, but in other respects the legislation fell wide of its mark. Ways are subject to abrogation by law; will is not. And where the will remains, the way is sure to be found. Subsequently, fixed geographical isolation yielded to fluid operational isolation and visibility, or rather invisibility, became the accepted ploy for coexistence. Streetwalkers were frequently arrested, hotel girls less, and call girls hardly at all. The poor suffered most as the "two-bit whore" was driven off the streets, and the impact on the criminal-justice system was enormous. By way of example, in 1969, over 40 per cent of the inmates of the District of Columbia Women's Detention Center were incarcerated for the offense of "soliciting prostitution." [37]

Besides the financial cost of processing these women through the system, maintaining them in prison, and apprehending them in the first place, the intangible cost in erosion of police morale was considerable, because the morally questionable practice of entrapment was often the only method possible. It becomes more conscionable for a vice-squad member to accept pay-offs from a pimp when he knows that call girls go unarrested and when many of the charges against the prostitutes he may arrest will be dismissed. Even if the policeman does not subscribe to one women's liberation leader's description of the prostitute as "the only honest woman," [38] he frequently feels that the investment of highly trained man-hours and expensive wiretapping equipment is disproportionate either to her crime or to the court's disposition to dismissal. Furthermore, the conscionable practice of accepting graft for this vice may influence his attitude to accept graft for other vices.

It is in deference to these practical as well as ethical considerations that many have sought a revision of procedures for handling the problem of prostitution. The alternatives which are being considered are decriminalization, regulation, and legalization, or some combination of these.

Decriminalization would in essence extend the practice of official tolerance already operative in many places, whereby unpopular laws drift into the category of unenforced laws. If history is any guide, this would be only a temporary expedient. Regulation, on the other hand, would require a quasi-legal reclassification that would permit official acknowledgment in the form of licensing. Proponents of this approach contend that it would diminish the cost to the criminal-justice system, the incidence of violent crimes linked to prostitution, street soliciting, and police pay-offs, as well as controlling the spread of venereal disease and the scope of activities of pimps and prostitutes.[39] In rebuttal, opponents have claimed that licensing might encourage prostitution by making it a requirement for certain jobs, such as being a cocktail waitress, that societal discrimination would reduce the part-time prostitute's chances of adjustment in other areas of her life, that pimps would become monopolistic brothel owners and drive or coerce independents out of business, and that venereal disease would become even more epidemic.[40] This latter conclusion is supported by public-health records which demonstrate a direct relationship between organized prostitution—even that which is medically supervised—and the incidence of venereal disease: "The American military experience in Europe proved that the greatest single source of infection among American troops in the area where licensing and medical inspection were standard practices was licensed houses." [41] The reasons are clear. The disease is clinically difficult to detect in women, blood tests or smears may produce false negatives in the presence of antibiotics, and the next patron may infect the prostitute, allowing her to spread disease to dozens of others before her next periodic examination. A Memphis study found that all the prostitutes implicated in the spread of disease possessed certificates showing them to be disease-free.[42] While a call girl, a part-timer, or a promiscuous amateur may be just as likely a carrier, the probability that she will accommodate only a small fraction of the number of patrons serviced by a brothel prostitute decreases her capacity for contagion.

Although the movement for legalization has not yet generated the major support which would be necessary for legislative passage, there is scattered evidence that it is no longer emotionally inconceivable nor politically suicidal. In 1971, a California poll subsequent to a legislative bill proposing state-licensed brothels showed a 50 per cent favorable response.[43] The fact that control rather than abolition of prostitution is the subject of public discussion indicates how far sentiment has swung toward acceptance, and it reflects not so much a changed reality as changed perceptions of reality. Several cogent realizations have invaded our individual and national consciousness—that sex is an innate and appetitive drive seeking discharge when it can, and causing problems when it can't; that sexual relations and psychological relationships may coexist but are, in fact, separate entities; that although sex may exist as a part of a total relationship and may give physiological expression to that relationship, it may also exist alone, an intrinsically satisfying experience unfettered by psychological bonds; and that sex is not, despite the traditional puritanical doctrine to the contrary, so innately evil or depraved that its only *raison d'être* is procreation, nor, as the latest edition of such an attitude suggests, need it necessarily be justified by love. Sometimes for most people, and most times for some people, sex can be simply sex, sought after and enjoyed for its own sake. There is a growing suspicion, supported by behavioral scientists and confirmed by history, that in a free society, a significant number of people will pursue certain sexual experiences regardless of societal proscriptions. Suppression of this minority has never really worked and, despite the recent sexual revolution, conversion of the majority is doubtful. In the past, dynamic societies such as ours have found that controlled expressions of otherwise antisocial drives permit sufficient discharge of a part to ensure stability for the whole. Some form of regulation, even to the point of legalization, is therefore being experimented with as a viable social compromise.

Currently, prostitution is illegal in every state except Nevada, where it is permitted in thirteen of its seventeen counties. There it thrives as a profitable business enterprise, attracting tourists and contributing to the financial well-being of the community. One large Nevada brothel, for example, pays eighteen thousand dollars a year in license fees to its county of residence.[44] At such "ranches," as they are currently euphemized, the going rate for a prostitute may start as low as ten dollars, considerably less than the prices charged by street and bar prostitutes in Reno or Las Vegas, where it is illegal. As with other services, prices increase in proportion to the time, effort, and skill required of the vendor. A customer with exotic tastes may enjoy the companionship of two women in a private room while he views a hard-core pornographic film by paying fifty to seventy dollars, depending on the women and the house. The

Mustang Branch Ranch, one of the largest legal houses of prostitution in Nevada, employs about thirty women, ages eighteen to thirty-five, who each net anywhere from three hundred to six hundred dollars a week. They gross twice that amount, but the split in most houses is fifty-fifty.

So far, at least, there appears to be an agreeable tripartite accommodation among the prostitutes, the customers, and the community. The prostitutes are protected from sadists, drug pushers, and unruly customers; the john is secure from blackmail, violence, being "rolled," and has whatever assurance strict health requirements can offer for minimizing venereal disease; the community separates the brothel from its other activities by restricting it from principal business streets and placing it beyond four hundred yards from the nearest schoolhouse or church. It is hoped that such legalization will provide safe access to a needed service, as well as increasing the effectiveness of the criminal-justice system, but it is also feared by many that the distinction between official permission and official approval will be blurred in the public's mind, and standards of morality will deteriorate.

Whether this permissiveness is construed as a rise or decline in moral standards depends entirely on the bias of the interpreter. If extramarital sexual abstinence is the criterion for virtue, then it must be conceded that men as a group have already fallen beyond redemption and have incurred a moral debt which cannot be forgiven unless compensatory allowances are made for their fallen partners. If the fiscal vending of sex is the criterion, it could be argued that the traditional practice of trading sexual for other favors within marriage is not entitled to a higher status than its frank commercialization. The bartering of services is no more honorable than their purchase. On the contrary, some have contended that in prostitution we have attained a higher level of honesty with regard to both sex and certain hitherto obfuscated aspects of male-female interactions.[45] Furthermore, the egalitarian principle that one man's money is as good as another's holds out to some physically and emotionally less attractive men the possibility of sexual satisfaction otherwise denied them. If the courts do not yet consider sexual satisfaction a right, some legislatures, at least, are recognizing it as a purchasable privilege.

Many of the people who now view female promiscuity and prostitution with alarm had previously tolerated similar male behavior with equanimity, if not pride—a fact which is characteristic of an institutionalized sexual dishonesty. It is not the behavior per se which is vilified—after all, boys will be boys and men will be men—but its assumption as a female prerogative which has generated the legal crisis of conscience. One suspects that the anticipated decline of the righteous neighborhood that men inhabit comes not from any change in its moral structure, but from a change in the zoning laws that have allowed women to move in.

As often happens in the transmigration from fads to fashions, vices to variations, and condemned to conventional, it is not a change in the behavior itself which improves its standing. Instead, it is the status of its practitioners, adherents, and followers who elevate it to a position of propriety, because acceptance in the social sphere often depends more on *who* than on *what*. It has been estimated that the proportion of males among prostitutes in America is at least one in ten, and that figure is rising.[46] Concurrently, a study of eighty cities in twenty-nine states reveals that the number of call girls is increasing and the number of streetwalkers is decreasing.[47] If the present trend continues, the status of prostitutes will rise because women of higher caliber and men (who by virtue of their maleness are accorded higher social standing than women) are entering the field. Matching this social influence is a legal development which will alter the perception, if not the practice, of prostitution. In New Jersey,[48] a court found that it was unconstitutional under the equal-protection clause and an obvious instance of sex discrimination to exclude men from being labeled a common scold. It is likely that this will be followed by challenges to statutes that exclude male prostitutes from coverage, and if both sexes are tarred with the same brush it might create a social dilemma. Should the rationale of this case be applied to prosecute male prostitutes and male customers in a manner similar to females, either prostitution would disappear, an unlikely possibility, or the penalties and opprobrium heaped on it would be lightened as befits the sensibilities of its most recent members.

Sentencing

While the foregoing discriminations restrict the woman's activities, the most severe threat to her freedom are the sentencing practices, which were conceived in nineteenth-century altruism and practiced in twentieth-century hypocrisy. For example, a legislative pronouncement embodied in the authoritarian legitimacy of Pennsylvania's Muncy Act [49] provided that "any female pleading guilty to or being convicted for a crime punishable by imprisonment for more than a year must be sentenced to confinement in the State Industrial Home for Women and that the sentence shall be merely a general one . . . and shall not fix or limit the duration thereof." Because the sentencing for women was not only different but in general more severe, the Act was challenged under the equal-protection clause.[50] In a divided opinion, the Pennsylvania Superior Court upheld the Muncy Act, declaring that it did not violate the equal-protection clause because of a discerned reasonable connection between the purpose of the legislation and the classification by sex. In a dissenting opinion, Judge Hoffman noted the Act's provision that "women sentenced for offences punishable by imprisonment for more than one year *must* be sentenced to the maximum permissible term. Men, on the other hand, may be sentenced to lesser terms." [51] He therefore reasoned that the Act constituted "an arbitrary and invidious discrimination against women offenders as a class." It was this view which was sustained by the Pennsylvania Supreme Court in reversing the lower court,[52] stating that there is no "reasonable and justifiable difference or deterrent between men and women which would justify a man being eligible for a shorter maximum prison sentence than a woman for the commission of the same crime, especially if there is no material difference in the records and the relevant circumstances." [53]

Burke observed that "laws, like houses, lean on one another": when one falls others are weakened. Such was the case with a Connecticut statute [54] struck down less than a year later in a federal district court decision.[55] As in Pennsylvania, the State had argued that the statute in question did not fall within the same category as statutes dealing with incarceration in penal institutions because it attempted to rehabilitate the women. Nevertheless, the district court rejected it, saying it constituted "an invidious discrimination against her which is repugnant to the equal protection of the laws guaranteed by the Fourteenth Amendment." [56]

While these cases clearly exemplified the judicial cognizance of sex-discriminatory practices, not all courts have seen fit to comply. New Jersey, for one, has not followed the Pennsylvania Supreme Court and the federal district court in Connecticut in declaring such laws unconstitutional. An example of disparate sentencing for men and women convicted of similar offenses, together with the judicial reason for failing to find it unconstitutional, is provided by an excerpt from an opinion by Judge Hall, of the New Jersey Supreme Court.

> Defendant could be held on the bookmaking conviction for as long as five years (although it is most unlikely that she would be). A first offender male, convicted of the same crime, would likely receive a State prison sentence of not less than one nor more than two years. He could not be confined for more than two years, less good behavior and work credits and, assuming maximum such credits, would be eligible for parole, and considering the nature of the offense, quite likely paroled in four months and twenty-eight days.
>
> . . . there are decisions in other jurisdictions concluding that disparate legislative sentencing schemes based upon sex are not constitutionally invalid. . . . These cases generally speaking reasoned that the legislature could legitimately conclude that female criminals were basically different from male criminals, that they were more amenable and responsive to rehabilitation and reform . . . which might, however, require a longer period of

confinement in a different type of institution . . . and that therefore the legislature could validly differentiate between sexes with
respect to the length of incarceration and the method of the
determination thereof.[57]

In other words, longer sentences for females could be justified if
they were based on special efforts to rehabilitate them. This chivalrous approach had its origins around 1869 when the State of Indiana
opened the first reformatory for women.[58] In conception it was
designed to combine an enlightened view of corrections with flexibility in sentencing in order to influence that group of prisoners
considered most malleable and responsive—women. Indeed, so
flexible was this approach that in the early twentieth century no
limits were set for minimum and maximum terms for females.
However, most states soon limited the maximum sentence to the
term prescribed by law for the particular offense. Still, considerable
sentencing disparities were tolerated. Iowa law, for example, permits women convicted of a misdemeanor to be confined up to five
years, whereas a male can only be imprisoned for a maximum of
one year unless the statute defining the particular offense states
otherwise.[59] Usually, statutes permit a judge to exercise his discretion in sentencing male offenders in order to impose a shorter
maximum sentence than that prescribed by law.[60]

In theory, such sex-based differential sentencing should have
resulted in generally shorter terms for females if they were, as
expected, more susceptible to rehabilitation than males. In practice, just the reverse occurred. What went wrong? The disappointing
results stemmed primarily from the failure of the rehabilitative
programs to materialize, and without these the implicit pledge of
early redemption tendered by flexible sentencing policies could only
become and, in fact, did only become extended periods of unpro-
ductive incarceration. Well-meaning intentions to the contrary
notwithstanding, the net effect was to penalize women with longer
confinements, more restricted privileges, and fewer opportunities
for training. The legislative voice may have been the voice of Jacob,
but the correctional hand was the hand of Esau. Women were

excluded from training courses, work-release programs, educational opportunities, halfway houses, and furloughs. Furthermore, their conditions of confinement were considerably more rigid than those of males, for historical and operational reasons which have been reviewed in Chapter 8. The legal basis for this continued discrimination has only recently been questioned because the rights of female prisoners, like those of male prisoners, must await judicial interpretations more favorable to individual rights. At present, there is no established "right to treatment" [61] for adult prisoners of either sex. In consequence, women have not been able to invoke such a right to compel their acceptance into the few male programs extant. However, a new approach is on the horizon. The progressive blurring of the constitutional distinction between "rights" and "privileges" [62] probably will be interpreted to mean that even though a state may not be required to provide programs for prisoners, once it does, whole classes of prisoners may not be excluded from participation solely on the basis of their sex.

Common-Law Limitations

As the goal of distant equality beckons closer and as each advance emboldens successive efforts, it is natural to focus on those rights and privileges which still elude women's reach, but in retrospect much of what they have been seeking has fallen within their grasp. In many areas the legal status of American women has improved so greatly that it approximates that of men. In many ways the old common-law limitations imposed on married women—"contractual incapacity, loss of rights to manage, control, and receive the income from real property owned prior to marriage, the complete transference to the husband of all premarital personal property" [63] —have been nullified by statute. Furthermore, the early judicial resistance which greeted the initial legislative reforms has vanished to the point where courts now support its spirit as well as its letter.

In fact, the entire common-law notion that a married woman, simply by the act of marriage, ceded her rights, privileges, and obligations as an individual to her husband has been consistently rejected by recent rulings. In taking exception to the common-law presumption of coercion, the Appellate Department of the California Superior Court, in 1949, offered the following compelling reasons:

> We conclude that the reign of the thousand-year-old presumption has come to an end. In our society, where almost no bride promises to obey her husband, and where it is not accepted as the usual that a wife does what her husband wishes by way of yielding obedience to a dominant will, the basis for the presumption has disappeared. A presumption that has lost its reason must be confined to a museum; it has no place in the administration of justice.[64]

Fifteen years later, another American challenge to male superiority, that version endorsed by the common-law doctrine of interspousal-conspiracy immunity, was mounted in California.[65] In overruling this doctrine, which the original colonists had transplanted from England and grafted onto American law, the California Supreme Court ruled that "when a husband and wife conspire only between themselves, they cannot claim immunity from prosecution for conspiracy on the basis of their marital status." [66] It must be remembered that while the language of the conspiracy debate is *they,* under the aegis of the doctrine of presumed coercion it is *her* incapacity which supports the immunity defense.

At the federal level, this issue of the incapability of marital partners to conspire together had already been rejected by the Supreme Court in 1960. In *United States v. Dege,* Mr. Justice Frankfurter, writing for the majority, stated that the Court would not "be obfuscated by medieval views regarding the legal status of women and the common law's reflection of them." According to him, the former rule was based on one of two assumptions: "either that responsibility of husband and wife for joint participation in a criminal enterprise would make for marital disharmony, or that a wife must be presumed to act under the coercive influence of her husband and, therefore, cannot be a willing participant. . . . The former assumption is unnourished by sense: the latter implies a view of American womanhood offensive to the ethos of our society." [67] While this legally anachronistic and philosophically discredited identity of husband and wife has not yet appeared before the courts of many states, its repudiation by California,[68] Colorado,[69] Illinois,[70] and Texas,[71] in addition to the United States Supreme Court, foretells its abandonment in the near future.

Although single women might well envy the social position of their married sisters, as the foregoing suggests, the reverse was true with regard to their respective legal positions. Immune from the twin maladies of paternalism and chivalry visited on women by the marriage ceremony, single women throughout Anglo-American legal history have enjoyed considerably more freedom. Presently, both groups have been making significant progress in narrowing the legal gap between themselves and American men. The Nineteenth Amendment swept aside legal obstacles to women's rights to vote, denial of jury duty has been denounced as unconstitutional,[72] the enactment of the sex-blind principle of equal pay for equal work and the enforcement of sanctions against sex-discriminatory hiring practices by employers and unions alike have improved the lot of all women.

Such help has been spiritual as well as material. The common law, which combined common lore and uncommon error with regard to women, chatellized them legally, morally, and, worst of all, psychologically. Its demise is unmourned by women because it had for too long ceased to embody the living truth, and it has for too long been embalmed as a decaying repository of damaging falsehoods. Such enlightened revisions of the marital contract as that contained in the "community property system," now utilized by eight states,[73] do more than simply recognize the marriage as an equitable partnership. By establishing the right of married women to claim commonly held marital property, they affirm her claim to hold independent views. It is no accident of language that "property" and "propriety" and "proper" all derive from the same Latin root—*"proprius,"* to own—for those who own goods are much more likely to own a good name and themselves as well. Control of the material objects of a society are as important to a woman in becoming her own person as they are to a man.

Abortion

But deeper than personal possessions and more basic than the acquisition of power, the *sine qua non* of personal liberty is the ownership of one's body and the control of its function. The still controversial issue of abortion has evoked intense feelings of outrage and kindled a sense of moral indignation on both sides of the issue. The arguments against abortion have generally emphasized the sanctity of life and defended the "right to life" of the unborn fetus. Those in favor of abortion have taken into consideration the *quality* of the life which awaits the newborn—would congenital defects, for example, render that life incapable of achieving an adequate degree of human satisfaction? Until the sixties, debates about abortion all centered on the fetus. Then came a new issue, hitherto lightly regarded, which was to become of overriding legal importance—the woman's right to an abortion. It still remains an issue of consummate moral and legal complexity—for two reasons: it pits the rights of the unborn fetus against the rights of its mother-to-be; and, despite the biological fact that both a man and a woman are responsible for conception, pregnancy is solely the burden of the woman—though both create, only one must bear the child. It is difficult to find another situation in which the paths of equality and equity are so divergent.

Until recently, the laws restricting abortions were hardly different from those of early nineteenth-century England, in spite of medical advances and social shifts which have occurred since then. The following section of the California Penal Code dealing with criminal abortion is typical of preliberalization antiabortion statutes in forty-one other jurisdictions:

> Every person who provides, supplies, or administers to any woman, or procures any woman to take any medicine, drug, or substance, or uses or employs any instrument or other means whatever, with intent thereby to procure the miscarriage of such a woman, unless the same is necessary to preserve her life is punishable by imprisonment in the State prison not less than two nor more than five years.[74]

This, notwithstanding estimates that over a million illegal abortions a year were performed in the United States and that anywhere from five to ten thousand women per year died as a result.[75] Even in the face of possibilities of death, mutilation, and prosecution, large numbers of women were risking criminal abortions rather than carry through their pregnancies to term. Doubtless, criminal abortion has always been practiced to some extent, but probably not in modern times on the scale reached in the sixties just prior to its legalization. This upsurge owed its impetus to public tolerance of extramarital coitus, public acceptance of the goal of zero population growth, and women's reassessment of their traditional obligations to society, their families, and themselves. In this changing climate it became possible for women to question the necessity of "living with a mistake" or the propriety of permitting the natural landmarks of menarche and menopause to define their life's purpose. The moral acceptance and widespread usage of oral contraceptives permitted women to redefine their child-bearing years within a more restricted range based on psychological rather than biological imperatives. To be worthwhile as a woman no longer required frequent evidences of fertility. On the contrary, the respectably rotund maternal figure began to look a bit dowdy beside the svelte form of the career woman, and the once universally revered image of prolific motherhood was indicted in some ecologic quarters for population pollution. In such a setting, it became emotionally easier for many women to admit that they did not want children and tactically easier to take the step from oral contraception to surgical abortion. This change in social mores found expression in the 1973 *Doe v. Bolton* [76] United States Supreme Court decision. The

Court held that the decision with regard to abortion in the first trimester resided solely with the woman and her physician. Thereafter, the state might interpose itself to prevent abortions. Compliance with the decision, as monitored by the Association for the Study of Abortions,[77] has not been uniform. Many hospitals have refused to allow the procedure until they are taken to court. There the trend is to force compliance by the public but not the private hospitals. A resolution of the issue by the Supreme Court is in the offing.

Job Opportunity

This seesaw scenario between the social sector and the legal sector involving alterations in behavior patterns, changes in the law, resistance, judicial clarification, and reluctant compliance was also played out in the events surrounding the Equal Pay Act of 1963 and Title VII of the Civil Rights Act of 1964. At the beginning of the twentieth century, there were five million women workers constituting 18 per cent of the American labor force.[78] After two world wars had drawn them into previously all-male occupations, the figures rose to over thirty-three million, constituting 37 per cent of the total. Impelled by the weight of numbers, the American tradition for fairness, and in no small part by the necessity to improve the lot of minority workers, a groundswell of sentiment arose in support of the concept of equal pay for equal work. First at the state level and finally, after eighteen years of persistent dogged efforts at the federal level, the Equal Pay Act of 1963 was passed.[79] This, together with the Civil Rights Act one year later and similar state laws enacted in its wake, struck down the legal bulwarks of sex discrimination and opened the way for a new era of renegotiating male-female relationships in American society. That women were indeed equal to the occasion and eager to improve their position is attested to by the fact that the Equal Employment Opportunity Commission, the federal agency created by the Act to process complaints of employment discrimination, reported that during its first year of operations over one-third of its complaints involved charges of sex discrimination.[80]

Equal Rights Amendment

Buoyed by their legislative successes and encouraged by the favorable judicial climate, women soon strove for and achieved equality in the right to sue for loss of consortium, the right to equal sentencing,[81] the right to engage in the profession of bartending,[82] the right to equal access to liquor establishments,[83] and the right to equal educational opportunities,[84] among many others. This tide of civil libertarianism, which ran so high in the sixties, inundated every area of the law with demands for equality. Women are now, or will soon be, able to enter previously all-male public schools, while married women will have some independent right to choose their domicile, have unrestricted property rights, and be allowed to retain their maiden name in every transaction including voter registration.[85] But equality necessarily cuts both ways and will draw from as well as add to the reservoir of women's rights. In states which provide alimony, men will become eligible under the same conditions which now govern women. Federal Social Security benefits will be extended to widowers of covered women workers. And women will be subject to jury service and perhaps military service as well. Some truly chivalrous exceptions may remain and be extended to men if it is established that they protect rather than prohibit. For example, properly trained women may no longer be restricted from hazardous jobs, but a North Carolina statute still makes it unlawful to require women to work in chain gangs.[86] If this is sustained, it may also have to encompass men.

The whole issue of the chivalrous treatment of women by the legal system has been confused by the competing claims of male self-interest with those of humaneness, but regardless of the intent, it has been misguided. Most subversion of equality under the law, even if promoted in the interests of justice, tends to perpetuate inequity because it creates a multitiered system of unwritten laws relying heavily on personal considerations and undercutting the very qualities of credibility, consistency, and fairness upon which the structure of justice must ultimately rest. When we circumvent certain deplorable procedures for only one class of persons instead of challenging them in the interests of all persons, the long-term struggle for justice as well as equality under the law can only be delayed. And yet the resolution of the difficulties created by one-sided chivalry may not be less but more chivalry, evenly dispensed to both sexes and motivated by the same forbearance usually reserved only for women. Recent legal developments may be inclining in that direction. Already the pursuit of equal protection for women has had a beneficial side effect for the rights of men, and may in the diffuse light of history be seen as the major ethical contribution of the movement to American life. By forcing an acceptance that women are legally no less than men, it has fostered the principle that men are no less than women. If a practice is undesirable for one, it is undesirable for the other, for the humanity which unites them is more important than the gender which divides them.

The deferential treatment of females begins with the arresting officer, positioned as the link between society and the criminal-justice system, and extends throughout the process of arraignment, hearing, trial, and sentencing. Sometimes these differences serve the women well and sometimes ill, but they always serve the criminal-justice system poorly. In the ordinary course of events, police tend to handle the minor offenses of young girls unofficially in order to spare them the social stigma associated with court appearance. It is not considered prestigious and may even lower a patrolman's or male detective's status to arrest a woman because of his own and his peer's confusion of social norms with professional norms. Women police officials would not suffer from a similar confusion, but they are rarely employed in a general apprehension and detection capacity. Long experience has taught frustrated prosecutors the difficulties involved in achieving convictions for women who are free of previous social stigmatization. Even the pursuit of such a conviction can be a source of embarrassment because judges and juries share a similar disinclination to find women offenders guilty. In the United States, as well as in other countries, court-room chivalry has time and again resulted in decisions for acquittal which were more faithful to accepted attitudes than accepted evidence. Misplaced manners and miscarried justice are often fellow travelers which have misled the public trust because they have followed where they should have beckoned.

Such handling—or rather, mishandling—of women has resulted in mistaken estimates of the number of women offenders. Officially, women have been thought to be seven to twenty times less involved in criminal behavior than men.[87] But if we correct for overlooking, excusing, forgiving, reluctance to report, unwillingness to hold, and general leniency all along the line from original complaint to imprisonment, the figures are likely to be more comparable to those of men. It is in just such circular ways that social prejudices reinforce and perpetuate themselves.

One might expect from the foregoing that women who were the recipients of such legal munificence would be inclined to be grateful to the social institutions which at every step had been biased on their behalf. Quite the contrary was found to be true by investigators [88] who studied attitudes toward the law and legal institutions among prisoners of both sexes. In seventy-two out of seventy-three instances, female prisoners demonstrated a more negative attitude than their male counterparts. These surprising results may stem from the fact that legal laxity throughout the system spares the best women offenders from the worst fate—imprisonment. And so only the most intransigent, negativistic, poorly socialized, and generally hard-core cases are likely to draw prison sentences. But there is another and darker side to chivalry which may be reflected by the attitudes of these women inmates. The prejudicial permissiveness with which society cloaks and protects most kinds of female deviancy is bitterly stripped away from those whose deviancy crosses a critical threshold of social tolerance. To these few, the bitterness of betrayal of social role expectations is manifested in treatment more harsh than that accorded males guilty of similar offenses. Hell hath no fury, to paraphrase Shakespeare, like society scorned!

According to the President's Commission on Law Enforcement and Administration of Justice,[89] more than half of the girls but only one-fifth of the boys were referred to juvenile court in 1965 for conduct which would not have been considered criminal if committed by adults. The findings of other studies [90] have confirmed that females, especially girls, may be dealt with more severely by the courts and are more likely than males to be incarcerated, even though they tend to have less extensive prior records of delinquency. With girls, as with women, such statistics probably reflect the twin factors of prior screening and female role incompatibility. The male perception of female deviancy, which up to now has been the prevalent perception, appears incapable of contemplating a balanced middle ground. Like the girl with the curl, when she is good—that is, compliant to traditional female standards—her goodness thwarts retribution. When she is bad—that is, rebellious—she is unredemptively horrid.

The importance of this caricatured depiction of women has not been fully appreciated by the criminological literature for the very good reason that most of the scholars, poets, and novelists who have written about women have been men. And until very recently, the whole profession of psychiatry suffered from a similar blind spot. It is almost always the case that the arresting officer is a man, the prosecuting attorney is a man, the presiding judge is a man, up until the mid-twentieth century the juries were almost exclusively male, and the legislators who enact the laws of the land are still usually men. No matter how fair-minded these men may try to be, it is difficult to conceive of a setup more likely to dispense unfairness than such a male-dominated superstructure. This is an area that is changing as law schools have increased their enrollment of female law students from 3 per cent to an estimated 10 per cent.[91] However, it may still take a generation or two before women achieve a more balanced representation among the ranks of district attorneys, judges, legislators, and politicians. When they do, we can expect a more realistic and less romanticized or burlesqued limning of women in the writing and adjudication of our laws.

But the momentum of social change pulses to a tempo of its own which may be slackened by legislative inertia, but once sprung, can hardly be stayed from its course. It does not stand waiting for laws, and in the case of equal rights for women has remained consistently in advance of the law. Changing technology in the kitchen and the factory have changed the job description of housewife and worker. Labor-saving devices, together with changed social patterns, have permitted women to exercise extraparturient options and command salaries commensurate with those of men. Alterations in social status and financial status demanded revised modes from lawmakers for regulating duties within the family and responsibilities for support. The traditional criminal nonsupport and desertion statutes, based upon the "Küche, Kirche, and Kinder" theory of a woman's role, are becoming early victims of legislative reappraisal. Similar legislative reviews are re-examining the appropriateness of laws against seduction of women and statutory rape in the light of rampant sexual permissiveness.

But women have long since passed the point where piecemeal, issue-by-issue legislation is any longer considered a worthy goal. The extent of their progress may be measured not only by what they have acquired but by what they are daring to demand. There have been many gains; there have also been many setbacks. The lesson seemed clear. In regard to sex discrimination, the judiciary is often unwilling to break ground in areas where legislators fear to tread, and the direction of future efforts would be more toward the Congress than the courts. In view of the seesaw progression of the Fourteenth Amendment strategy, the surest and fastest route to equality would seem to be passage of the Equal Rights Amendment. This plan is not entirely new, because proposals of this kind have been introduced in each Congress since 1923.[92] What is different about the present effort is that it will most likely be ratified this time and, if not, certainly in the near future. The Twenty-seventh Amendment was passed by Congress March 22, 1972:

Section 1.   Equality of rights under the law shall not be denied or abridged by the United States or by any State on account of sex.

Section 2.   The Congress shall have the power to enforce, by appropriate legislation, the provisions of this article.

Section 3.   This amendment shall take effect two years after the date of ratification.

The states have until March 22, 1979, to ratify it. After ratification, the state legislatures will have two years to change or eliminate all statutes found to conflict with the new amendment.

The laws which will come under the most careful scrutiny are those which have in the past been considered chivalrous but in the present are construed as sexist. They include the laws related to obscenity, slander, seduction, support, assault and battery, abduction, adultery, prostitution, and pandering, to mention only a few. When sex-based discrimination is found to exist, the legislatures will have to decide between rewriting the laws so that they apply equally or striking them completely from the books. For example, the present statutes dealing with seduction are based on the premise that women are emotionally more fragile and naïve than men and thus their "honor" (as sexual abstinence used to be quaintly characterized) must be protected by the state. Not only is "honor" now a broader concept and chastity less of a prize than previously, but also the fact that sexual relations have occurred no longer justifies the inference that the man has done something to the woman. To be compatible with the Equal Rights Amendment, seduction statutes will either have to be amended to extend protection against seduction to men or, in recognition of the difficulties associated with fixing responsibility between two consenting adults, repealed altogether. In the philosophic climate of the present day, the time-honored institution of chivalry will either be completely dead or be alive for the nourishment of both sexes.

As the most comprehensive and decisive statement on equality, the Twenty-seventh Amendment is expected to affect the following areas of American life:

1. *Protective Labor Laws:* Those laws which discriminate against women workers would be voided while those which protect women would be extended to benefit men as well.

2. *Alimony:* Men would be eligible under the same conditions that govern women. However, since alimony is only awarded in a small percentage of divorce cases and since in those instances a woman's capacity for self-support is considered, the effect of this extension will be minimal.

3. *Government Pensions:* Women in the same job categories as men will have to receive the same retirement benefits. Currently, those of women are frequently smaller.

4. *Social Security:* Not only will men and women be entitled to the same benefits at the same age, but widowers will also be eligible for spouses' benefits just as widows are now.

5. *Military Benefits:* Contrary to present policy, women veterans will receive the same benefits under the G.I. Bill as men. Should the present voluntary-enlistment policy for the armed forces be abandoned and the draft reinstituted, women would be eligible for military conscription. However, Congress would probably exempt mothers.

6. *Miscellaneous:* Laws governing rape will not be abolished nor, in deference to the citizen's right to privacy, will there be any change in the separation of the sexes in military barracks, prisons, and public restrooms.

Ratification of the Equal Rights Amendment before the deadline of March 22, 1979, is almost certain. It has been endorsed by the President of the United States, both the Democratic and Republican parties, organized labor, and a broad spectrum of religious and civic groups. In addition, it is being shepherded through state legislatures by a sophisticated, well-organized campaign conducted by the National Women's Party, the National Organization for Women (NOW), the National Federation of Business and Professional Women's Clubs, and the League of Women Voters.

Support for this from the male electorate may also be expected because it would be shortsighted to conclude that the successful struggle for equality would benefit only women. At this point in history it must be granted that women would realize the greater gains because they are currently the more disadvantaged group. But discrimination has an uncomfortable habit of shifting allegiances, and there is no assurance that future inequities would not fall on groups presently favored. Therefore, the support for abolition of sex-discriminatory laws which has come from men has stemmed as much from enlightened self-interest as adherence to altruistic principles. Perhaps at root they are the same. It could be argued that, like proverbial honesty, fairness in law is the best policy, because in the long run it is the only policy which can sustain itself.

Although the political currents of women's rights and civil rights have originated from demographically different segments of the American mainstream, they have been historically confluent because of the recognition, on the part of women, at least, that their goals are identical. What is wrong with sex-based discriminatory laws is not simply that they handicap women but that they subvert the principles of equality and, therefore, law itself. From this larger perspective, it is irrelevant to point out (though it is true) that some laws favor women over men. Compensatory favoritism is innately incommensurate with the principles of justice.

In the final analysis, the march of political organizations, legislative passage, and even ratification itself is dwarfed and diminished beside the colossal social transformations which have already negotiated the American culture landscape. In the ordinary course of events, social and legal norms are considered happily engaged when the idea whose time has come is enacted into the law whose obedience is assured. Such a time has already come for women's rights—and become passé, superseded by vocational, social, and psychological events which overshadow the limited efforts of law to alter or restrict. Gradually at first, but with increasing intensity, women have been enjoying a common-law dalliance with equality which statutory law may belatedly sanction but will not dare sever. Women have learned their lessons slowly, but they have learned them well. In Antisthenes' fable of the Council of the Beasts, when the hares began clamoring for equality, the lion's tart reply was, "Where are your claws and teeth?" To women's detractors as well as to women's supporters, the claws and teeth are everywhere in evidence. The political atmosphere is charged with the electric excitement of restored confidence and anticipation. A quiet revolution has been transforming despair to hope and grief to anger. Almost unheralded, almost unheeded, almost without honor, this quiet revolution has been stirring in the kitchens and bedrooms and nurseries of America. In the depths of long-silent women, stifled aspirations have been groping subliminally toward awareness and inchoate emotions struggling for expression. The long-suffering are no longer willing to suffer; the long-winded are no longer content to sigh in the breeze; for the imminence of equality draws closer, and no law can block its way.

Liberation and Beyond

But I have promises to keep,
And miles to go before I sleep.

—Robert Frost
"Stopping by Woods
on a Snowy Evening"

For all its considerable accomplishments, the chief effects of the women's liberation movement are still potential, still unrealized, and even now an unfulfilled promise. But the increasing flow of traffic in both directions across the sex-role barriers gives evidence that fulfillment is imminent. The goal of spanning the full spectrum of male activities has become for women their social manifest destiny.

The historical roots of this particular liberation are intertwined with the American allegiance to individual rights proclaimed by the Declaration of Independence in 1776, rededicated by the Civil War in 1865, and extended by the civil-rights movement of the 1950s and 1960s. These successive and cumulative waves established the principle of equality on which the women's liberation movement built, but it was finally the force of their vocational, political, and social militancy which established their determination to be accepted as equals. The *Sturm und Drang* of the 1960s, with its "freedom riders," sit-ins, campus unrest, and national disillusionment, infected women with the virulent strain of civil disobedience which was encouraging other minority groups—intellectuals, blacks, and juveniles—to reassess their traditional roles. In addition, other un-

related events were conspiring to make women particularly susceptible to the forces of social change. A post–World War II population explosion had discredited the once sacrosanct status of motherhood. Technology altered the necessity and social and political
developments challenged the desirability of a total female commitment to homemaking. Freed by medical advances from the burden
of unwanted pregnancies, encouraged by opportunities, and goaded
by economic obligations, women in droves left their kitchens and
carriages to take their chances in the wide world. They became
soldiers, sailors, sky marshals, stevedores, doctors, lawyers, and
executives. From such advantageous platforms many of them also
launched careers in burglary, larceny, auto theft, forgery, counterfeiting, and embezzling. There were few activities, criminal or noncriminal, which they did not embrace with avid interest and ample
ability.

Juvenile girls followed their elders into deviancy in some areas
and led them in others. All-girl gangs made their debut in New
York City while the "granny bashers" were terrorizing parts of
London with razor blades and knives. In prostitution, miniskirted
teeny-hookers paraded with bored housewives and unemployed
actresses on downtown streets. They peddled their prurient pubescence on public thoroughfares already abandoned by the professionals who had moved on to posh rooms in luxurious hotels. The
predicament of the juvenile girls was particularly distressing because the normal turmoil of adolescence could no longer find safe
refuge in traditional female social roles.

Thus the middle third of the twentieth century witnessed the
rise and fall of women in ways hardly imaginable to their Victorian
ancestors. It was the lack of imagination concerning women's true
abilities and the erroneous myths supporting their infirmities that
kept women so long in vassal. Even women believed in their own
frailty because for centuries it had been given to them on the best
authority: Aristotle, Hippocrates, Homer, Tennyson, even Freud
admonished them to huddle safely behind the barriers which men
had erected for their protection. But false confessions and con-

trived disabilities depend on the compliance of the victim, and by the mid–twentieth century the victims were no longer willing to be penalized for an offense of which they were innocent. Embryologists, anthropologists, behavioral scientists, and eventually politicians were discovering that women were inherently equal to, if not exactly the equal of, men. Much of the hallowed erudition and established thinking about women through the ages was a scientific hoax if not a pernicious male conspiracy designed to indenture women to the lifelong servitude of men. Women were awakening to the fact that they were the human race's greatest unused resource.

But their abilities would certainly have remained latent and largely useless without the judicial, legislative, and social changes which brought them to realization. In landmark decisions stretching from Mr. Justice Bradley's denial of a license for a woman to practice law in 1872 to Mr. Justice Fortas's extension of equal treatment in 1968, the courts have evolved a sex-blind philosophy of justice. Hand in hand with this have gone legislative changes which have transformed the position of women from that of chattel, in which they were held by feudal practice and common law, to that of partners, with almost equal rights and responsibilities. The vocational and educational opportunities which accompanied these shifts, together with the financial independence they made possible, altered the mental set which was the final barrier to liberation. Full integration awaits passage of the Equal Rights Amendment, but the compelling testimony of broken barriers confirms a trend whose successful completion is a foregone conclusion. There is Angela Davis leading a new leftist alliance in America, there is Françoise Giroud heading a new cabinet department as State Secretary for *La Condition Féminine* in France, there are law-school courses devoted to law and sex bias, there are girls in woodshops, boys in home economics, girls who want to be doctors, and boys who want to be nurses. There are even women enrolled in a federal service academy. But what is a promise in one context can be a threat in another. There is the British millionaire's daughter convicted of stealing art for the Irish Republican Army, the American heiress kidnap-victim-turned-kidnaper, the thirteen-year-old girl who robbed a Greenwich Village bank of over two thousand dollars; the skyrocketing increase in the rate at which women steal cars, burglarize stores, forge checks, embezzle funds, run away from their husbands, and engage in prostitution. While they have demonstrated ability to drive tractor trailers, climb telephone poles, lay bricks, carry mail, perform surgery, defend clients, and judge cases, they have also shown no greater potential than males to remain law-abiding.

The extent to which women have become comfortable with themselves and confident enough to defend their special interests is illustrated by the inauguration of the First National Hookers Convention held in the Glide Memorial Methodist Church in June 1974. It was sponsored by an organization of prostitutes calling themselves COYOTE, an acronym for Call Off Your Old Tired Ethics. Masks were supplied at the registration desk but few were worn, and official convention T-shirts proclaimed "1974, Year of the Whore." The aim of the seventy-five-hundred-member organization is to make prostitution a respectable service, to decriminalize it, and to ensure for women the same *de facto* freedom to solicit as that enjoyed by men. While of no special significance in itself, the fact that such a gathering could occur at all and that it received press coverage rather than indictments is convincing evidence of how times have changed.

But such indicators are merely the litmus test of potential future change and should not be confused with the transformation itself. It is not the high jinks of such affairs nor the histrionics of burning bras, nor even the more earnest litigious efforts to desegregate all-male establishments which will mark this era for posterity. Nor is it in the factories or universities or legislatures that the most consequential events are occurring. The Rubicons which women must cross, the sex barriers which they must breach, are ultimately those that exist in their own minds. And that is why the task, though begun, is only half finished. And that is why for the present generation of women, equality will remain more social than psychological.

Like a distant planet, it has moved within their ken but will forever elude their grasp. It will remain for another generation of women, a generation who, as girls, will think it perfectly natural to become carpenters or architects or steeplejacks or senators, a generation who will dream of running away from home to join the circus or growing up to become desperados or gunslingers. This is the generation which will have achieved not the only equality but that equality from which all others issue. It is the equalization which occurs in the hopes and aspirations, perceptions and cognitions of girls and boys in their maturing awareness of each other or themselves that will ultimately fulfill the promise of liberation. Andrew Fletcher, an eighteenth-century Scottish patriot, declared that if a man could write the ballads of a nation it would not matter who made its laws. The lyrics of those ballads are printed large on the front pages of newspapers across the nation every day, they are belted out at teen-age concerts, and their sounds reverberate through the echo chambers of the pop culture. The message is changing our cultural medium to accommodate to the new woman —who is really the old original one newly discovered.

The forces behind equal employment opportunity, women's liberation movements, and even public-health problems like lung cancer and heart disease have been causing and reflecting a steady erosion of the social and psychological differences which have traditionally separated men and women. It would be natural to expect parallel developments in female criminality. The increasing similarity of social attitudes toward and activities by both men and women in areas as diverse as politics, liquor consumption, smoking habits, industry, choice of profession, and sexual proclivities will eventually enable us to delineate how the biological (as distinct from the cultural) differences between the sexes will be manifested. Until there is complete social equality it will not be possible to tell with any certainty which of the demonstrated differences between the sexes are biological and which cultural. But what is clear is that as the position of women approximates the position of men, so does the frequency and type of their criminal activity. It would, therefore, seem justified to predict that if present social trends continue women will be sharing with men not only ulcers, coronaries, hypertension, and lung cancer (until recently considered almost exclusively masculine diseases) but will also compete increasingly in such traditionally male criminal activities as crimes against the person, more aggressive property offenses, and especially white-collar crime. As women invade the business world, there is no reason to expect them to be any more honest than men, and to the extent that crime is related to motivation and opportunity, the incidence of such white-collar offenses as embezzlement and fraud should achieve par with men. It is not only in men's private clubs and taverns that males are being forced to make way for females. The separate lady's entrance at the tavern may remain separate but ladies are demanding more and more room at the bar.

What, then, are the changes that we can anticipate in the criminal-justice system? First, as women gain greater equality with men, the male-dominated judicial process will likely treat them with less deference and impose more stringent sanctions; the condition of being a woman in a man's world will carry less protection. The other aspect of increasing equality will manifest itself in the larger number of women police officers, magistrates, prosecutors, and judges. What effect the elimination of the sexual differences between the judge and the judged will have among women cannot be certain, but if the experience in the present system with men judging men has any transfer value we would expect decisions to be based more on the facts of a case and less on emotional considerations. While it is true that some of what is considered female crime—e.g., prostitution—will probably be eliminated by fiat, what remains may be prosecuted with more rigor and less compassion.

Although women have inhabited the earth as long as men, benign and despotic paternalisms have made her something of a stranger to herself. She is in consequence almost an extraterrestrial visitor in her native habitat and it will be a while before she stakes out her claims in her new territory. But like rivers diverted by dams and dikes from their original beds, the flood tide of liberation has carried them over the artificial banks and returned them to their ancient courses. New opportunities have linked up with old abilities and women are no longer content to be men's symbols of femininity or virtue or sexuality. They want to be themselves, whatever that is or can become. For the present they are passing through a stage in which they are imitating men's roles because identification is the most expedient way to learn. But it is unlikely that they will be content to become smaller, weaker, softer men. There is evidence that women will fashion from their uniqueness psychosocial creations sufficiently attractive to induce men to emulate them—socially and antisocially. The best and the worst are still to come and the shape of the final configuration is still amorphous. But it is as certain as sunrise that after a long and frustrating historical sojourn, women have finally come home to themselves and they are home to stay.

References

Chapter 1. Changing Patterns

1. I. Devore, "Mother-Infant Relations in Free-Ranging Baboons," in *Maternal Behavior in Mammals,* ed. H. L. Rheingold (New York: John Wiley & Sons, 1965).
2. I. Devore, "Male Dominance and Mating Behavior in Baboons," in *Sex and Behavior,* ed. F. A. Beach (New York: John Wiley & Sons, 1965).
3. For a more explicit theoretical discussion of cultural goals and institutionalized means see, Robert K. Merton, *Social Theory and Social Structure* (New York: The Free Press, 1967 [originally published in 1949]), p. 146.
4. Reproduced from "The Economic Role of Women," in *The Economic Report of the President, 1973,* United States Department of Labor (Washington, D.C.: U.S. Government Printing Office, 1973).
5. For example, see Mirra Komarovsky, "Cultural Contradictions and Sex Roles: The Masculine Case," *American Journal of Sociology,* January 1973, 78:873–84. Also, Marianne A. Ferber and Jane W. Loeb, "Performance, Awards, and Perceptions of Sex Discrimination Among Male and Female Faculty," *American Journal of Sociology,* January 1973, 78:995–1002; and Talcott Parsons and R. F. Bales, *Family, Socialization and Interaction Processes* (New York: The Free Press, 1955), p. 158.
6. *American Journal of Sociology,* January 1973, Vol. 78.
7. Nicholas Gage, *The Mafia Is Not an Equal Opportunity Employer* (New York: McGraw-Hill, 1971), p. 95.
8. Crime in the United States, Uniform Crime Reports, United States Department of Justice (Washington, D.C.: U.S. Government Printing Office, 1972), p. 124.
9. For a critique of the Uniform Crime Reports, see Marvin E. Wolfgang, "Uniform Crime Report: A Critical Appraisal," *University of Pennsylvania Law Review,* April 1963, III:708–738.
10. Uniform Crime Reports, *op. cit.,* p. 124.
11. Marvin E. Wolfgang, *Patterns in Criminal Homicide* (New York: John

Wiley & Sons, 1958), Chapter 11. For a further discussion of the victim/offender relationship, see David Ward, Maurice Jackson, and Renee Ward, "Crimes of Violence by Women," in *Crimes of Violence*, eds. Donald Mulvihill, *et al.* (Washington, D.C.: U.S. Government Printing Office, 1969).

12. Edwin H. Sutherland and Donald R. Cressey, *Principles of Criminology* (Philadelphia: J. B. Lippincott Co., 1966 [originally published 1924]), p. 139.

13. *Ibid.*, p. 139. See also, H. vonHentig, "The Criminality of the Colored Woman," *University of Colorado Studies*, Series C. I. No. 3 (1942). For a discussion of the black female role in society, see, for instance, Lee Rainwater, "Crucible of Identity: the Negro Lower Class Family," *Daedalus*, Winter 1966, 95:172–216; also, Elliott Liebow, *Tally's Corner* (Boston: Little, Brown and Co., 1966).

14. Uniform Crime Reports, *op. cit.*, p. 124.

15. *Ibid.*, p. 139.

16. *Ibid.*, p. 159.

17. "Ten Most Wanted Fugitives" Program, United States Department of Justice, Federal Bureau of Investigation, Washington, D.C., December 28, 1968.

18. Among them: Bernardine Rae Dohrn, Katherine Ann Power, Susan Edith Saxe, Angela Yvonne Davis.

19. John Pascal and Francine Pascal, *The Strange Case of Patty Hearst* (New York: The New American Library, 1974), p. 92.

20. *The New York Times*, May 9, 1972.

21. *Girl Offenders Aged 17 to 20 Years*, a Home Office Research Unit Report (London: Her Majesty's Stationery Office, 1972), p. 3.

22. *Time*, October 16, 1972. In London, girl gangs are known as "bovver" (cockney for "bother," which means "fight") birds.

23. Albert Schrut, M.D., and Toni Michels, "Adolescent Girls Who Attempt Suicide—Comments on Treatment," *American Journal of Psychotherapy*, 1969, 23:243–51.

24. Walter R. Gove and Jeanette F. Tudor, "Adolescent Sex Roles and Mental Illness," *American Journal of Sociology*, January 1973, 78:812–35.

25. For a history of the National Organization for Women, see Jo Freeman, "The Origins of the Women's Liberation Movement," *American Journal of Sociology*, January 1973, 78:792–811.

26. Herbert M. Adler, M.D., and Van Buren O. Hammett, M.D., "Crisis, Conversion, and Cult Formation: An Examination of a Common Psychosocial Sequence," *American Journal of Psychiatry*, August 1973, 138:861–64; and Herbert M. Adler, M.D., and Van Buren O. Hammett, M.D., "The Doctor-Patient Relationship Revisited," *Annals of Internal Medicine*, April 1973, 78:595–98.

27. Figures calculated from data of Uniform Crime Reports, *op. cit.*, p. 124.

28. For a comprehensive discussion of shoplifting, see Mary Owen Cameron, *The Booster and the Snitch* (New York: The Free Press, 1964). See also, T. C. N. Gibbens and Joyce Prince, *Shoplifting* (London: The Institute for the Study and Treatment of Delinquency), 1962.

Chapter 2. Female Passivity:
Genetic Fact or Cultural Myth?

1. Caesar Lombroso, *The Female Offender* (New York: The Wisdom Library, 1958 [originally published in 1899]), pp. 2–3.

2. Edith R. Spaulding, "The Results of Mental and Physical Examinations of Four Hundred Women Offenders—with Particular Reference to Their Treatment During Commitment," *Journal of the American Institute of Criminal Law and Criminology*, 1914–15, V:704–717; V. V. Anderson, "The Immoral Woman as Seen in Court," *Journal of the American Institute of Criminal Law and Criminology*, 1917–18, VIII:902–910; Albert S. B. Guibord, "Physical States of Criminal Women," *Journal of the American Institute of Criminal Law and Criminology*, 1917–18, VIII:82–95.

3. Sheldon and Eleanor T. Glueck, *Five Hundred Delinquent Women* (New York: Alfred A. Knopf), 1934; and Otto Pollack, *The Criminality of Women* (Philadelphia: The University of Pennsylvania Press, 1950).

4. Margaret Mead, *Male and Female* (New York: Dell Publishing Co., 1972 [originally published in 1949]), p. 168.

5. These conclusions are discussed extensively in the psychoanalytic literature. See, for example, Sigmund Freud, *Female Sexuality*, Collected Papers, Vol. V (London: Hogarth, 1950 [originally published in 1931]).

6. See, for example, Judd Marmor, "Changing Patterns of Femininity: Psychoanalytic Implications," in Salo Rosenbaum and Ian Alger (eds.), *The Marriage Relationship* (New York: Basic Books, 1968), Chapter 3. See also, Naomi Weisstein, " 'Kinder, Kuche, Kirche' as Scientific Law: Psychology Constructs the Female," in Robin Morgan (ed.), *Sisterhood Is Powerful* (New York: Random House, 1970), pp. 205–220.

7. For example, Freud, in his early writings (1905), appeared to equate femininity and passivity, masculinity and activity. See, Sigmund Freud, "Three Contributions for the Theory of Sex," in *Basic Writings of Sigmund Freud*, ed. A. A. Brill (New York: Modern Library, 1938 [originally published in 1905]).

8. For descriptions of embryonic development see: Robert W. Gay, "Organizing Effect of Androgen on the Behavior of Rhesus Monkeys," in *Endocrinology and Human Behavior*, ed. Richard P. Michael (London: Oxford

University Press, 1968), pp. 12–31. See also, J. Money, "Psychosexual Differentiation," in *Sex Research: New Developments,* ed. J. Money (New York: Holt, Rinehart & Winston, 1965); R. E. Whalen, "Differentiation of the Neural Mechanisms Which Control Gonadotropin Secretion and Sexual Behavior," in *Perspectives in Reproduction and Sexual Behavior,* ed. Milton Diamond (Bloomington, Ind.: Indiana University Press, 1968); and Milton Diamond, "Genetic-Endocrin Interactions and Human Psychosexuality," *ibid.,* pp. 417–43.

9. Julia A. Sherman, *On the Psychology of Women* (Springfield, Ill.: Charles C. Thomas, 1973), p. 3.

10. See, B. Childs, "Genetic Origins of Some Sex Differences Among Human Beings," *Pediatrics,* 1965, 35:798–812.

11. B. Childs, *ibid.* Also, Amram Scheinfeld, *Women and Men* (New York: Harcourt Brace, 1944).

12. J. M. Tanner, *Growth at Adolescence* (second ed., Springfield, Ill.: Charles C. Thomas, 1962).

13. Simone de Beauvoir, *The Second Sex* (New York: Alfred A. Knopf, Inc., 1953), p. 28.

14. For hand differences see Tanner, *op. cit.,* pp. 40–42.

15. Sherman, *op. cit.,* p. 9.

16. L. W. Sontag, "Physiological Factors and Personality," *Child Development,* 1947, 18:185–89.

17. Scheinfeld, *op. cit.*

18. Anne Anastasi, *Differential Psychology* (New York: Macmillan, 1949).

19. See, N. W. Ellis and S. L. Last, "Analysis of the Normal Electroencephalograms of Normal Children," *Monograph of the Society for Research in Child Development,* 9, No. 3; and S. M. Smith, "Discrimination Between Electroencephalograph Recordings of Normal Females and Normal Males," *Annals of Eugenics,* 18:344–50.

20. David A. Hamburg and Donald T. Lunde, "Sex Hormones in the Development of Sex Differences," in *The Development of Sex Differences,* ed. Eleanor E. Maccoby (Stanford, Cal.: Stanford University Press, 1966).

21. R. Dorfman and F. Ungar, *Metabolism of Steroid Hormones* (New York: Academic Press, 1965).

22. de Beauvoir, *op. cit.,* p. 28.

23. For a comprehensive analysis of learned and innate aspects of aggression, see, Marvin E. Wolfgang and Franco Ferracuti, *The Subculture of Violence* (London: Tavistock Publications, 1967), pp. 192–201.

24. Dorthea McCarthy, "Language Development of the Preschool Child," in *Child Behavior and Development,* eds. R. G. Barker, J. S. Kounin, and R. F. Wright (New York: McGraw-Hill, 1943).

25. Leona E. Tyler, *The Psychology of Human Differences* (New York: Appleton-Century-Crofts, 1965).

26. Roberta M. Oetzel, Annotated Bibliography in *The Development of Sex Differences,* ed. Eleanor E. Maccoby (Stanford, Cal.: Stanford University Press, 1966).

27. Arden N. Frandsen and James R. Holder, "Spatial Visualization in Solving Complex Verbal Problems," *Journal of Psychology,* 73:229–33.

28. For finger differences see Tanner, *op. cit.,* pp. 40–42.

29. Anthony Barnett, *The Human Species* (Middlesex, England: Penguin Books, 1961), p. 189.

30. I. Werdelin, *Geometrical Ability and the Space Factors in Boys and Girls* (Lund, Sweden: University of Lund, 1961).

31. Sherman, *op. cit.,* p. 14.

32. Jerome Kagan, "Acquisition and Significance of Sex Typing and Sex Role Identity," in *Review of Child Development Research,* eds. M. L. Hoffman and Lois W. Hoffman (New York: Russell Sage Foundation, 1964), pp. 137–67. Also, Tyler, *op. cit.*

33. Sherman, *op. cit.,* p. 14.

34. Eleanor E. Maccoby, "Sex Differences in Intellectual Functioning," in *The Development of Sex Differences,* ed. Eleanor E. Maccoby (Stanford, Cal.: Stanford University Press, 1966).

35. Sherman, *op. cit.,* p. 14.

36. M. Lewis, J. Kagan, and J. Kalafat, "Patterns of Fixation in the Young Infant," *Child Development,* 37:331–41.

37. E. M. Bennett and L. R. Cohen, "Men and Women: Personality Patterns and Contrasts," *Genetic Psychology Monographs,* 1959, 59:101–55.

38. *Ibid.*

39. *Ibid.*

40. Alfred C. Kinsey, Wardell B. Pomeroy, Clyde E. Martin, and Paul H. Gebhard, *Sexual Behavior in the Human Female* (New York: Pocket Books, 1965).

41. Alexander Pope, Moral Essays, Epistle II, To Mrs. M. Blount, 270.

42. Sigmund Freud, quoted by Dr. Ernest Jones, *The Life and Works of Sigmund Freud,* London: The Hogarth Press, 1957.

43. Gregory Bateson, *et al.,* "Toward a Theory of Schizophrenia," *Behavioral Science,* 1956, 1:251.

44. For a discussion of the formulation of sex-role differences, see the chapter on "The Formative Years: Childhood," in de Beauvoir, *op. cit.,* pp. 249–306. Also, Eleanor E. Maccoby, "Role Taking in Childhood and its Consequences for Social Learning," *Child Development,* June 1959, 30:239–52; and Eleanor

E. Maccoby, "The Taking of Adult Roles in Middle Childhood," *Journal of Abnormal and Social Psychology,* November 1961, 63:439–503.

45. For an elaborate discussion of the stigmatized, see Erving Goffman, *Stigma* (Englewood Cliffs, N.J.: Prentice-Hall, 1963).

46. Robert R. Sears, Eleanor E. Maccoby, and Harry Levin, *Patterns of Child Rearing* (Evanston, Ill.: Row, Peterson and Co., 1957), pp. 401–407. Also, de Beauvoir, *op. cit.,* pp. 249–306.

47. Jerome Kagan, "The Child's Sex Role Classification of School Objects," *Child Development,* 1964, 35:1051–56.

48. Sears, Maccoby, and Levin, *op. cit.,* pp. 401–407, and de Beauvoir, *op. cit.,* pp. 249–306.

49. There is a plethora of literature on identification. The term has been used in different ways by various authors. For instance, the psychoanalytic interpretation can be found in Sigmund Freud, *Group Psychology and the Analysis of the Ego* (New York: Liveright, 1951); Justin Aronfreed ("The Concept of Internalization" in *Handbook of Socialization Theory and Research,* ed. D. A. Goslin [Chicago: Rand McNally, 1969], pp. 263–324) explains the internalization of a cognitive template; Albert Bandura ("Social-Learning Theory of Identificatory Processes" in Goslin, *op. cit.,* pp. 213–62, and "Social Learning Through Imitation," in *Nebraska Symposium on Motivation* [Lincoln: University of Nebraska Press], pp. 211–69) stresses observational learning; and Talcott Parsons and Robert F. Bales (*Family Socialization and Interaction Process* [Glencoe, Ill.: The Free Press, 1955]) relate internalization to the structure of the nuclear family. For a recent publication containing several articles with reviews and bibliographies, see Goslin, *op. cit.*

50. See Sears, Maccoby, and Levin, *op. cit.,* pp. 405–6 and de Beauvoir, *op. cit.,* pp. 249–306.

51. Jerome Kagan and H. A. Moss, *Birth to Maturity* (New York: John Wiley & Sons, 1962).

52. Orville G. Brim, Jr., "Family Structure and Sex Role Learning by Children: A Further Analysis of Helen Koch's Data," *Sociometry,* September 1958, 21:343–64.

53. Parsons and Bales, *op. cit.,* p. 23.

54. de Beauvoir, *op. cit.,* p. 249.

55. M. R. Rosenzweig and E. A. Bennett, "Effects of Differential Environments on Brain Weights and Enzyme Activities in Gerbils, Rats and Mice," *Developmental Psychology,* 1969, 2:87.

56. Jane Goodall and The World of Animal Behavior: The Wild Dogs of Africa, documentary film produced by Metromedia Producers Corp., 1974.

57. See, Jean-Claude Ruwet, *Introduction to Ethology* (New York: International Universities Press, 1972), p. 192; David A. Hamburg, "Aggressive Behavior

of Chimpanzees and Baboons in Natural Habitats," *Journal of Psychiatric Research,* 1971, 8:385–98; Jane van Lawick Goodall, "The Behavior of Chimpanzees in Their Natural Habitat," *The American Journal of Psychiatry,* January 1973, 130:1–12.

58. L. H. Matthews, "Visual Stimulation and Ovulation in Pigeons," *Proceedings Soc Lond* (Biol), 1939, 12:557–61.

59. Konrad Lorenz, "Companionship in Bird Life," in *Instinctive Behavior,* ed. Claire H. Schiller (New York: International Universities Press, 1957).

60. Jan van Lawick-Goodall, "The Behavior of Chimpanzees in Their Natural Habitat," *The American Journal of Psychiatry,* January 1973, 130:1–12.

61. E. A. Beeman, "The Effect of Male Hormones on Aggressive Behavior in Mice," *Physiological Zoology,* 1947, 20:373–405; R. R. Hutchinson, R. E. Ulrich, and N. H. Azren, "Effects of Age and Related Factors on the Pain-Aggression Reaction," *Journal of Comparative Physiological Psychology,* 1965, 59:365–69.

62. Hamburg and Lunde, *op. cit.*

63. Jane van Lawick Goodall, *In the Shadow of Man* (Boston: Houghton Mifflin Co., 1971).

64. J. H. Reynierse, "Submissive Postures During Shock," *Animal Behavior,* 1971, 19:102–107.

65. Margaret Mead, *Sex and Temperament in Three Primitive Societies* (New York: William Morrow & Co., 1963 [originally published in 1935]), p. XIV.

66. *100 Great Kings, Queens and Rulers of the World,* ed. John Cunning (New York: Taplinger Publishing Co., 1968), p. 442.

67. Pollak, *op. cit.,* pp. 62–66.

68. *Ibid.*

69. For a discussion of these envies and their relationship to puberty behavior, see, Gerhard O. W. Mueller, *Delinquency and Puberty: Examination of a Juvenile Delinquency Fad* (CLEAR Center, New York University, 1971), pp. 102–109. See also, Judd Marmor, "Changing Patterns of Femininity and Masculinity" in *Woman in a Man-Made World,* eds. Nona Glazer-Malbin and Helen Youngelson Waehrer (Chicago: Rand McNally, 1972), pp. 68–73; and Bruno Bettelheim, *Symbolic Wounds: Puberty Rites and the Envious Male* (London: Thames and Hudson, 1955).

70. Catherine Milton, *Women in Policing* (Washington, D.C.: The Police Foundation, 1972).

71. For the fate of those women who have been unable to find outlets for their assertive strivings see the interpretation of Jacob Chwast, "Socio-Psychological Aspects," in "Special Problems in Treating Female Offenders," *International Journal of Offender Therapy,* 1971, 15:24–27.

72. For a discussion of traditional female roles and their relationship to tradi-

tional female crimes, see Pollak, *op. cit.;* also, Ann D. Smith, *Women in Prison: A Study of Penal Methods* (London: Stevens, 1962), Chapter 2. For a discussion of traditional juvenile offenses see, Albert J. Reiss, "Sex Offenses: The Marginal Status of the Adolescent," *Law and Contemporary Problems,* Spring 1960, XXV:309–333; see also, Albert K. Cohen and James F. Short, Jr., "Research in Delinquent Subcultures," *Journal of Social Issues,* 1958, XIV:20–37; Don C. Gibbons, *Delinquent Behavior* (Englewood Cliffs, N.J.: Prentice-Hall, 1970); Gordon H. Barker and William T. Adams, "Comparison of the Delinquency of Boys and Girls," *Journal of Criminal Law, Criminology and Police Science,* December 1962, 53:471–72; and Ruth R. Morris, "Female Delinquency and Relational Problems," *Social Forces,* 1964, 43:82–89.

73. Lionel Tiger and Robin Fox, *The Imperial Animal* (New York: Dell Publishing Co., 1971), p. 5.

Chapter 3. The Oldest and Newest Profession

1. Charles Winick and Paul M. Kinsie, *The Lively Commerce* (Chicago: Quadrangle Books, 1971), p. 41.
2. *Ibid.,* p. 137.
3. *Ibid.,* p. 132.
4. Edwin M. Lemert, *Social Pathology* (New York: McGraw-Hill, 1951), pp. 257–58.
5. Ellen Strong, "The Hooker," in Robin Morgan (ed.), *Sisterhood Is Powerful,* (New York: Random House, 1970), pp. 289–96.
6. Lemert, *op. cit.,* pp. 257–58.
7. William E. H. Lecky, The Priestess of Humanity in a History of European Morals, reprinted in *The Cry for Justice,* Upton Sinclair (Philadelphia: The John C. Winston Co., 1915), pp. 168–69.
8. Alfred C. Kinsey, Wardell B. Pomeroy, Clyde E. Martin, and Paul H. Gebhard, *Sexual Behavior in the Human Female* (New York: Pocket Books, 1970 [originally published in 1953]), p. 323.
9. *Ibid.,* p. 300.
10. *Ibid.,* p. 298.
11. Winick and Kinsie, *op. cit.,* p. 186.
12. Kinsey, *et al., op. cit.,* p. 661.
13. Winick and Kinsie, *op. cit.,* p. 16.
14. Kinsey, *et al. op. cit.,* p. 300.
15. Winick and Kinsie, *op. cit.,* p. 16
16. *Ibid.,* p. 33–34.
17. *Ibid.,* p. 19.

18. Kingsley Davis, "Sexual Behavior," in *Contemporary Social Problems,* second edition, Robert K. Merton and Robert A. Nisbet (eds.) (New York: Harcourt, Brace and World, 1966), p. 352.

19. *Ibid.,* p. 365.

20. *Ibid.,* p. 366.

21. *Ibid.*

22. Winick and Kinsie, *op. cit.,* p. 4.

23. *Ibid.,* p. 5.

24. *Ibid.,* p. 97.

25. *Ibid.,* p. 109.

26. Will Levington Confort, "The Police—Court Reporter" from *Midstream,* reprinted in Sinclair, *op. cit.,* pp. 165–66.

27. John H. Gagnon, "Prostitution," *International Encyclopedia of the Social Sciences,* ed. David L. Sills (New York: The Macmillan Co. and the Free Press, 1968), 12:592–598.

28. W. A. Bonger, *Criminality and Economic Conditions* (Boston: Little, Brown and Co., 1916), pp. 321–56.

29. Robert E. Park and Ernest W. Burgess, *Introduction to the Science of Sociology* (Chicago: University of Chicago Press, 1921).

30. Kingsley Davis, "The Sociology of Prostitution," *American Sociological Review,* October 1937, 2:744–55.

31. Lemert, *op. cit.,* p. 233.

32. Frank S. Caprio, *Female Homo-Sexuality* (New York: Grove Press, 1954).

33. See for example, Edward Glover, *The Psychopathology of Prostitution* (London: Institute for the Study and Treatment of Delinquency, 1957). See also, Harold Greenwald, *The Elegant Prostitute* (New York: Walker & Co., 1970 [originally published in 1958]).

34. Otto Fenichel, *The Psychoanalytic Theory of Neurosis* (New York: W. W. Norton & Co., 1945).

35. Sigmund Freud, "Contributions to the Psychology of Love," *Collected Papers* v. 4 (New York: Basic Books Inc., 1959, originally published in 1924).

36. Lemert, *op. cit.,* p. 247.

37. Winick and Kinsie, *op. cit.,* p. 86.

37A. *Time,* June 5, 1972.

38. Christina Milner and Richard Milner, *Black Players, The Secret World of Black Pimps* (Boston: Little, Brown and Co., 1972).

39. L. F. Chapman and H. G. Wolff, "The Cerebral Hemispheres and the Highest Integrative Functions of Man," *A.M.A. Archives of Neurology,* 1959, 1:357.

40. Herbert M. Adler and Van Buren O. Hammett, "Crisis, Conversion, and Cult Formation: An Examination of a Common Psychosocial Sequence," *American Journal of Psychiatry,* August 1973, 130:861–64.

41. James H. Bryan, "Apprenticeships in Prostitution," *Social Problems,* Winter 1965, 12:287–97.
42. David Ward and Gene G. Kassebaum, *Women's Prison* (Chicago: Aldine Publishing Co., 1965), p. 131.
43. Winick and Kinsie, *op. cit.,* p. 67.
44. Greenwald, *op. cit.,* pp. vii–viii.
45. Stephanie Greenberg and Freda Adler, "Crime and Addiction: An Empirical Analysis of the Literature, 1920–1973," *Contemporary Drug Problems,* Summer, 1974, pp. 221–270.
46. Similar statements have been made by hotel personnel in smaller cities and towns also.
47. Mary K. Linsday, "Prostitution—Delinquency's Time Bomb," *Crime and Delinquency,* 1970, 16:151–57.
48. *Time,* June 27, 1969.
49. *Ibid.*
50. Davis, "Sexual Behavior," *op. cit.,* p. 352.
51. J. D. Frank, "The Role of Cognitions in Illness and Heating in Research," in *Psychotherapy,* eds. H. H. Strupp and L. L. Luborsky (Baltimore, Md.: French-Bray Printing Co., 1962), pp. 1–12.
52. Talcott Parsons, *The Social System* (Glencoe, Ill.: The Free Press, 1951).
53. W. H. Masters and V. E. Johnson, *Human Sexual Inadequacy* (Boston: Little, Brown and Co., 1970).
54. An idea developed by Greenwald, *op. cit.,* p. xix.

Chapter 4. Minor Girls and Major Crimes

1. Both sets of figures cited in James F. Short, Jr., "The Study of Delinquency," in *International Encyclopedia of the Social Sciences,* ed. David L. Sills (New York: Macmillan Co. and the Free Press, 1968), 4:74–81.
2. Ruth S. Cavan, *Juvenile Delinquency* (Philadelphia: J. B. Lippincott Co., 1962), p. 24.
3. Frederick B. Sussman, *Law of Juvenile Delinquency* (New York: Oceana Publications, 1959), pp. 21–22.
4. Albert K. Cohen and James F. Short, Jr., "Juvenile Delinquency," in *Contemporary Social Problems,* eds. Robert K. Merton and Robert A. Nisbet, (New York: Harcourt, Brace & World, 1966 [originally published in 1961]).
5. *Ibid.*
6. Barbara Allen Babcock, "Introduction: Women and the Criminal Law," *The American Criminal Law Review,* Winter 1973, 11:291–94; and Nancy Barton Wise, "Juvenile Delinquency Among Middle Class Girls," in *Middle-*

Class Juvenile Delinquency, ed. Edmund W. Vaz (New York: Harper & Row, 1967).

7. Ira L. Reiss, "Sexual Codes in Teen-Age Cultures," *The Annals of the American Academy of Political and Social Science,* November 1961, 338: 53–62.

8. For a discussion of deviation from sex-role expectation see, Albert K. Cohen, *Delinquent Boys* (New York: The Free Press, 1955); Ruth R. Morris, "Female Delinquency and Relational Problems," *Social Forces,* 1964, 43:82–89; and Richard A. Cloward and Lloyd E. Ohlin, *Delinquency and Opportunity* (New York: The Free Press, 1960).

9. James S. Coleman, *The Adolescent Society* (New York: The Free Press of Glencoe, 1963). See also Elaine Walster, Vera Aronson, Darcy Abrahams, Leon Rottman, "The Importance of Physical Attractiveness in Dating Behavior," *Journal of Personality and Social Psychology,* 1966, 4:508–16. In the latter study it was found that the only important determinant of a boy's liking for his date was her physical attractiveness.

10. In an early work (1923) William I. Thomas viewed the sexually delinquent female as an "unadjusted" girl who used sex as capital in an attempt to satisfy her dominant wishes for security, recognition, new experience and response: W. I. Thomas, *The Unadjusted Girl* (New York: Harper & Row, 1967 [originally published in 1923]). Seymour L. Hallbeck, *Psychiatry and the Dilemmas of Crime* (New York: Harper & Row, 1967), p. 138.

11. Albert K. Cohen and James F. Short, Jr., "Research in Delinquent Subcultures," *Journal of Social Issues,* 1958, 14:20–37; Albert J. Reiss, "Sex Offenses: The Maryland Status of the Adolescent," *Law and Contemporary Problems,* Spring 1960, 25:309–33.

12. Clyde B. Vedder and Dora B. Somerville, *The Delinquent Girl* (Springfield, Ill.: Charles C Thomas, 1970), p. 89.

13. James F. Short and Fred L. Strodtbeck, *Group Process and Gang Delinquency* (Chicago: University of Chicago Press, 1965), p. 38.

14. W. W. Wattenberg and F. Saunders, *"Sex Differences Among Juvenile Offenders,"* Sociology and Social Research, Sept.–Oct. 1954, 39:24–31; John Cowie, Valerie Cowie, and Eliot Slater, *Delinquency in Girls* (London: Heinemann, 1968); J. D. Atcheson and D. C. Williams, "A Study of Juvenile Sex Offenders," *American Journal of Psychiatry,* 1954, 3:366–70; Gordon H. Barker and William T. Adams, "Comparison of the Delinquency of Boys and Girls," *Journal of Criminal Law, Criminology and Police Science* (December, 1962), 53:471–72.

15. Walter Reckless, *The Crime Problem* (New York: Appleton-Century-Crofts, 1961), p. 83.

16. Yona Cohn, "Criteria for the Probation Officer's Recommendation to the Juvenile Court," in *Becoming Delinquent,* eds. Peter G. Garabedian and Don C. Gibbons (Chicago: Aldine Press 1970); see also, Robert Terry, "Discrimination in the Handling of Juvenile Offenders by Social Control Agencies," in Garabedian and Gibbons, *op. cit.*

17. Wattenberg and Saunders, *op. cit.;* Halleck, *op. cit.,* p. 141.

18. Cohn, *op. cit.*

19. John P. Clark and Edward Haurek, "Age and Sex Roles of Adolescents and Their Involvement in Misconduct: A Reappraisal," *Sociology and Social Research,* 1966, 50:496–508; Wise, *op. cit.;* Martin Gold, *Delinquent Behavior in an American City* (Belmont, California: Brooke, Cole Publishers, 1970).

20. Harry Elmer Barnes and Negley K. Teeters, *New Horizons in Criminology* (Englewood Cliffs, N.J.: Prentice-Hall, 1943), p. 923; Anthony Platt, *The Child Savers* (Chicago: University of Chicago Press, 1969).

21. Elizabeth Hurlock, *Adolescent Development* (3rd ed., New York: McGraw-Hill, 1967); in another study 2000 adolescents in grades 6, 9, and 12 showed significant increases in opposite-sex preference choice in a sociometric test given in 1963 and compared to 1942: Raymond G. Kuhlen and Nancy B. Houlihan, "Adolescent Heterosexual Interest in 1942 and 1963," *Child Development,* 1963, 36:1049–52.

22. See note 19.

23. Wise, *op. cit.,* pp. 179–80.

24. *Ibid.,* p. 180; Gold, *op. cit.,* pp. 63–64.

25. Wise, *op. cit.,* pp. 181, 188.

26. Gisela Konopka, *The Adolescent Girl in Conflict* (Englewood Cliffs, N.J.: Prentice-Hall, 1966).

27. *Ibid.*

28. *Ibid.*

29. Halleck, *op. cit.,* p. 142.

30. Uniform Crime Reports, Crime in the United States, United States Department of Justice (Washington, D.C.: U.S. Government Printing Office, 1972), p. 124.

31. Reginald G. Smart and Dianne Fejer, *Changes in Drug Use in Toronto High School Students Between 1972–1974,* Project J 183, Addiction Research Foundation, Toronto.

32. James F. Short, Jr., "Introduction: On Gang Delinquency and the Nature of Subcultures," in *Gang Delinquency and Delinquent Subcultures,* ed. James F. Short, Jr. (New York: Harper & Row, 1968).

33. Hanus J. Grosz, Herbert Stern, and Edward Feldman, "A Study of Delinquent Girls Who Participated in and Who Abstained from Participating in a Riot," *American Journal of Psychiatry,* April 1969, 125:1370–79.

34. *The Philadelphia Inquirer,* February 4, 1973.

35. *The New York Times,* May 9, 1972.

36. *Time,* October 16, 1972.

37. *Ibid.*

38. Talcott Parsons, "Certain Primary Sources and Patterns of Aggression in the Social Structure of the Western World," *Psychiatry,* May 1947, 10:167–81; Parsons, "Age and Sex in the Social Structure of the United States," *American Sociological Review,* October 1942, 7:604–16.

39. For data on Japan see Jackson Toby, "Affluence and Adolescent Crime," in the President's Commission on Law Enforcement and Administration of Justice, Task Force on Juvenile Delinquency: Task Force Report: *Juvenile Delinquency and Youth Crime,* Washington, D.C., U.S. Government Printing Office, 1967, p. 132. For Argentina see Lois B. DeFleur, *Delinquency in Argentina* (Pullman, Wash.: Washington State University Press, 1970). For Sweden see Toby, *op. cit.* For the Netherlands see Jackson E. Baur, "The Trend of Juvenile Offenses in the Netherlands and the United States," *Journal of Criminal Law, Criminology, and Police Science,* 1964, 55:359–69. For England and Russia see T. R. Fyvel, *Troublemakers: Rebellious Youth in an Affluent Society,* New York: Schocken Books, 1964.

40. Fyvel, *op. cit.,* p. 123.

41. Robert Merton, "Social Structure and Anomie," *American Sociological Review,* 1938, 3:672–82.

42. Cloward and Ohlin, *op. cit.*

43. Marvin E. Wolfgang and Franco Ferracuti, *The Subculture of Violence* (London: Tavistock Publications Ltd., 1967).

44. Edwin H. Sutherland and Donald R. Cressey, *Principles of Criminology* (Seventh Ed., Philadelphia: J. B. Lippincott Co., 1966).

45. Ruth S. Cavan and Jordan T. Cavan, *Delinquency and Crime: Cross-Cultural Perspectives* (Philadelphia: J. B. Lippincott Co., 1968), p. 227.

46. Albert K. Cohen, "Middle-Class Delinquency and the Social Structure," in Vaz (ed.) *op. cit.*

47. Thorsten Sellin, *On Cultural Conflict and Crime: A Report of the Subcommittee of Delinquency of the Committee on Personality and Culture* (New York: Social Science Research Council, 1938).

Chapter 5. Women in Wonderland: The Psychotropic Connection

1. Frances K. Oldham, F. E. Kelsey and E. M. K. Geiling, *Essentials of Pharmacology* (Philadelphia: J. B. Lippincott Co., 1951 [originally published in 1947]), p. 115.

2. *Drug Use in America: Problems in Perspective,* Second Report of the National Commission on Marihuana and Drug Abuse (Washington, D.C.: U.S. Government Printing Office, 1973), p. 29.

3. Raymond M. Glasscote, James N. Sussex, Jerome N. Jaffe, John Ball, and Leon Brill, *The Treatment of Drug Abuse* (Joint Information Services of the American Psychiatric Association, 1972), p. 17.

4. Walter R. Cuskey, T. Premkumar, and Lois Sigel, "Survey of Narcotic Addiction and Drug Abuse Among Females in the United States Between 1850 and 1970," *Public Health Reviews,* 1972, 1:5–39.

5. Charles E. Terry and Mildred Pellens, *The Opium Problem* (Montclair, N.J.: Patterson Smith, 1970 [originally published in 1928]), p. 5.

6. *Ibid.,* p. 5.

7. *Ibid.,* p. 17.

8. *Ibid.,* p. 11.

9. *Ibid.,* pp. 33–34.

10. A. K. Shapiro, "Factors contributing to the placebo effect, their implications for psychotherapy," *Am. J. Psychother.,* 1964, 18:73–88.

11. John A. Clausen, *Drug Addiction in Contemporary Social Problems,* eds. Robert K. Merton and Robert A. Nesbit (New York: Harcourt, Brace and World, Inc., 1966 [originally published in 1961]).

12. *Ibid.*

13. J. Olds, "Hypothalamic substrates of reward," *Physiol. Rev.,* 1962, 42:554–604.

14. Cuskey, *et al., op. cit.*

15. Bingham Dai, *Opium Addiction in Chicago* (Shanghai: Commercial Press, 1937).

16. Cuskey, *et al., op. cit.*

17. Glasscote, *et al., op. cit.,* p. 19.

18. *Ibid.,* p. 21.

19. For a summary of the psychiatric approaches see Marie Nyswander, *The Drug Addict as a Patient* (New York: Grune and Stratton, 1956), Chapter 4; Alfred R. Lindesmith, *Drug Addiction: Crime or Disease* (Bloomington, Ind.: Indiana University Press, 1961); Paul H. Hock and Joseph Zubin, *Problems of Addiction and Habituation* (London: Grune and Stratton, 1958).

20. Abraham Wikler, *Opiate Addiction: Psychological and Neurophysiological Aspects* (Springfield, Ill.: Charles C Thomas, 1952), p. 54.

21. Vincent Dole and Marie Nyswander, "Rehabilitating Heroin Addicts After Blockade with Methadone," *New York State Journal of Medicine,* August, p. 2011; H. E. Hill, C. A. Haertzen, and R. Glaser, "Personality Characteristics of Narcotic Addicts as Indicated by the MMPI," *Journal of General Psychiatry,* 1960, 62:127.

22. J. A. O'Donnell, "Social Factors and Follow-Up Studies in Opiate Addiction," *Res. Pub. Ass. Res. Nev. Mental Dis.*, 1968, 46:333.

23. Alfred R. Lindesmith, "The Drug Addict as Psychopath," *American Sociological Review*, 1940, 51:920.

24. Isadore Chein, *et al.*, *The Road to H* (New York: Basic Books, 1964), pp. 273–74; also, B. M. Spinley, *The Deprived and the Privileged: Personality Development in English Society* (New York: Humanistic Press, 1953), p. 79.

24A. Robert K. Merton, *Social Theory and Social Structures* (Glencoe, Ill.: Free Press, 1957), pp. 153–54.

25. Stephanie Greenberg and Freda Adler, "Crime and Addiction: An Empirical Analysis of the Literature, 1920–1973," *Contemporary Drug Problems*, Summer 1974, pp. 221–70.

25A. Richard A. Cloward and Lloyd E. Ohlin, *Delinquency and Opportunity* (New York: Free Press, 1960), pp. 178–186.

26. Harold Finestone, "Cats, Kicks and Colors," *Social Problems*, July 1957, 15:3–13.

27. Erich Goode, *Drugs in American Society* (New York: Alfred A. Knopf, 1972), p. 168.

28. Dai, *op. cit.*, p. 173; also, Chein, *op. cit.*, pp. 84, 151.

29. Clausen, *op. cit.*

30. Harold Finestone, "Narcotics and Criminality," *Law and Contemporary Social Problems*, 1957, 22:69–85.

31. Cloward and Ohlin, *op. cit.*, pp. 178–179.

32. Walter R. Cuskey, Arthur D. Moffett, Happa B. Clifford, "Comparison of Female Opiate Addicts Admitted to Lexington Hospital in 1961 and 1967," *H.S.M.H.A. Health Reports*, April 1971, 86:332–40.

33. Charles Winick and Paul M. Kinsie, *The Lively Commerce* (Chicago: Quadrangle Books, 1971), p. 67.

34. Goode, *op. cit.*, p. 169.

35. Winick and Kinsie, *op. cit.*, p. 72.

Chapter 6. The Link Between Opportunity and Offense: Race

1. Robert W. Fogel and Stanley L. Engerman, *Time on the Cross* (Boston: Little, Brown and Co., 1974).

2. Moses Grandy, *Narrative of the Life of Moses Grandy, Late a Slave in the United States of America* (Boston: O. Johnson Publishing Co., 1844), p. 11.

3. Speech, Illinois, September 11, 1858.

4. James Baldwin, *The Fire Next Time* (New York: Dial Press, 1963).

5. Marvin Wolfgang, *Patterns in Criminal Homicide* (New York: John Wiley & Sons, 1966), p. 56.

6. Freda Adler, "The Female Offender in Philadelphia" (unpublished doctoral dissertation, University of Pennsylvania, 1971).

7. Charles Winick and Paul M. Kinsie, *The Lively Commerce* (Chicago: Quadrangle Books, 1971), p. 216.

8. *Ibid.,* pp. 216–17.

9. Edwin H. Sutherland and Donald R. Cressey, *Principles of Criminology* (Seventh Ed., Philadelphia: J. B. Lippincott Co., 1966), pp. 139–40.

10. Lucy Chase Manuscript, American Antiquarian Society, Worcester, Mass.

11. Walter B. Miller, "Lower Class Culture as a Generating Milieu of Gang Delinquency," *Journal of Social Issues,* 1958, 1415–19.

12. Robert Coles, *Children of Crisis* (Boston: Little, Brown and Co., 1964), pp. 368–69.

13. Lee Rainwater, "Crucible of Identity: The Negro Lower-Class Family," *Daedelus,* Winter 1966, 95:172–216.

14. Toni Morrison, "What the Black Woman Thinks About Women's Lib," *The New York Times Magazine,* August 22, 1971, p. 63.

15. Harry Bailey, Jr. (ed.), *Negro Politics in America* (Columbus, Ohio: Charles E. Merrill Books, 1967), p. 164.

16. Chuck Stone, *Black Political Power in America* (Indianapolis: Bobbs-Merrill Co., 1968), p. 10.

17. Donald Matthews and James Prothro, *Negroes and the New Southern Politics* (New York: Harcourt, Brace & World, 1966), p. 11.

18. Hanes Walton, Jr., *Black Politics* (Philadelphia: J. B. Lippincott Co., 1972), p. 35.

19. Claude Brown, *Manchild in the Promised Land* (New York: Signet Books, 1965), p. 8.

20. Lewis A. Coser, "Some Functions of Violence," *The Annals of the American Academy of Political and Social Science,* March 1966, p. 10.

21. *Negro Women in the Population and in the Labor Force,* United States Department of Labor, Wage and Labor Standards Administration, December 1967, pp. 1, 17.

22. Laura S. Haviland, *A Woman's Life-Work, Labors and Experiences* (Chicago: Publishing Association of Friends, 1889), pp. 300-301.

23. From a Report of the Joint Select Committee to Inquire into the Condition of Affairs in the Late Insurrectionary States, 42nd Congress, 2nd Session (Washington, D.C.: U.S. Government Printing Office, 1872), Vol. 6, pp. 400–403.

24. United States Department of Commerce, Bureau of the Census, Current Population Report, No. 85, p. 60.

25. "Women in the Labor Force," June 1972–73, issued by the Employment Standards Administration, United States Department of Labor.

26. Facts on Women Workers of Minority Races, June 1972, Employment Standards Administration, United States Department of Labor, Women's Bureau, Washington, D.C.

27. Cynthia Fuchs Epstein, "Positive Effects of the Multiple Negative: Explaining the Success of Black Professional Women," *The American Journal of Sociology*, January 1973, 78:927.

28. President's Committee on Equal Economic Opportunity, Preliminary Report, 1964.

29. *The Negro Family*, United States Department of Labor, Office of Planning and Research, Washington, D.C., March 1965, pp. 29–40, 52–53.

Chapter 7. The Link Between Opportunity and Offense: Class

1. Edwin H. Sutherland, "White-Collar Criminality," *American Sociological Review*, 1940, 5:1–12.

2. Frederick Pollock and Frederic William Maitland, *History of English Law* (Boston: Little, Brown and Co., 1909), Vol. 2, p. 535.

3. Quoted by Hermann Manheim, *Criminal Justice and Social Reconstruction* (London: Routledge, 1946), p. 121.

4. Alpheus T. Mason, *Harlan Fiske Stone: Pillar of the Law* (New York: The Viking Press, 1956), p. 380.

5. Albert Morris, *Criminology* (New York: Longmans, Green and Co., 1935), pp. 152–58.

6. See Sutherland, "White-Collar Criminality," *op. cit.;* see also, Edwin H. Sutherland, "Crime and Business," *Annals of the American Academy of Political and Social Science*, 1941, CCXVII:112–18; also, Edwin H. Sutherland, "Is 'White-Collar Crime' Crime?," *American Sociological Review*, 1945, 10:132–39.

7. Richard Austin Smith, "The Incredible Electrical Conspiracy," *Fortune*, April 1961, pp. 132–80; May 1961, pp. 161–224.

8. Abe Fortas, "America's Electrical Price Conspiracy," *The Oxford Lawyer*, 1962, 5:29–32.

9. Smith, *op. cit.*

10. President's Commission on Law Enforcement and the Administration of Justice, *Crime and Its Impact—An Assessment* (Washington, D.C.: U.S. Government Printing Office, 1967).

11. Sutherland, "White-Collar Criminality," *op. cit.*

12. *Ibid.*
13. Smith, *op. cit.*
14. Edward Ross, *Atlantic Monthly*, January, 1907, 99:44–55.
15. Elizabeth Waldman, "Changes in the Labor Force Activity of Women," in *Women in a Man-Made World*, eds. Nona Glazer-Malbin and Helen Young-elson Waehrer (Chicago: Rand McNally, 1972), pp. 30–38.
16. The Economic Role of Women, Women's Bureau, Employment Standards Administration, United States Department of Labor, 1973, p. 91.
17. Arthur Hayward (ed.), *Lives of the Most Remarkable Criminals* (New York: Dodd, Mead and Co., 1927), p. 376.
18. Mary Owen Cameron, *The Booster and the Snitch* (London: The Free Press of Glencoe, 1964), pp. 145–50.
19. *Ibid.*, p. 59.
20. *Manpower Report of the President: A Report on Manpower Requirements, Resources, Utilization, and Training* (Washington, D.C.: U.S. Government Printing Office, 1973).
21. *Ibid.*, p. 127.
22. *Ibid.*, p. 164.
23. *Time*, May 6, 1974.
24. *Manpower Report, op. cit.*, p. 141.
25. The Economic Role of Women, *op. cit.*, p. 101.
26. *The New York Times*, January 20, 1974.
27. *Manpower Report, op. cit.*, p. 66.
28. *The New York Times*, January, 20, 1974.
29. *Ibid.*
30. *The New York Times*, Tuesday, September 26, 1967.
31. *The Evening Bulletin*, Friday, February 22, 1974.
32. *The New York Times*, Sunday, October 20, 1968.
33. *The New York Times*, Friday, March 31, 1967.
34. *The New York Times*, Wednesday, November 24, 1971.

Chapter 8. New Crimes and Old Corrections

1. A. F. C. Wallace, "Mazeway Resynthesis: A Biocultural Theory of Religious Inspiration," New York Academy of Sciences, May 1956, 18:626–38.
2. Freda Adler and John C. Ball, "Drug Abuse Treatment Programs as a Natural Criminology Laboratory: A Pennsylvania Study," *International Journal of Offender Therapy and Comparative Criminology*, 1972, 16:13–17.
3. According to Barbara Allen Babcock, the problems of women in prison were hidden until the recent general interest in the rights of the female: see Bab-

cock, "Introduction: Women and the Criminal Law," *The American Criminal Law Review*, Winter 1973, 11:291–94.

4. Harry Elmer Barnes and Negley K. Teeters, *New Horizons in Criminology* (New York: Prentice-Hall, 1943), p. 573.

5. William Nagel, *The New Red Barn* (New York: Walker & Co., 1973), p. 31.

6. Linda R. Singer, "Women and the Correctional Process," *The American Criminal Law Review*, Winter 1973, 11:295–308.

7. Nagel, *op. cit.*, pp. 31, 117; see also *Dawson v. Carberry* no. C-71-1916 (N.D. Cal. filed Sept. 1971) in which female jail inmates challenged their exclusion from a work furlough program; for a discussion of offender rehabilitation through job training, see Marcia Hovey, "The Forgotten Offenders," *Manpower*, January 1971, pp. 38–40.

8. Hovey, *op. cit.*

9. Gresham Sykes and Sheldon L. Messinger, "The Inmate Social Code," in *The Sociology of Punishment and Correction*, eds., Norman Johnson, Leonard Savitz, Marvin Wolfgang (Second Ed., New York: John Wiley & Sons, 1970), pp. 401–408.

10. Herbert M. Adler and Van Buren O. Hammett, "Crisis, Conversion, and Cult Formation: An Examination of a Common Psychosocial Sequence," *American Journal of Psychiatry*, August 1973, 130:861–64.

11. Howard Polsky, *Cottage Six* (New York: Russell Sage Foundation, 1962), pp. 69–81, and Clarence Schrag, "Leadership Among Prison Inmates," *American Sociological Review*, February 1954, 19:37–42.

12. See, for example, Clarence Schrag, "Some Foundations for a Theory of Correction" in *The Prison*, ed. Donald Cressey (New York: Holt, Rinehart & Winston, 1961), pp. 346–57.

13. David A. Ward and Gene G. Kassebaum, "Homosexuality: A Mode of Adaptation in a Prison for Women," *Social Problems*, Fall 1964, 12:159–77; homosexuality among adolescents is discussed in: Seymour L. Halleck and Marvin Hersko, "Homosexual Behavior in a Correctional Institution for Adolescent Girls," *American Journal of Orthopsychiatry*, October 1962, 32:911–17.

14. David A. Ward and Gene G. Kassebaum, *Women's Prison* (Chicago: Aldine Publishing Co., 1965; Rose Giallombardo, *Society of Women: A Study of a Women's Prison* (New York: John Wiley & Sons, 1966).

15. *Attica*, The Official Report of the New York State Special Commission on Attica (New York: Bantam Books, 1972).

16. Sykes and Messinger, *op. cit.*

17. Giallombardo, *op. cit.*

18. See, Carolyn Engel Temin, "Discriminatory Sentencing of Women Offenders: The Argument for ERA in a Nutshell," *The American Criminal Law*

Review, Winter 1973, 11:355–72; also, Leo Kanowitz, *Women and the Law* (Albuquerque: University of New Mexico Press, 1969).

19. Singer, *op. cit.*, and Nagel, *op. cit.*, pp. 31–117.

20. Hanus J. Grosz, Herbert Stern, and Edward Feldman, "A Study of Delinquent Girls Who Participated in and Who Abstained from Participation in a Riot," *American Journal of Psychiatry*, April 1969, 125:370–79.

21. "Report by District of Columbia on the Status of Women" as read into the *Congressional Record* by Hon. Donald M. Fraser (R.–Minn.), May 22, 1972.

22. *Manpower Research Monograph No. 28*, A Review of Manpower R & D Projects in the Correctional Fields, 1963–1973, United States Department of Labor, p. 33.

23. There are 800 women in two federal prison facilities at Alderson and Terminal Island, Calif. State institutions house approximately 6000 women and about 8000 more are found throughout the country and municipal prisons (statistics provided by Department of Labor).

24. Of the thirty major federal and state facilities which house females, twenty-four are essentially male institutions headed by male wardens. See statement of Elizabeth Duncan Koontz, Women's Bureau, United States Department of Labor, before the District of Columbia Commission on the Status of Women, November 4, 1971.

25. Sheldon Glueck and Eleanor Glueck, *Five Hundred Delinquent Women* (New York: Alfred A. Knopf, 1934).

26. Statistical Report, 1972, Bureau of Women, United States Department of Labor.

27. Marcia Hovey, "The Forgotten Offenders," *Manpower*, January 1971.

28. Nagel, *op. cit.*, p. 163.

29. National Advisory Commission on Criminal Justice Standards and Goals Report, Washington, D.C., 1973.

30. Maxwell Jones, *The Therapeutic Community: A New Treatment Method in Psychiatry* (New York: Basic Books, 1953).

31. Philip Rieff, *The Triumph of the Therapeutic* (New York: Harper Torchbooks, 1968), p. 70.

Chapter 9. Ladies and the Law

1. *Bradwell v. the State*, 16 Wall. 130 (U.S. 1872).

2. 4 Blackstone, Commentaries 28.

3. *O'Donnell v. State*, 73 Okla. Cr. 1, 117 P. 2d 139 (1941).

4. Perkins, Criminal Law 800 (1957).

5. Moore, "The Diverse Definitions of Criminal Adultery," 30 U. Kan. City Law Review, 29 (1962).

6. *Macbeth*, Act II, Sc. 3, Line 22.

7. In re Carey, 57 Cal. App. 297, 304 (1922).

8. Mr. Justice Fortas, dissenting in *Avery v. Midland County, Texas*, U.S. 88 S. Ct. 1114, m. 2 (1968).

9. *Strauder v. West Virginia*, 100 U.S. 303, 310, (1880).

10. Washington was the second state to allow women jurors (1911) and Kansas the third (1913).

11. Lois J. Frankel, "Sex Discrimination in the Criminal Law: The Effect of the Equal Rights Amendment," *The American Criminal Law Review*, Winter 1973, 11:469–510.

12. Hearings were held by the House and Senate Judiciary Committees in 1948 and 1956, respectively. See, Hearings of the Equal Rights Amendment to the Constitution and Commission on the Legal Status of Women, House Committee on the Judiciary, Subcommittee No. 1, 80th Congress, 2d Session (1948); Hearings on Equal Rights, Senate Committee on the Judiciary, Subcommittee on Constitutional Amendments, 84th Congress, 2nd Session (1956).

13. Simone de Beauvoir, *The Second Sex* (New York: Alfred A. Knopf, 1952).

14. Leo Kanowitz, *Women and the Law* (Albuquerque: University of New Mexico Press, 1969), p. 3.

15. See, for example, Martin E. P. Seligman, Steven F. Maier, and James H. Gear, "Alleviation of Learned Helplessness in the Dog," *Journal of Abnormal Psychology*, 1968, 73:256–62; J. Bruce Overmeir and Martin E. P. Seligman, "Effects of Inescapable Shock Upon Subsequent Escape and Avoidance Responding," *Journal of Comparative and Physiological Psychology*, 1967, 63:28–33.

16. *Frontiero v. Richardson*, U.S. 93 S. Ct. 1764, 1769 (1973).

17. Margaret Mead, *Sex and Temperament in Three Primitive Societies* (New York: William Morrow & Co., 1963 [originally published in 1935]).

18. *Goesart v. Cleary*, 335 U.S. at 466.

19. Kanowitz, *op. cit.*, p. 200.

20. *Ibid.*

21. P. Cutright, Testimony before the Commission on Population Growth and the American Future, May 27, 1971.

22. *Lamb v. Brown*, 456 F. 2d 18 (10th Cir. 1972).

23. *Ibid.*

24. *White v. Crook*, 251 F. Supp. 401, 408 (M.D. Ala. 1966).

25. Since 1963, when the Committee on Civil and Political Rights of the President's Commission on the Status of Women was organized, there have been

increasing constitutional challenges of sex-based discriminatory laws.

26. *Ibid.*, pp. 36–37.
27. Charles Rosenbleet and Barbara Pariente, "The Prostitution of the Criminal Law," *The American Law Review*, Winter 1973, 11:373–427.
28. *Ibid.*
29. *Ibid.*
30. *Ibid.*
31. B. J. George, Jr., "Legal, Medical and Psychiatric Considerations in the Control of Prostitution," in 60 Mich. L. Review (1962).
32. San Francisco Commission on Crime, A Report on Non-Victim Crime in San Francisco, June 1971.
33. *Ibid.*
34. *Physician's World* (December 1973) 1:64.
35. George E. Worthington and Ruth Topping, *Specialized Courts Dealing with Sex Delinquency* (Montclair, N.J.; Patterson Smith, 1969), pp. 154–55.
36. Charles Winick and Paul Kinsie, *The Lively Commerce* (Chicago: Quadrangle Books, 1971), p. 212.
37. District of Columbia Department of Corrections, Movement and Characteristics of Women's Detention Center Admissions, No. 39 (1969).
38. *The New York Times*, May 29, 1970, p. 30.
39. For a discussion of legalization, illegalization, and decriminalization see, "Prostitution: A Non-Victim Crime?," *Issues in Criminology*, Fall 1973 8:137–61.
40. Lentino, "Medical Evaluation of a System of Legalized Prostitution," *Journal of the American Medical Association*, 1955, 158:20.
41. *Ibid.*
42. McGinnis and Packer, "Prostitution Abatement in a V.D. Control Program," *Journal of Social Hygiene*, 1941, 27:355.
43. *Physician's World*, December 1973, 1:61.
44. *Ibid.*, p. 64
45. *The New York Times*, May 29, 1970, p. 30.
46. Sherwin and Winick, "Debate: Should Prostitution Be Legalized?," *Sexual Behavior*, January 1972.
47. *Ibid.*
48. *New Jersey v. Palendrano*, No. 408–71 (Monmouth County, N.J., Superior Court, July 13, 1972).
49. Pa. Stat. Ann tit. 51 § 566 (1964).
50. *Commonwealth v. Daniels*, 210 Pa. Super. 156,232 A 2d 247 (1967).
51. *Ibid.* 210 Pa. Super. 156, 160–161, 232 A 2d 247, 251–252 (1967).
52. 37 U.S. L.W. 2063 (1968).
53. *Ibid.* 2064.

54. Conn. gen. Stat. Ann. § 17–360 (1960).
55. *United States ex rel. Robinson v. York,* 281 F. Supp. 8 (D.C. Vonn. 1968).
56. 281 F. Supp. at 17.
57. *State v. Costello,* 59 N.J. 334, 282 A 2d 748 (1971).
58. Carolyn Engel Temin, "Discriminatory Sentencing for Women Offenders: The Argument for ERA in a Nutshell," *American Criminal Law Review,* Winter 1973, 11:355–72.
59. Iowa Code Ann. § 245 7 (1969).
60. Temin, *op. cit.*
61. Linda R. Singer, "Women and the Correctional Process," *American Criminal Law Review,* Winter 1973, 11:295–308.
62. See, e.g., *Board of Regents v. Roth,* 92 S. Ct. 2701, 2706 (1972); *Morrissey v. Brewer,* 92 S. Ct. 2593 (1972); *Graham v. Richardson,* 403 U.S. 365,374 (1971).
63. Kanowitz, *op. cit.,* p. 197.
64. *People v. Stately,* 91 Cal. App. 2d Supp. 943, 948, 206 P. 2d 76, 81 (1949).
65. *People v. Pierce,* 61 Cal. 2d 879, 40 Cal. R ptr. 845, 395 P. 2d 893 (1964).
66. *Ibid.*
67. *United States v. Dege,* 364 U.S. 51 (1960).
68. See Note 65.
69. *Dalton v. People,* 68 Colo. 44, 189 P. 37 (1920).
70. *People v. Martin,* 4 Ill. 2d 105, 122 N.E. 2d 245 (1954).
71. *Marks v. State,* 144 Tex. Crim. 509, 164 S.W. 2d 690 (1942).
72. *White v. Crook,* 251 F. Supp. 401, 408 (M.D. Ala., 1966).
73. Kanowitz, *op. cit.,* p 61.
74. Cal. Penal Code § 274.
75. Leavy and Kummer, "Criminal Abortion: A Failure of Law," 50 A.B.A.J. 52 m.2 (1964).
76. 410 U.S. 179, 1973.
77. *Medical Economics,* April 1, 1974, p. 17.
78. Margolin, "Equal Pay and Equal Employment Opportunities for Women," N.Y.U. 19th Conference on Labor 297, 302 (1967).
79. *Ibid.*
80. Release of Equal Employment Opportunity Commission, July 2, 1966.
81. E.g. *United States ex. rel Summrell v. York,* 288 F. Supp. 955 D. Conn., 1968; *United States ex. rel Robinson v. York,* 281 F Supp. 8, 16 (D. Conn. 1968).
82. *Sail'er Inn, Inc. v. Kirby,* 5 Cal. 3d 1, 485 P. 2d 529, 95 Cal. R ptr. 329 (1971).
83. *Seidenberg v. McSorley's Old Ale House, Inc.,* 308 F. Supp. 1253 (S.D. N.Y. 1969).

84. *Kirstein v. Rector and Visitors of the University of Virginia,* 309 F. Supp. 184 (E.D. Va. 1970).

85. Hartford, Connecticut, Superior Court Ruling, 1974.

86. N.C. Gen. Stat. § 14-262 (1969).

87. Walter C. Reckless and Barbara Ann Kay, *The Female Offender* (consultants' report presented to the President's Commission on Law Enforcement and the Administration of Justice (1967).

88. Barbara Ann Kay and Christine G. Schultz, "Divergence of Attitudes Toward Constituted Authorities Between Male and Female Felony Inmates," in Walter C. Reckless and Charles L. Newman (eds.), *Interdisciplinary Problems in Criminology: Papers of the American Society of Criminology, 1964* (Columbus: College of Commerce and Administration, Ohio State University, 1965), pp. 209–216.

89. *The Challenge of Crime in a Free Society* (President's Commission on Law Enforcement and Administration of Justice 56, 1967).

90. See, for example, Olson, *op. cit.;* Robert M. Terry, "Discrimination in the Handling of Juvenile Offenders by Social Control Agencies," *Journal of Research in Crime and Delinquency* (1967) 4:218–30; Don C. Gibbons and Manzer J. Griswold, "Sex Differences Among Juvenile Court Referrals," *Sociology and Social Research,* November–December 1957, 42:106–110.

91. Marlynn Marter, "More Women Are Studying Law," *The Philadelphia Inquirer,* April 27, 1973.

92. Nick Thimmesch, "The Sexual Equality Amendment," *The New York Times Magazine,* June 24, 1973.

Index

Abortions, 213, 235–237
  adolescent girls, 216–217
  arguments against, 235
  woman's right to, 235–237
Acerra, Lucy, 19
Activism, 208
Adam and Eve, 37, 39, 206
Addams, Charles, 23
Adler, Alfred, 42
Adler, Polly, 66
Adolescents, 28, 42–43, 85–110
  aggressive drives, 130–131
  competition with boys, 94
  crime rates, 19–20, 22
  drug addiction, 95–96, 106–107, 126–127, 132
  female criminality, 87–88, 248
  female role changes, 92–95
  gangs, 96–97, 248
  identity problems, 94–96
  legal status changes, 216–217
  political demonstrations, 101
  prostitution, 248, 250
  rise in illegitimacy, 216–217
  runaways, 71, 90, 95
  teen-age girls, 28, 89–90, 96–97
  unemployment, 87
  violence-oriented crimes, 22
  youth cultural system, 107
  (See also Juvenile delinquency)
Adultery, 205–206, 213
Affluent society, 124–125
  influence on youth, 104–105
Aggressive behavior, 37, 42–43
  androgenic hormones and, 2, 42, 44
  black women, 182–183
  development of, 41–42
  in female prisons, 182–185
  sex differences, 2
Alcoholics Anonymous, 200
Alcoholism, 61, 95, 112, 173, 200
Alderson Federal Reformatory for Women (West Va.), 178–181
American Social Health Association, 64, 223
American Telephone and Telegraph Co., 167
Amphetamines, 95, 112
Animal studies, 41
  aggression, 43–44
  dominance and status, 10, 41–42, 208

Anti-trust violations, 156, 159–160
Anti-war protests, 25, 101–103
Aristotle, 35
Arrests, 16, 19–20, 49
  for major crimes, 19–20
Arrington, Marie Dean, 20
Assassinations, 21
Assaults, 3, 27
  (See also Murder and aggravated assault)
Attica (New York) prison riot, 178, 181
Auden, W.H., 178
Australia, female crime, 17
Auto thefts, 18, 248–250

Bachelor women, 29
Baldwin, James, 137
Ballads and lyrics, 5, 251
Bank robbery, 6–7, 14
Barbiturates, 111–112
Bartels, William, 79
Beauvoir, Simon de, 26, 41
Bedford Hills (New York) Correctional Facility, 199
Behavior, 2, 10, 177–179
  female passivity, 2–3, 31–53
  male, 2, 176–177
  prison codes of, 176–179
  social differences, 39–53
  (See also Aggressive behavior; Deviant behavior)
Biological basis of criminality, 31–33, 135
Black males, 29, 137–138
  crime rate, 17
Black Muslim movement, 177
Black power, 144–145
Black women, 29, 133–154
  aggressive behavior, 182–183
  biological differences, 135
  crime rates, 17
  criminal-justice system and, 143–154
  criminality, 17, 138–139, 153–154, 169
  criminologic influences, 134–135, 138, 140, 150–151, 153–154
  deviant behavior, 150–152
  educational deprivation, 147–148
  effects of slavery, 135–136
  family responsibilities, 134, 136, 141–142, 150

Black women (*cont.*):
　historical factors, 135–137
　leadership and power, 169
　liberation and, 152–153
　low income levels, 148–150, 154
　migration to cities, 146–147
　myths concerning, 133–135
　racial basis in hiring, 149
　self-image, 143–144
　sex-role, 133
　social-role, 133–134, 139–140, 152–153
　stereotypes, 133
　white-collar crime, 169
Blackstone, William, 205
Blue-collar crimes, 134, 156, 169
Bottero, Pasquale, 23
Bradley, Justice, 249
Bradley, Omar, 26
Brainwashing, 72
Burglary, 3, 22, 248
　crime rate, 16, 18
Business theft, 156–158, 160
　(*See also* White-collar crime)

Call girls, 55, 65, 72, 74, 76, 79, 223, 225, 228
Capone, Al, 77, 156
Carmichael, Stokely, 146
Carpenter, Ken, 192
Catherine, Empress of Russia, 46
Changing status of women, 5–30
Chicago: Cook County jail for women, 182–183, 187, 193–194
　Democratic Convention (1966), 101–102
Child-rearing practices, 124
　female-dominated, 103–104
Chivalry and paternalism, 32, 207, 234, 238–241
Civil Rights Act of 1964, 206, 216, 219, 237
Civil-rights movement, 1, 25–26, 144–146, 153, 247
Class differences, female delinquency, 7–8, 21, 28, 109
　white-collar crime, 156–158, 162, 165
Cleopatra, 46
Cocaine, 112, 130
Codeine, 112, 118
Comfort, Will Levington, 67
Community property system, 234–235
Community relationships, 200–201
Community treatment centers for offenders, 190–201
　public resistance to, 194–195

Confidential magazine, 60
Conformist behavior, 42–43, 53, 173, 208
Constitution of United States, 212, 217–218, 220
　Fourteenth Amendment, 220, 230, 242
　(*See also* Equal Rights Amendment)
Consumer fraud, 156–157
Contraceptives, oral, 58, 236,
Contractual and property rights, 206–207
　community property system, 234–235
Counterfeiting, 29, 248
Crime: definition, 155, 172
　linked to social roles, 17, 27–28
　(*See also* Female criminality)
Crime rates, 8, 29
　adolescents, 17–20, 85, 87–88, 95
　arrests for index crimes, 16, 19–20, 29
　black males vs. females, 17, 138–139
　male vs. female, 15–17, 139, 153–154
　trends in, 16
　Uniform Crime Reports, 15–16, 28, 52
Criminal justice system, 211–219
　effect of prostitution on, 224
　future trends, 252
　juvenile courts, 88, 91–92
　legal status of women, 239–243
　male bias, 214–215
　sentencing, 229–232
　women offenders, 239–243
Criminality (*see* Female criminality)
Cultural differences between men and women, 33–35, 44–45
Custody of minor children, 209–210

Dandridge, Dorothy, 144
Davis, Angela, 144, 249
Davis, Kingsley, 80–81
DeFreeze, Donald, 21
Democratic Convention riots (1966), 101–102
Dependent traits, 41, 111
DeQuincey, Thomas, 118
Deterrence role of prisons, 173, 175
Deviant behavior, 23, 53
　black women, 150–152
　controlling, 171–201
　social role and, 28–29
　stress-related ailments and, 23–24
　treatment of, 171–173
Dickens, Charles, 161

Discriminatory laws and practices, 12, 219
  male bias, 204–211
  (*See also* Sex-discrimination)
Divorces, 23–24, 210
  alimony and, 210
  custody of children, 209–210
  family desertions and, 24
Doe v. Bolton, 236
Dole, Vincent, 123
Dominance and status, 10, 34, 44–45
  cultural factors, 44–45, 52
  differences between men and women, 41–42
  submissiveness and, 50–51
Double standard, 207–209
  prostitution and, 80–81
Drug addiction, 95–96, 111–132, 173
  adolescents, 106–107, 126–127, 130–132
  causes, 121–122
  dependency on drugs, 111–112, 122, 126
  drug overuse, 114, 123
  group pressures and, 126–128
  historical background, 114–118
  laws and penalties, 119–120
  personality studies, 123–124
  prostitutes and, 73, 77–78, 130
  psychoactive drugs, 114
  pushers, 113, 118, 120
  shifts in socioeconomic status, 129
  social factors, 128–130
  tolerance to drugs, 111, 123
  withdrawal symptoms, 111–112, 122
Drug subculture, 114
"Due Process" principle, 218, 220
Durkheim, Emile, 33
Dylan, Bob, 5

Economically motivated offenses, 14, 16, 18, 29, 188
Egalitarianism, 208
Eisemann-Schier, Ruth, 20
Electrical conspiracy, 159–161
Elizabeth I, queen of England, 46
Embezzlement, 3, 27, 29, 156, 161–162, 248, 250, 252
  crime rate, 16
Emotional security, 10
Employment: equal opportunity in, 237, 251
  sex-discrimination, 206, 216
Equal Opportunity Commission, 167, 237
Equal opportunity for women, 12–14

Equal Pay Act of 1963, 237
Equal pay for equal work, 237–238
"Equal protection" principle, 218, 220
Equal Rights Amendment, 218, 238–246, 249
  provisions, 207, 238–239, 243–244
  ratification of, 207, 243–245
  sex-based legal inequities, 207
  women offenders, 239–243
Equal-rights movement, 25–26, 92, 108, 155, 210, 249
  effect on youth, 216–217
  sexual freedom, 80
Ethical systems, 172, 206
Europe, female criminality, 17
Extortion, crime of, 14, 22, 97

Families: black, 141–142
  changing status of, 13, 94–95, 104
  desertions, 24
Fanny Hill, 60
Federal Bureau of Investigation (FBI), 12
  "ten most wanted" list, 20
  Uniform Crime Reports, 15–16, 28, 52
Federal Bureau of Prisons, 190–191
Female criminality, 5–30, 249–250
  abilities and opportunities, 28–30, 251–253
  adolescents, 17–18
  biological basis theories, 31–33, 35
  black vs. white, 153–154
  causes of, 24–25, 53
  changing patterns, 2–30
  cultural differences, 33–35, 44–45
  development of, 19–20
  in Europe and Australia, 17
  future trends, 247–253
  increasing faster than male criminality, 1–3, 11, 15–17, 19, 29
  linked to social roles, 17, 27–28
  "masculinization" of female behavior, 42
  new breed of offenders, 3, 6–7, 177–179, 182–183, 188
  new concepts, 33–34
  physical characteristics, 6–7, 31–33
  social vs. sex roles, 27–29
  stereotypes, 43, 45
  versus male criminality, 1–3, 11, 15–17, 19, 29, 33–35
  white women, 152–153
  World War II, 46–47
Female passivity, 2, 31–53
  physical differences, 35–37

Female passivity (*cont.*):
  psychological differences, 37–39
  social differences, 39–53
Feminine Mystique, The (Friedan), 26
Femininity, 30, 204
  attitude of adolescents, 86
  conformity to male standards, 10, 253
  decline of, 169
  "new feminism," 26–27
  revolutionary feminism, 20
Fight vs. flight behavior, 37, 44, 120–121, 125
Fletcher, Andrew, 251
Ford Foundation, 150
Forgery, 29, 248, 250
Fortas, Justice Abe, 249
Fortune magazine, 159
Frankfurter, Justice Felix, 212, 233
Fraud, 29, 157, 252
  (*See also* Consumer fraud)
Freud, Sigmund, 9, 33, 35, 38, 42, 48
Friedan, Betty, 26
Frustrations and discontent, 209

Gage, Nicholas, 14–15
Gambling, 61, 218
Gandhi, Indira, 46
Gang violence, 3, 22, 96–97, 106
  all-girl gangs, 22, 100–101, 248
  "granny-bashers," 22, 248
  in London, 22, 100–101, 106, 248
  in New York City, 100, 106
  organized warfare, 98–101
General Motors, 160
Genetic studies, 35–36
Giroud, François, 249
Goals and motivation, 9, 104–105
Goldsmith, Oliver, 9
Goodman, Judge Budd G., 222
Goodrich, Edna, 195–200
Goodwin, Sue, 97–98
Grandy, Moses, 136
"Granny-bashing," 22, 248
Greek hetaerae, 56, 61–63, 82
Group behavior, 28, 177
Group sex, 74–76
Guerrilla warfare, 20
  girl gangs, 100–101
Guns and weapons, 43

Hack, Al, 51, 102–103
Halfway houses, 191, 193–195
Hall, Camilla, 20
Hardy, Thomas, 29
Harrison Act (1914), 119, 122

Hashish, 112
Hearst, Patricia, 20
Heroin, 95, 111, 112, 118, 123, 130
Hickey, Daniel C., 78
Hiring practices, 167
Hoffman, Judge, 229
Holmes, Oliver Wendell, 203
Homemaking, diminishing status, 5, 12, 48, 242, 248
Homosexuality, 8, 82, 174
Hooker, General Joseph, 55
Hookers, 23, 55
  convention of, 250
Horne, Lena, 144
Horney, Karen, 9
Hotel Association of New York City, 78

Ibsen, Henrik, 9
Identity problems, 94, 253
Image of women, 7–8
  new self-image, 27–29
Indiana, sentencing disparities, 231
Indiana Correctional Institution for Girls, 174, 183–184
Indiana Reform Institute for Women, 174
Indochina war protests, 92
Inferiority female theories, 31–35

Japanese geisha girls, 56
Job opportunities for women, 12–14
  equal, 12–14, 167, 237
  legal status of women, 237–238
  occupational skills and, 10, 12–13
Johnson, Virginia, 60, 82
Jones, Maxwell, 200
Judicial interpretations, 203, 211–219, 249
  (*See also* Criminal justice system)
Jury service, 234
  sex-discrimination, 206–207
Juvenile delinquency, 85–110
  causes, 103–105, 108
  criminal subculture, 105–106
  definition, 89
  female criminality, 108–109, 188
  gang activities, 96–97
  increase in, 87–88, 95
  population explosion and, 108
  sexual misbehavior, 90–91, 95, 108
  social changes and, 87, 108–110
  state laws, 88–89
  teen-age girls, 89–91
  unemployment and, 87
  (*See also* Adolescents)

Kidnapping, 20
King, Martin Luther, Jr., 150
Kinsey, Alfred C., 58–60
Ku Klux Klan, 148

Labor, Department of, 163–167
    prison training programs, 187
Labor force, women in, 12–13, 163–167
Labor laws, protective, 209
Laissez-faire doctrine, 157, 160–161
Larceny, 18, 248
    crime rate, 16, 18
Law Enforcement Assistance Administration (LEAA), 192
Law enforcement authorities
    male bias, 49–50, 213
    white-collar crime and, 156–157
Lawrence, D. H., 60
Lawyers, women, 12, 249
Leadership and power, 43, 45–47, 109
    black women, 109
    radical political groups, 21
Lecky, William, 57
Legal status of women, 203–246
    abortions, 235–237
    biblical concepts, 205
    changes in social customs and, 207–213
    common-law limitations, 205, 232–235
    community property system, 234–235
    contractual and property rights, 206–207
    criminal-justice system, 239–243
    custody of minor children, 209–210
    discriminatory treatment, 204–210
    divorce and alimony cases, 209–210
    doctrine of presumed coercion, 205–206, 233
    equal pay for equal work, 237–238
    "equal protection" and "due process" clause, 218, 220
    Equal Rights Amendment, 207, 238–246
    historical experiences, 204
    job opportunities, 237–238
    judicial interpretation, 203, 211–219
    jury service, 206–207, 234
    legislative acts, 203, 249
    married women, 232–233
    prostitution, 213, 220–228
    protective labor laws, 209
    public opinion and, 203

sex-discrimination, 207
    in employment, 206, 216, 218–219
    jury service, 206–207
    sentencing practices, 206, 222, 229–232
    sexual conduct, 213–214
    single women, 205, 234
    trends, 204–211
    voting rights, 206, 234
    woman's acceptance of double standard, 207–210
Lesbianism, 8, 174
"Liberation movement," 7–8
    (*See also* Women's liberation movement)
Lincoln, Abraham, 136
Loan-sharking operations, 14, 19, 158
Lombroso, Caesar, 31–33, 53
London gangs, 22, 100–101, 248
    Bovver Birds, 22, 100–101, 106
    "granny-bashing," 22, 248
Loock, Fred F., 161
Lorenz, Konrad, 42
Los Angeles Times, 79
LSD, 95, 112

McCone Committee, 159
McCormick, Claudia, 182, 187, 193–194
McLaughlin, Virginia, 181–182, 186
Mafia, role of women, 14–15
Makeba, Miriam, 144
Males: bias of, 5, 48–49, 205
    characteristics, 42–43
    chauvinism, 14
    competition with women, 48
    dominance and status, 5, 8–9, 34, 44–45
    power structure, 1–3, 9–10
    protection of sexual privileges, 205–206
    psychosomatic illnesses, 23–24
Man-woman relationships, 9–10
    social differences, 39–53
Maria Theresa of Austria, 46
Marijuana, 95, 112
Marriage, changing status of, 13
    sex-differentiated age for, 212–213
Married women, legal status, 206, 232–233
Married Women's Property Acts, 206
Marx, Karl, 25, 68, 112
Maryland Correctional Institution for Women, 189
"Masculinization" of female behavior, 1, 39, 40, 42, 106

Masters, William H., 60, 82
Mead, Margaret, 34, 45
Meir, Golda, 46
Mental illness, 23, 173, 200
Mental sets, 3, 28–29
  regarding women, 9
Methadone, 112
Militancy of female offenders, 182–183
Miller, Henry, 60
Morality and social taboos, 55
Morphine, 118, 122
Morris, Albert, 157
Morrison, Toni, 142
Motherhood, changing status of, 5, 48, 248
Motivation and goals, 9, 104–105
Muggings, 14, 22–23
  by female gangs, 22–23, 100–101, 248
  by prostitutes, 22–23, 77–78
Muncy (Pa.) State Prison for Women, 97–98, 183–185
Murder and aggravated assault, 14, 20, 23, 252
  by adolescents, 18
  crime rate, 16, 18
Myths concerning women, 12, 46, 184, 248–249

Narcotic addicts, 19
  (See also Drug addiction)
National Achievement Scholarship Program, 150
National Advisory Commission on Criminal Justice Standards and Goals, 191
National Association for the Advancement of Colored People (NAACP), 145
National Women's Party, 244
Nevada, legalized prostitution, 79, 83, 226–227
"New feminism," 26–27
New York City: gang activities, 22–23, 97–100, 248
  The Black Persuaders, 100
  Sedgewick Sisters, 100, 106
  police force, 18–19, 50–51
  prostitutes, 23, 77–78, 95
News media, 3, 13, 29
Niantic (Conn.) Women's Prison, 184, 189
Nineteenth Amendment, 234
Nixon Administration, 192

NOW (National Organization for Women), 26, 244
Nyswander, Marie, 123

Occupational skills, 10, 12–13
Opium, 111, 114–120, 122
  legislation prohibiting, 119
  properties of, 116–117
  (See also Drug addiction)
Organized crime: prostitution and, 77
  role of women, 14–15
Orman, Jim, 48–49

Passivity, female, 2, 31–53
  physical characteristics, 35–37
  psychological characteristics, 37–39
  social characteristics, 39–53
Paternalism, benign and despotic, 252
Peace demonstration, 101–103
Pennsylvania: Muncy Act, 229–230
  Muncy State Prison for Women, 97–98, 183–185
  Program for Women and Girl Offenders, 193
Permissiveness, 172, 207, 242
Perry, Nancy Ling, 20
Philadelphia, gang violence, 98–99
Philadelphia House of Correction, 183
Physical characteristics, 31–33, 35–37, 43
Physical strength, 43
Physiological sex differences, 2
Pimps, 65–67, 71–72, 95, 225
  ethnic backgrounds, 66
  role of, 67–68
Playboy magazine, 60
Ploscowe, Morris, 60
Police, 18–19
  attitudes toward female criminals, 18–19, 42–43, 48–49
  pay-offs and graft, 224
Policewomen, 12, 19, 49–50, 252
  prejudice of police toward, 50–51
Polikoff, Gladys, 97
Political activism, 101, 129–130
Political graft, 158
Population explosion, 5, 48, 108, 248
Pornographic literature, 60–61
Power, desire for, 9–10
Pregnancy: changing attitudes, 10, 52
  rise in illegitimacy, 216–217
President's Commission on Law Enforcement and the Administration of Justice, 161, 241

President's Commission on the Status of Women, 219
Prisons and prisoners, 7–8, 171–201
adolescent girls, 183–184
Alderson prison riot, 178–179, 184, 186
antisocietal subculture, 175–177
architecture, 185
Attica riot, 178, 181
black prisoners, 151, 177
changing social and criminal patterns, 173–201
coed, 24–25
community treatment centers, 190–201
correctional programs, 173, 180–182, 190–191
deterrence role, 173, 175
educational opportunities, 179, 185, 187–188
environmental conditions, 180–181, 185
female aggression and militant behavior, 3, 182–183
female code of behavior, 177–179
halfway houses, 191, 193–195
"humanization" of system, 190–201
isolation from community, 180–181, 190
juvenile delinquents, 97–98
liberation movement within, 7–8
male code of behavior, 176–177
moratorium on new building, 191–192
new type of female offenders, 6–7, 177–179, 182–183, 188
punishment, 173, 190
Purdy (Washington), 195–201
recidivism, 151, 188–189, 192, 200
recreational facilities, 179, 185, 187
rehabilitation, 172–173, 188, 190–191, 231–232
riots and violence, 98, 178–186
sentencing, discriminatory practices, 206, 222, 229–232
single-sex, 174
staff, 175, 198–199
training programs, 175, 178–179, 185–188, 196–197
treatment of prisoners, 190–200
visitors, 199–200
Property rights of women, 206–207
community property, 234–235
Prostitution, 3, 15, 27, 55–83, 248
adolescents, 59, 95, 248, 250

arrest rates, 28, 64
"baby pros," 59
books and plays, 60
"brainwashing" prostitutes, 72
brothels, 55, 58, 61, 65–66
call girls, 55, 65, 72, 74, 76, 79, 223, 225, 228
changes in, 56, 58
classes of prostitutes, 61
convention of prostitutes, 250
"daytimers," 65
decline of commercial, 65
decriminalization of, 224–225, 250, 252
definition, 68–69, 223
deviants, 73, 79
discriminatory legal treatment, 213, 220–228
double standard, 28, 80–81
drug addiction and, 73, 77–78, 130
economic factors, 64–65, 70–73, 76, 81
effect of liberation movement, 73, 81–82
failure to arrest males, 28
financial return from, 64–65, 70–73, 76, 81
geographical isolation, 223
Greek hetaerae, 56, 61–63, 82
group sex and, 74–76
historical background, 55–58, 61–63, 82–83
hookers, 23, 55, 250
illegal status, 61, 220–221
impact on criminal-justice system, 224
juvenile runaways, 71, 73
madams, 65–66
"massage parlors," 56
nonprofessional females, 58
organized, 223
part-time housewives, 64–65, 72–74, 76, 79
pimps, 65–68, 71–72, 95, 225
pornographic literature, 60–61
prevalence of, 64
privacy argument, 220–221
profession or trade, 58, 62–63
psychological basis, 69–72
public attitudes, 56, 58–60, 63, 73, 79–83
reasons for entering, 68–69, 75–76
"red-light districts," 55, 61, 223
regulation and legalization of, 79–80, 224–227

Prostitution (*cont.*):
  shifts in sexual behavior, 56, 58–60, 63–64, 72
  social function of, 57–58, 61–62, 72–74
  streetwalkers, 55, 61, 73, 78–79, 81, 223, 228
  violence-oriented crimes and, 22–23, 77–78
Protestant Reformation, 56–57
Protestant work ethic, 62
Psychological differences, 9, 37–39, 251–253
Psychosomatic illnesses, 23–24
Public-health problems, 251–252
Public opinion, 203, 218–219
Purdy (Tacoma, Washington) Treatment Center for Women, 195–201

Quinn, Peter, 18

Racial differences, 133–154
Radical movements, 20–22
  leadership of, 21
Rape, 213–216
  antiquated laws, 214–216
  effect on victim, 214–216
  women's lib and, 215–216
Reddy, Helen, 5
Rehabilitation of prisoners, 172–173, 188, 190–191
Repeaters, 15
Repression, 172
Revolutionary feminism, 20
Rieff, Philip, 201
Risk-taking, 42
Rites of passage, 24, 94, 126
Robbery, 3, 14, 27
  by adolescents, 17–18
  crime rate, 16–18
  mixed teams, 18
Role expectations, 40–41
Role models, parents as, 94–95
Role playing, 11
Runaways, 71, 90, 95

St. Augustine, 2, 57
San Francisco Commission on Crime, 222
Saroyan, William, 60
Seduction, legal statutes, 243
Sentencing practices, 229–232
  disparate schemes, 230–231
  sex discrimination, 206, 222, 229–232

Separate-but-equal philosophy, 1, 48, 205
Sex-discrimination, 167, 203–246
  criminal-justice system, 252
  in employment, 205, 216
  legal position of women, 203–246
  in sentencing practices, 206, 222, 229–232
Sexual behavior: group sex, 74–76
  legal system discrimination, 213–214
  shifts in, 56, 58–60, 63–64, 72
Sexual differences, 8–9, 33–35, 41, 45
  blurring of, 153
  cultural variations, 44–45
  physical differences, 35–37
  physiological differences, 2, 37–39
  social differences, 39–53
Sexual factors in crime, 27–29
Sexual freedom, 63–64
Shaw, George Bernard, 70
Sherman Act (1890) violations, 159
Shoplifting ("boosting"), 3, 6, 15, 27, 164–165
Single women, legal status, 205, 234
Smith, Edward, 71
Smith, Richard Austin, 159
Smith v. Alwright (1944), 145
Social changes, 39–53, 249
  juvenile delinquency and, 87, 108–110
  legal status of women, 207–213
  prisons and prisoners, 173–201
  prostitution, 57–58, 61–62, 72–74
Social differences between men and women, 39–53
  effect of World War II, 46–47
  sex-role personality traits, 41, 45
  social-role expectations, 40–41, 43–47, 53
Social equality, 251–253
Social factors, 27–28
  stability and change, 86
Social movements, 5, 93
  changing patterns, 5–30
Social position, changing status, 13
Social-role expectations, 40–41, 43–47, 53
  World War II, 46–48
Social Security benefits, 238
Social taboos and morality, 55
Social values, male-oriented, 213
Socioeconomic factors, 7–8
  drug addiction, 132
Socrates, 85–87, 109
Soltysik, Patricia, 20–21

Southern Christian Leadership Conference, 145
Springman, Connie, 191
Status of women, 12–13
  drive for, 10–11
  male model, 106
  (*See also* Dominance and status)
Steinbeck, John, 60
Stereotypes, 43, 45, 51, 204
  black women, 133
Stickney, A. B., 161
Stone, Chief Justice, 157
Strauss, Franz Josef, 23
"Streetwalkers," 23, 55, 223, 228
Strength of women, 10–11
Stress-related ailments, 23–24
Student Nonviolent Coordinating Committee (SNCC), 145–146
Student strikes, 20
Suicide attempts, 23–24
Supreme Court decisions, 249
  on abortion, 236–237
  on sex-discrimination, 210
Sutherland, Edwin, 156
Swinger parties, 74–75, 79
Symbionese Liberation Army, 20–22

Taxi drivers, 18–19
Tennyson, Alfred Lord, 10, 31
Tranquilizers, use of, 112–113, 120, 123, 130
Trauig, Harry, 189
Twenty-seventh Amendment (*see* Equal Rights Amendment)

Uniform Crime Reports, 15–16, 28, 52
Unisexual styles, 5, 93, 169
United States v. Dege, 233
Upper-class crime, 28, 156–158
Upward mobility, 29, 104–105

Value system, 155
  of female criminals, 7–8
Velimesis, Margery L., 193
Venereal disease, 225
Victimless crimes, 64, 173, 218
Violence-oriented crimes, 3, 14, 16–17, 22
  adolescent females, 22–23, 100–101

gangs, 22, 96–101, 106, 248
prostitutes, 22–23, 77–78
Voter-registration drives, 144–146
Voting rights of women, 206, 234

Washington, D.C.: gang activities, 96–98, 102–103
  peace demonstrations, 102–103
  police force, 48–51, 71, 102–103
  Rape Crisis Center, 216
  Women's Detention Center, 224
Watergate scandals, 160, 162
Weapons and guns, 10–11, 43
"Weather Underground," 20
White-collar crime, 155–169
  by black women, 134, 140, 144, 169
  concept of, 158
  definition, 158
  equality of opportunity and, 252
  incidence and scope of, 160–162
  opportunities for, 156–157, 163–169, 252
  profit motive and, 160
  public alarm over, 157–159
  types of, 156–159
  upper-class practitioners, 156–158
Wilde, Oscar, 175
Williams, Tennessee, 60
Women's-liberation movement, 2, 8, 26–27, 34–35, 153, 247–253
  activists, 129
  attitude of women criminals, 7–8, 25
  black women and, 140, 152–153
  crime rate and, 8
  effect on prostitution, 73, 81–82
  effect on rape cases, 215–216
  forces for social change, 248
  future trends, 247–253
  historical roots, 247
  legal changes and, 209
  male liberation and, 11
  social revolution, 25–27
  women's rights, 26–27
Work ethic, 62, 121
World War II, 46–48
  increase in female crime, 46–47
  shift in male attitudes, 48
  social and criminal roles, 46–48
  women assume male roles, 47

About the Author

Freda Adler is Associate Professor of Criminal Justice at Rutgers University, as well as a faculty member of the National College of State Judiciary, and a consultant to the United Nations crime prevention and criminal justice section. She received her B.A., M.A., and Ph.D. degrees at the University of Pennsylvania, and was subsequently Research Director of the Drug and Alcohol Abuse program at the Medical College of Pennsylvania, and a professor in the Department of Psychiatry at the University of Pennsylvania.

She has lectured on criminology in Europe and South America, served as a consultant to several government agencies, served on the editorial board of *Criminology: An Interdisciplinary Journal,* and written numerous journal articles. In 1972 she received the Herbert Bloch Award for service to the American Society of Criminology. Among her previous works are *Medical Lollipop, Junkie Insulin, or What?; A Systems Approach to Drug Treatment;* and *Crime and Addiction.*

Dr. Adler has three children and lives in New York City.